Ableton Live 101

An Introduction to Ableton Live 10

To access the online video
visit www.halleonard.com/mylibrary
Enter Code
6224-2117-2415-2458

Ableton Live 101
An Introduction to Ableton Live 10

Eric Kuehnl
Andrew Haak

with contributions by

Frank D. Cook

NextPoint Training, Inc.
Ableton Live 10

Rowman & Littlefield
Lanham • Boulder • New York • London

Published by Rowman & Littlefield

An imprint of The Rowman & Littlefield Publishing Group, Inc.

4501 Forbes Boulevard, Suite 200, Lanham, Maryland 20706

www.rowman.com

6 Tinworth Street, London SE11 5AL, United Kingdom

Library of Congress Cataloging-in-Publication Data available

ISBN 978-1-5400-4686-4 (paperback)

ISBN 978-1-5381-3470-2 (eBook)

♾™ The paper used in this publication meets the minimum requirements of American National Standard for Information Sciences– Permanence of Paper for Printed Library Materials, ANSI/NISO Z39.48-1992.

Contents

Acknowledgments

The authors would like to extend special thanks to the following individuals who have provided support, feedback, technical information, editorial input, and other contributions for this version of the book: Mark Anderson, John Cerullo, Andy Cook, Frank D. Cook, Matt Donner, Mark Garvey, Greg Gordon, Bruce Tambling, Michael Tanamachi, Simon Pennington.

Eric would like to thank his wife and children for their support and understanding: Amanda Goodroe, Thom, and Freddie.

Andrew would like to thank Casey, Eric Kuehnl, Steve Heithecker, Matt Donner, the Pyramind community at large, and Football the cat.

Welcome to Ableton Live

Congratulations on beginning work under the NextPoint Training Digital Media Production program. Within this program, you have the opportunity to pursue certification in Ableton Live and other digital media applications.

Ableton Live's award-winning technology is embraced by recording artists and audio production professionals around the world. The material in this course book will help you to join their ranks, unleashing the power and productivity of your own Ableton Live system.

This book represents the first step on a journey toward mastering Ableton Live software. The information, exercises, and projects you will find here are written for Ableton Live systems running version 10.1 software. However, the vast majority of the book applies equally to earlier software versions, including Ableton Live 9.x. Whether you are interested only in self-study or you would like to pursue formal training through a NextPoint Training Certification Partner, this book will develop your core skills and introduce you to the awe-inspiring power of Ableton Live.

About This Book

This book provides a course outline for the audio enthusiast with relatively little Ableton Live experience. This text and the associated Ableton Live 101 instructor-led training course were developed by NextPoint Training, Inc. (NPT) as part of our Digital Media Production program and certification offerings. While this course book can be completed through self-study, we recommend the hands-on experience available through an instructor-led class with an NPT Certification Partner.

For more information on the classes offered through the NextPoint Training Digital Media Production program, please visit http://NextPointTraining.com/certification.

Ableton Live 10 Edition

This edition of the Ableton Live 101 course has been written to address recent software changes up through the Ableton Live 10.1 release. The material is focused on the principles that you need to understand to complete an Ableton Live project, from initial setup to final export. Whether your project involves recording audio, preparing MIDI sequences for virtual instruments, or editing and mixing audio files, Ableton Live 101 will teach you the steps required to succeed.

The Download Media

This book makes use of media files for the included exercises and the final project. The media files can be accessed by visiting www.halleonard.com/mylibrary and entering your access code, as printed on the opening page of this book. From there, you can download the Media Files 2019 folder for this course. Instructions for downloading the media files are provided with the exercises and final project, as needed.

The downloadable Media Files 2019 folder includes three subfolders for use with this book.

Sample Files for Exercises

The 01 Completed Exercises folder within the Media Files 2019 folder provides sample Set files of each completed Ableton Live exercise (Exercises 4 through 10). These are provided primarily for reference purposes. Sample files 4 though 9 can also be used as starting points for subsequent work in Exercises 5 through 10, as needed.

Exercise Media

The 02 Exercise Media folder provides the audio and MIDI files you will import to complete the work in Exercises 5 through 10, following the instructions included in this book.

Files for the Final Project

The 03 Final Project Media folder provides content for the final project that you will complete in the second part of this book. This folder includes a Set file and associated media required to complete the project, following the step-by-step instructions in the Final Project section of the book.

Course Prerequisites

Most Ableton Live enthusiasts today have at least a passing familiarity with operating a computer. If you consider yourself a computer novice, however, you should review some basics before beginning this course. You will need to know how to complete such tasks as:

- Starting up your computer

- Using the mouse to navigate through folders and select files

- Using standard menus and menu commands

- Using common keyboard commands for standard operating system operations

- Locating, moving, and renaming files and folders

- Using standard cut, copy, and paste commands

- Opening, saving, and closing files

This course focuses on using Ableton Live in a digital audio recording and production environment. The work requires a basic understanding of MIDI and audio recording techniques, processes, and equipment, such as the following:

- MIDI devices

- Microphones and miking techniques

- Audio interfaces

- Mixer signal flow

- Audio monitoring equipment

If you are a beginner in the field of audio production, you can supplement this text with independently available literature or courses on audio recording tools and techniques.

Course Organization and Sequence

This course has been designed to familiarize you with the practices and processes you will use to complete a recording, editing, and mixing project.

Chapters and Exercises

The first part of the book includes ten primary chapters and ten associated short exercises. The first three chapters provide information on Ableton Live's background and history, installation and startup procedures, and the current user interface. The subsequent chapters present specific processes and techniques, in the general order that you will use them to complete a project—from creating a new Set, to recording and editing, and on through to mixing and completing a final export.

Each of the chapters is followed by a brief exercise that gives you practice applying what you have learned.

Final Project

The second part of this book is the final project. This section includes instructions for completing an unfinished project included in the **Media Files 2019** folder. The project in this section can be completed at any point as you progress through the ten primary chapters.

Appendices

This edition of the book includes two appendices. Appendix A provides information on the audio and MIDI Effects devices that are included with Ableton Live. Appendix B provides details on the Software Instrument devices that are included with Ableton Live.

The NPT Digital Media Production Program

This Ableton Live 101 book has been written as a textbook for teaching and learning Ableton Live software. In addition to being an off-the-shelf guide for consumers, this book is also the official text for NextPoint Training's professional certification in Ableton Live. By completing the coursework in this text, you are taking an important step toward certification. And consider this: Having a certification from NextPoint Training just might help you land that next gig, find others with similar skills and interests, or even obtain your dream job in the industry.

To become certified in Ableton Live, you must register at ElementsED.com, where you can complete additional study in Ableton Live, review coursework (as desired), take practice quizzes, and take the Ableton Live Certified Professional Exam. Detailed information on current requirements is available from the NextPoint Training website at http://NextPointTraining.com/certification.

Curriculum and Certification Levels

NextPoint Training currently offers certification in Ableton Live software, Pro Tools|First software, and Steinberg Cubase software. (Visit NextPointTraining.com/certification for the latest information.) The certification credential associated with the Ableton Live 101 course is Ableton Live Certified Professional I.

The Certified Professional program prepares individuals to operate an Ableton Live system in an independent production environment. This certification requires successful completion of the Ableton Live 101 instructor-led course at an NPT Certification Partner school and a passing score on the associated Ableton Live certification exam.

Other Courses Offered in the Digital Media Production Program

NextPoint Training offers several additional certification courses to help you become proficient using a wide range of audio production tools.

- *Audio Production Basics with Pro Tools|First* teaches the basics of recording, editing, mixing, and processing audio using Pro Tools | First software. It offers an introduction to digital audio for students aspiring to work in music or video production, audio engineering, broadcast, or new media.

- *Steinberg Cubase 101* provides the foundational skills needed to operate a Steinberg Cubase system in an independent production environment. The goal of this course is to help individuals start working effectively on their own projects in Cubase Artist or Cubase Pro software.

NextPoint Training Course Configuration

NextPoint Training uses a version–specific approach to course design, enabling students and educators to access classes based on the products and software versions that meet their particular needs and training environments.

Audio Curriculum

The NextPoint Training audio coursework includes programs supporting certification in several areas, including Ableton Live, Avid Pro Tools, Steinberg Cubase, and more. The Ableton Live certification path is described above. Course components are designed to be completed as individual product-focused classes; however, the same content may be made available through different class configurations.

Other Media Courses

Details on of each of the courses offered through the NextPoint Training Digital Media Production program are available in the NPT Certification Program Guide.

How Can I Learn More?

Additional resources are available to help you explore the topics covered in this book, review key points in each chapter, and test your knowledge of the material. The **Ableton Live 101 Study Guide** module available through the Elements|ED online learning platform (ElementsED.com) allows learners to review key concepts and information from this course through visual examples and to assess their learning using practice quizzes. This module is particularly useful to help students prepare for the Ableton Live Certified Professional exam.

Conventions and Symbols Used in This Book

Following are some of the conventions and symbols used in this book, and throughout the books in the NextPoint Training Series.

Keyboard Shortcuts and Modifiers

Menu choices and keyboard commands are typically capitalized and written in bold text. Hierarchy is shown using the greater than symbol (>), keystroke combinations are indicated using the plus sign (+), and mouse-click operations are indicated by hyphenated strings, where needed. Brackets ([ ]) are used to indicate key presses on the numeric keypad.

Convention	Action
File > Save Set	Choose Save Set from the File menu.
Ctrl+N	Hold down the Ctrl key and press the N key.
Command-click (Mac)	Hold down the Command key and click the mouse button.
Right-click	Click with the right mouse button.
Press [1]	Press 1 on the numeric keypad.

Icons

The following icons are used in this book to call attention to tips, shortcuts, listening suggestions, warnings, and reference sources.

 Tips provide helpful hints and suggestions, background information, or details on related operations or concepts.

 Shortcuts provide useful keyboard, mouse, or modifier-based shortcuts that can help you work more efficiently.

 Warnings caution you against conditions that may affect audio playback, impact system performance, alter data files, or interrupt hardware connections.

 Cross-References alert you to another section, book, or resource that provides additional information on the current topic.

 Online References provide links to online resources and downloads related to the current topic.

Chapter 1

Background Information

This chapter introduces you to Ableton Live's capabilities and uses for audio production, MIDI workflows, mixing, and video post-production. You will learn about the evolution of Ableton Live and get an introduction to the characteristics of analog and digital audio. You will also get an overview of the latest developments in Ableton Live 10 software and learn about the different Ableton Live configurations available today.

 ## Learning Targets for This Chapter

- Identify common industry uses for Ableton Live software

- Recognize the contributions of historical developments in sampling and sound editing, MIDI technology, computer I/O, and recording technology to today's digital audio workstation

- Understand the relationship between sample rate and frequency response in digital audio

- Understand the relationship between bit depth and dynamic range in digital audio

- Recognize components and features of various Ableton Live configurations

 Key topics from this chapter are illustrated in the Ableton Live 101 Study Guide module available through the Elements|ED online learning platform. Sign up for free at ElementsED.com.

The Ableton Live Digital Audio Workstation

Ableton Live is one of the most widely used applications for music production in the world today, integrating capabilities in audio and MIDI recording, editing, mixing, and mastering, as well as support for desktop video. As such, Ableton Live empowers a wide range of producers—from hobbyist to professional—to easily achieve all of their production tasks within an intuitive yet powerful environment.

At its core, Ableton Live is a multi-track software-based music production system. When the first version of Ableton Live was introduced back in 2001, it's unique approach to audio and MIDI composition revolutionized the music production world.

Today's Ableton Live offers audio recording, graphical audio editing, MIDI sequencing, digital signal processing, and mixing through a single, integrated system. With the ability to incorporate QuickTime video files, Ableton Live has also established itself as viable option for composing for visual media such as film and television.

Audio Processing

Ableton Live works with audio that is stored electronically in digital format. The software records audio performances and saves them as files on a storage drive. Like a digital photograph that is comprised of a collection of discrete pixels, the audio files created by Ableton Live are made up of a collection of discrete *samples*. Ableton Live supports audio formats with resolutions up to 32-bit floating point and sample rates up to 192 kHz.

Just as you can use an image editor to modify, enhance, and otherwise alter your digital photographs in creative ways, you can use Ableton Live to edit your digital audio. Working in the digital realm makes it easy to copy, paste, move, delete, process, and otherwise manipulate parts of your recordings. Ableton Live lets you resize and split waveforms, convert audio data to MIDI data, change the timing and feel of performances, rearrange song sections, and much, much more.

MIDI Production

Ableton Live's built-in sequencing technology enables you to record and edit MIDI data along with your audio recordings. MIDI recordings differ from their digital audio counterparts in that they capture performance event data rather than sound samples. You can record MIDI signals from an external controller (such as Ableton Push) through a MIDI interface or USB port and then edit the data using Live's Clip View.

Ableton Live's MIDI features include MIDI tracks, MIDI effects, grid and groove quantize functions, velocity editing, and more. Furthermore, some editions of Ableton Live come bundled with several great-sounding virtual instrument plug-ins.

Mixing and Automation

Beyond recording, editing, and arranging, Ableton Live offers a software-based mixing environment that provides control over signal routing, effects processing, signal levels, panning, and more. The mixing operations in Ableton Live can be automated and stored with your Set file, enabling you to recall, edit, and refine your mixes over time. When you save an Ableton Live Set, all routing, automation, mixing, and effects settings are stored in their present state and will recall in that state whenever the Set is reopened.

Additionally, Ableton Live can be combined with hardware from third-party manufacturers in various configurations to provide multiple channels of simultaneous input and output for your projects. Large Sets including dozens of simultaneous audio and MIDI tracks can be managed without audio degradation. Ableton Live systems can range from very simple to extremely advanced and powerful.

Audio for Video Post-Production

Ableton Live also provides a powerful audio platform for video post-production tasks. You can import QuickTime movies and use the Ableton Live Video window for quick visual reference or full-screen display as you compose a music score, edit dialog, and/or create sound effects. When completed, your finished movie file can be exported with the final audio mix embedded.

Ableton Live History and Evolution

In the 1990s, two musicians named Gerhard Behles and Robert Henke spent much of their time performing minimal techno around Berlin under the moniker *Monolake*. Out of necessity, the two developed custom performance software using the Max music programming language to trigger audio loops and samples in their shows. By the end of the 1990s, Behles and Henke made the decision to convert their messy Max code into a streamlined commercial application that could be sold to other musicians. After several years of development, the first version of Ableton Live was released in 2001. The software was an immediate success thanks to its intuitive interface and innovative sample manipulation and playback features.

Over the years since, Ableton has released a steady stream of updates that have each improved the functionality of Ableton Live. One of the most important early updates was Ableton Live 4 (2004), which introduced MIDI sequencing and VST plug-in support. Ableton Live 5 (2005) introduced track freeze and MP3 support. Ableton Live 6 (2006) introduced QuickTime video support and allowed users to produce music for film and video from within Live for the first time.

Max for Live

In 2007, Ableton announced that they were working with Cycling '74 to integrate the Max music programming language directly into Ableton Live. In 2009, the two companies released Max for Live software, which made it possible to use Max patches directly inside of Ableton Live. Ableton acquired Cycling '74 in 2017, and beginning with Ableton Live Suite 10, the Max for Live application is now integrated into Ableton Live at no additional cost.

Control Surfaces

In 2009, Ableton worked with Akai Professional to release the first dedicated Ableton Live controllers. The result was the APC40, which closely approximated the Ableton Live software interface in an intuitive hardware format. The APC functionality included the ability to launch clips and scenes and adjust mixer and device settings from a hardware controller.

In 2013, Ableton again teamed up with Akai Professional to create the Push hardware instrument. Push took the APC concept to the next level and offered access to almost every aspect of Ableton Live from the controller, including note entry, step sequencing, and much more.

In 2017, Ableton designed and built Push 2 completely in-house. Push 2 expanded on the capabilities of the original Push by adding a larger display and higher quality pads.

Figure 1.1 Ableton Push 2 hardware instrument

Getting the Most from Your System

To make the most of your experience with Ableton Live 10 and to optimize your results using the platform, it is helpful to understand some audio basics and to familiarize yourself with the software options available with Ableton Live. The remainder of this chapter focuses on these topics.

Audio Basics: Waveform, Frequency, and Amplitude

To work effectively with sound, it is helpful to understand what sound is and what gives a sound its character. When we hear a sound, what we actually experience is a variation in the air pressure around us. This variation results from vibrations in material objects—whether a knock on a tabletop, a running car engine, or a plucked guitar string. When a vibrating object moves through a back-and-forth motion, the variation in air pressure that it produces becomes an auditory event. If the object is vibrating at a frequency that falls within the range of human hearing, we perceive the varying air pressure as a sound.

The nature of the sound we hear is determined by the waveform, frequency, and amplitude of the vibration.

Waveform

The waveform of the sound pressure variations that reaches our ears creates our perception of the sound's source, be it a tabletop, a car engine, or a guitar string. The waveform is the "shape" of the sound—or, more accurately, the shape of the vibration that produced the sound. As a vibrating object moves through its back-and-forth motions, its path is not smooth and continuous. Instead, the cycles of vibration are typically complex and jagged, creating a sound that is influenced by the physical material that the object is composed of and the resonance induced by the object's surroundings. Each object vibrates differently; the waveform of the vibration gives the sound its unique character and tone.

Frequency

The frequency of the sound pressure variations that reaches our ears creates our perception of the pitch of the sound. We measure this frequency in *cycles per second* (CPS), also commonly denoted as *Hertz* (Hz). These two terms are synonymous—15,000 CPS is the same as 15,000 Hz. Multiples of 1,000 Hz are often denoted as kilohertz (kHz). Therefore, 15,000 Hz is also written as 15 kHz.

As the frequency of vibration increases, the pitch of the sound goes up—numerically higher frequencies produce higher pitches, while numerically lower frequencies produce lower pitches. Each time the frequency doubles, the pitch rises by one octave.

By way of example, the open **A** string on a guitar vibrates at 110 Hz in standard tuning. Playing the **A** note on the 12th fret produces vibrations at 220 Hz (one octave higher).

 The range of human hearing is between 20 and 20,000 cycles per second, or stated another way, from 20 Hz to 20 kHz.

Amplitude

The intensity or amplitude of the sound pressure variations that reaches our ears creates our perception of the loudness of the sound. We measure amplitude in *decibels* (dB). The decibel is a logarithmic unit that is used to describe a ratio of sound pressure; as such, it does not have a linear relation to our perception of loudness.

As the amplitude of pressure variations increases, the sound becomes louder. Doubling the intensity of sound-pressure variations creates a gain of 3 dB; however, we do not perceive this change as doubling the sound's loudness. An increase of approximately 10 dB is required to produce a perceived doubling of loudness. By way of example, the amplitude of ordinary conversation is around 60 dB. Increasing the amplitude to 70 dB would essentially double the loudness; increasing amplitude to 80 dB would double it again, quadrupling the original loudness.

Recording and Playing Back Analog Audio

The task of a recording microphone is to respond to changes in air pressure—the waveforms, frequencies, and amplitudes that make up a sound—and translate them into an electronic output that can be captured or recorded. A microphone functions as a *transducer*, converting acoustic energy into an electrical current.

The continuous electrical signal produced by a microphone is an alternating current with a waveform, frequency, and amplitude that directly corresponds to, or is analogous to, the original acoustic information. This electrical signal is thus considered to represent *analog audio*.

If this continuous analog signal is captured on traditional recording media, such as magnetic tape, it can be played back by directly translating the electrical waveform, frequency, and amplitude back into analogous variations in air pressure through the means of an amplifier and a loudspeaker.

Converting Audio to Digital Format

Before you can record or edit with Ableton Live, the analog audio (electrical signal) relayed by a microphone, guitar pickup, or other device must be translated into digital numeric information (binary data). This conversion is necessary so that the signal can be stored, read, and subsequently manipulated by a computer.

The process of translating electrical signals to binary data is referred to as *analog-to-digital conversion*, commonly abbreviated as *A/D conversion*. Two essential factors affect the A/D conversion process: *sample rate* and *bit depth*.

The Importance of Sample Rate

Sampling is the process of taking discrete measurements of an electrical signal at various moments in time. Each measurement, or sample, is a digital representation of the signal voltage at that instant. Played back in succession, these samples approximate the original signal, much like a series of photographs played back in succession approximates movement in a film or video.

The sample rate is the frequency with which these digital measurements are collected.

Nyquist Theorem

A fundamental law of analog-to-digital conversion, commonly referred to as the Nyquist Theorem, drives the sample rate required for digital audio.

The Nyquist Theorem states that in order to produce an accurate representation of a given frequency of sound, each cycle of the sound's vibration must be sampled a minimum of two times. If the sample rate is any lower, the system will read the incoming frequencies inaccurately and produce the wrong tones. (In concept, this is much like the effect seen in early motion pictures, where a wagon wheel will appear to rotate backward due to the low frame rates being used.) In digital audio, the false tones produced by this type of frequency distortion are known as *alias tones*.

Minimum Sample Rate

Because the range of human hearing is generally accepted to be 20 Hz to 20 kHz, the Nyquist Theorem tells us that a sampling rate of at least 40 kHz (twice the upper range of human hearing) is required to capture full-frequency audio.

Most professional digital recording devices today offer sample rates of at least 44.1 kHz (often as much as 96 kHz or higher). The digital information on an audio CD is stored at a standard sample rate of 44.1 kHz.

The Importance of Bit Depth

Computers use binary digits called *bits* (0s or 1s) to represent each sample measurement that is collected. The number of bits used for each sample is referred to as the *binary word length*, or bit depth.

The more binary digits included in the bit depth, the greater the accuracy of each sample measurement. The relative amplitude (or loudness) of each sample is *quantized*, or rounded to the closest available whole-number value within the word length.

 The range of numeric values available for each sample at a given bit depth is equal to 2 to the nth power (2^n), where n is the number of bits in the binary word.

By way of example, consider a 4-bit binary word. This word length can represent only 16 different amplitude levels (2^4). As such, a 4-bit binary word would record audio using only 16 discrete amplitude levels. By contrast, a 16-bit digital word could represent 65,536 discrete amplitude levels (2^{16}), creating a much more continuous dynamic response. A 24-bit digital word could define more than 16 million discrete amplitude levels (2^{24}).

Larger binary words are able to quantify variations in amplitude with much greater accuracy. Therefore, a 24-bit audio file will always more accurately reflect the dynamic range of the original sound than its 16-bit counterpart.

 Thirty-two-bit floating-point files represent discrete amplitude levels in the same way as 24-bit files. The 8 additional bits provide exponent biasing and allow for headroom above full-scale 24-bit audio.

Calculating Dynamic Range

A very general rule of thumb can be used to calculate the dynamic range capability of an A/D system. By multiplying the word size by six, you can estimate the useful dynamic range of a fixed-point system. For example, a system with an **8-bit** binary word would produce a dynamic range of about 48 dB (8 × 6), while a **16-bit** system would accommodate a 96-dB dynamic range (16 × 6). A **24-bit** system would have a theoretical dynamic range of 144 dB (24 × 6).

In theoretical terms, the dynamic range (or signal-to-quantization noise ratio) increases by approximately 6 dB for each bit added to the binary word length.

Minimum Bit Depth

The useful dynamic range of speech and music is generally considered to be from 40 to 105 dB. To capture this range, an A/D converter must be able to accurately represent differences in amplitude of at least 65 dB; stated another way, it must have a minimum 65-dB dynamic range. This would require at least 11 bits in the binary word.

To provide an adequate dynamic range to minimize the impact of the noise floor at the low end of the spectrum, and to allow a healthy amount of headroom at the high end, Ableton Live uses a minimum word length of 16 bits. Greater bit depths can be used to increase precision and accommodate a wider dynamic range.

Sample Rate, Bit Depth, and File Size

A consequence of files with higher sample rates and greater bit depths is the higher storage capacity required to record them. Each minute of 16-bit/44.1-kHz mono audio occupies about 5 MB of storage space. Higher sample rates increase the storage requirement. At 96 kHz, each minute of 16-bit mono audio requires about 11 MB of storage space.

Increasing the bit depth has the same effect. For example, one minute of 24-bit/44.1-kHz mono audio occupies about 7.5 MB of hard-drive storage space, while the same audio in a 32-bit float file (at 44.1 kHz) will require about 10 MB of hard-drive space per minute.

 Stereo files require twice as much storage space as mono files, since each file includes two channels of audio (left and right).

Recording in Digital Format

When you are recording into Ableton Live using audio that is already in a digital form (from DAT or CD, for example), you don't need to translate the audio before bringing it into the system. The process of converting from digital to analog and back to digital can introduce distortion and degrade the original signal.

Digital Transfers

To prevent audio degradation, unnecessary conversions should be avoided. Keeping audio information in the digital domain while transferring between machines or devices will retain its sonic integrity with no discernible signal degradation.

Digital Audio Connections

On the rear panel of many audio interfaces are connections for accomplishing digital transfers. Common digital connections include *S/PDIF*, which uses RCA jacks (sometimes called *coaxial jacks*), and *AES/EBU*, which uses XLR-type connectors. S/PDIF is the *Sony/Philips Digital Interface* standard, a consumer format, and AES/EBU is the *Audio Engineering Society/European Broadcast Union* digital interface standard, a professional format.

Although the formats are nearly identical in audio quality, if given the choice, you should use the AES/EBU format over S/PDIF. As a professional format, AES/EBU is technically more stable, and it filters out any copy protection encoded in the digital audio stream.

Ableton Live Configurations

The requirements for your digital audio recording projects will determine the edition of Ableton Live that you will need to use. Ableton Live 10 is available in three editions: Ableton Live Intro, Ableton Live Standard, and Ableton Live Suite.

Software Editions

Ableton Live Intro (and the similar Ableton Live Lite) is a basic version of Ableton Live, with limitations on editing features, track count, scene count, and input and output (I/O) capabilities.

Ableton Live Standard provides the full editing feature set, unlimited tracks and scenes, and up to 256 channels of I/O. This book focuses on Ableton Live Standard software features.

Ableton Live Suite offers all of the Ableton Live Standard features, and includes additional virtual instruments, audio and MIDI effects, and Max for Live.

 For more information about the various editions of Ableton Live, see "Ableton Live Edition Comparison" in Chapter 2 of this book.

All Ableton Live editions are available for both Mac and Windows operating systems.

Ableton Live Intro vs. Ableton Live Standard vs. Ableton Live Suite

Throughout this book, we use the term **Ableton Live** to refer generically to all available software editions and the terms **Ableton Live Intro**, **Ableton Live Standard**, and **Ableton Live Suite** to refer to specific editions of Ableton Live software, where needed for differentiation.

Host-Based Systems Versus DSP-Accelerated Systems

Ableton Live systems can either be host-based, meaning they rely solely on the processing power of the host computer for routing, mixing, and processing of audio signals, or DSP-accelerated systems, meaning that the computer's processor is supplemented by additional processor chips dedicated to digital signal processing (DSP) for mixing and real-time processing.

DSP-accelerated Ableton Live systems can be constructed using third-party products that feature DSP processing. The most common examples are the Apollo interfaces and UAD Satellite units by Universal Audio.

Audio Interface Options

An audio interface provides the analog-to-digital conversion required for recording to Ableton Live, as well as the digital-to-analog conversion required for playback from Ableton Live to your analog speakers or headphones. Ableton Live can be run without an audio interface, using your computer's built-in speakers or headphone jack for playback; however, recording options may be limited or unavailable.

Examples of Audio Interfaces

All versions of Ableton Live support a range of audio hardware:

■ **Basic Interfaces**—Ableton Live supports a variety of hardware I/O options on both Mac and Windows computers. These may include your computer's built-in audio hardware or an external interface that connects via USB, FireWire, or Thunderbolt. Many of these peripherals can be powered by the computer's FireWire or USB bus, enabling portability for laptop systems.

Figure 1.2 Focusrite's Scarlett 2i4 is an excellent entry-level interface

When considering the purchase of an external interface, it's important to remember that Ableton Live Intro supports a maximum of eight input and output channels. Although interfaces with more inputs and outputs can be used with Ableton Live Intro, you'll need to select a maximum of eight inputs and outputs at one time.

■ **Mid-Range Interfaces**—Ableton Live Standard and Ableton Live Suite support up to a maximum of 256 channels of input and output, so much larger interfaces (or combinations of interfaces) can be used. You should consider a mid-range interface if you need more than just a couple of channels of input and output. You should also consider stepping up to a mid-range interface if you're looking for better quality microphone preamps and analog-to-digital and digital-to-analog convertors.

Figure 1.3 MOTU's UltraLite Mk3 is an affordable, mid-range interface

- **High-End Interfaces** – If you're looking for an interface with a large number of inputs and outputs, you'll most likely want to consider a high-end interface from manufacturers such as Antelope Audio, Apogee, Focusrite, or Universal Audio. These interfaces offer as many as 64 channels of input and output to accommodate the largest recording configurations. You may also want to step up to a high-end interface if you're looking for the absolute best quality in terms of microphone preamps and convertors.

Figure 1.4 Antelope Audio's Orion Studio is high-end interface with 32 channels of I/O

Cross-Platform Issues

Ableton Live editions are available for both Mac and Windows systems. Most Ableton Live controls, tools, procedures, and menus are similar on both systems. There are, however, some differences in keyboard commands and file-naming conventions that can impact your work when moving between different platforms.

Keyboard Commands

Many keyboard commands in Ableton Live use *modifier keys*, which are keys pressed in combination with other keys or with a mouse action. Modifiers and other equivalent keys can have different names on each platform. Table 1.1 below summarizes the modifier keys that are commonly used in shortcut operations on Mac and Windows computers.

Table 1.1 Modifier keys on Mac and Windows systems

Mac	Windows
Command key	Ctrl (Control) key
Option key	Alt key
Control key	Start (Win) key
Return key	Enter key on main (not numeric) keypad
Delete key	Backspace key

File-Naming Conventions

A few differences exist in the way files are named and recognized by Mac and Windows.

File Name Extensions

For cross-platform compatibility, all Ableton Live files in a project must have a three-letter file extension added to the file name. Ableton Live Set files use the *.als* extension. WAV files have the *.wav* file extension, and AIFF files have the *.aif* file extension.

Incompatible ASCII Characters

Ableton Live file names cannot use ASCII characters that are incompatible with a supported operating system. The following characters should be avoided in order to maintain cross-platform compatibility:

/ (slash)

\ (backslash)

: (colon)

* (asterisk)

? (question mark)

" (quotation marks)

' (apostrophe)

< (less-than symbol)

> (greater-than symbol)

| (vertical line or pipe)

You should also avoid any special characters typed with a modifier key on Mac or Windows systems.

Review/Discussion Questions

1. Name and describe four types of production tasks that Ableton Live can be used for. (See "The Ableton Live Digital Audio Workstation" beginning on page 8.)

2. What is the frequency range of human hearing? (See "Audio Basics: Waveform, Frequency, and Amplitude" beginning on page 10.)

3. What does the frequency of a sound wave affect in terms of how we perceive the sound? How is frequency measured? (See "Audio Basics: Waveform, Frequency, and Amplitude" beginning on page 10.)

4. What does the amplitude of the sound wave affect? How is amplitude measured? (See "Audio Basics: Waveform, Frequency, and Amplitude" beginning on page 10.)

5. How does the sample rate of a system relate to the frequency of audio it can capture? What is the name of the law that specifies the relationship between sample rate and audio frequency? (See "The Importance of Sample Rate" beginning on page 12.)

6. How does the bit depth of a system relate to the dynamic range of audio it can capture? How can you estimate the dynamic range of a system? (See "The Importance of Bit Depth" beginning on page 13.)

7. What are some common digital connections available on audio interfaces? What type of connector jack does each use? (See "Recording in Digital Format" on page 14.)

8. Name some audio interfaces that are available for use with Ableton Live. (See "Audio Interface Options" beginning on page 16.)

 To review additional material from this chapter and prepare for certification, see the Ableton Live 101 Study Guide module available through the Elements|ED online learning platform at ElementsED.com.

Selecting Your Audio Production Gear

🎧 Activity

In this exercise, you will define your audio production needs and select components for a home studio based around Ableton Live software. By balancing your wants and needs against a defined budget, you will be able to determine which hardware and software options make sense for you.

🕐 Duration

This exercise should take approximately 10 minutes to complete.

⊕ Goals/Targets

- Identify a budget for your home studio

- Explore microphone options

- Explore audio interface options

- Explore speakers/monitoring options

- Consider other expenses

- Identify appropriate components to complete your system

Getting Started

To get started, you will create a list of needs and define an overall budget for your home studio setup. This budget should be sufficient to cover all aspects of your initial needs for basic audio production work. At the same time, you'll want to be careful to keep your budget realistic so that you can afford the upfront investment. Keep in mind that you can add to your basic setup over time to increase your capabilities.

Use the table below to outline your basic requirements and to serve as a guide when you begin shopping for options. Place an **X** in the appropriate column for your expected needs in each row.

Do not include MIDI gear in this table, as we will address that separately.

 This exercise assumes that you own a compatible computer with built-in speakers for playback. Do not include a host computer in this table.

Function or Component	Not Required	Minimum Configuration	Maximum Configuration for Ableton Live Intro
Audio Interface: Output Channels (Playback)	–	1-2 Inputs	8 Inputs
Audio Interface: Input Channels (Recording)	–	2 Outputs (for stereo playback)	8 Outputs (for stereo playback and output to external gear)
Output Device(s)	Built-in Computer Speakers	Headphones	Stereo Monitor Speakers
Input Device(s) (Microphones)	–	USB Microphone	XLR Microphone(s) (specify type and number)
Accessories and Other (List or Describe) (Stands, Soundproofing, Software Add-Ons, etc.)			

Available Budget for the Above: _____

Identifying Prices

Your next step is to begin identifying prices for equipment that will meet your needs. Using the requirements you identified above as a guide, do some Internet research at an online music retailer of your choice to identify appropriate options for each of the items listed in the table below. You may also want to browse some manufacturers' websites for more information.

Component	Manufacturer and Model	Unit Cost
Audio Interface		
Microphones		
Headphones		
Monitor Speakers		
Accessories/Other		
	TOTAL	

Finishing Up

To finalize your purchase decisions, compare the total in the table above to the budget you allocated. If you find that your budget is not sufficient to cover the total cost, you will need to determine which purchase items you can postpone or consider bundle options. On the other hand, if you have money left over in your budget, you can consider upgrade options.

Chapter 2

Getting Started with Ableton Live

This chapter covers the basic requirements to get up and running with Ableton Live. It reviews the Ableton Live software components and installers, as well as the file structure used for Ableton Live Sets. It also introduces the basic user interface for the software and reviews menu operations. The second half of this lesson provides an overview of the main views in Ableton Live.

◈ Learning Targets for This Chapter

- Understand the components included with an Ableton Live system and how to access installers

- Recognize the basic Ableton Live project file structure

- Understand basic Ableton Live software and plug-in options

- Power up an Ableton Live system

- Navigate the Ableton Live menu system to locate common commands

- Recognize and work in the main Ableton Live views

Key topics from this chapter are illustrated in the Ableton Live 101 Study Guide module available through the Elements|ED online learning platform. Sign up for free at ElementsED.com.

This chapter presents an overview of basic Ableton Live operations and functions. You will be introduced to the filing structure that Ableton Live uses for its Sets and backups, the steps required to start up an Ableton Live system, and the primary elements of the main Ableton Live views.

Target Systems

Although most of the concepts discussed in this book are applicable to all Ableton Live systems, the book is specifically written for Ableton Live 10.1 *Standard* software. While any Ableton Live system can be used with this book, certain menus, commands, and functions may differ from one configuration to another. Additionally, Ableton Live Suite users will have access to various features and devices that may not represented in this book.

Because many users will be new to Ableton Live 10, new features introduced in Ableton Live 10 are generally identified as such in the text. All descriptions are based on the user interface and functionality in Ableton Live 10.1, unless otherwise noted.

> You can try Ableton Live 10 free for 30 days by visiting the Ableton website at https://www.ableton.com/trial/.

Registering Your Software

Before you can install Ableton Live, you'll need to create an account on Ableton.com and enter your product registration code. If you purchased a boxed version of Ableton Live or Push, your registration code will be included in the box. If you purchased a digital download of Ableton Live from a reseller, your registration code can be found in your confirmation email.

> If you purchased Live through Ableton.com, the software will already be registered to your account.

If you've never registered an Ableton product, do the following:

1.   Go to Ableton.com and create an account. You will be taken directly to the product registration page shown in Figure 2.1.

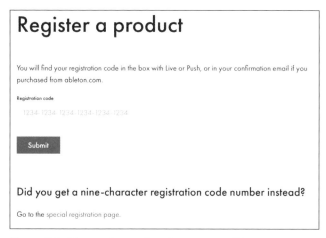

Figure 2.1 The product registration page on Ableton.com

2.   Enter your registration code and click the **SUBMIT** button.

If you've previously registered an Ableton product, do the following:

1.   Go to Ableton.com and log in to your account.

2.   Click on the **ACCOUNT** link in the upper right corner of the webpage. The Account page will appear, displaying a Licenses pop-up near the top.

Figure 2.2 The Licenses pop-up menu in the user's Account page at Ableton.com

3.   Click on the pop-up menu next to Licenses and choose **REGISTER A PRODUCT**. You'll be taken to the registration page (shown in Figure 2.1) where you can register your new or upgraded product.

Software Installation and Operation

Ableton uses separate installers for each version and edition of Ableton Live. Each Ableton Live installer also installs a variety of included software devices providing additional functionality. Supplemental devices and content (known as "packs") may be included as well, but these will require separate installation through the Ableton website or directly within the Ableton Live application (Ableton Live 10 and later only).

Ableton uses the term *version* to differentiate numbered versions of the software such as Live 9 or Live 10. Ableton uses the term *edition* to differentiate between the different flavors of Live, such as Intro, Standard, and Suite.

To access the installers for Ableton Live, do the following:

1. Go to Ableton.com and log in to your account.

2. Click on the **ACCOUNT** link in the upper right corner of the webpage. The Account page will appear.

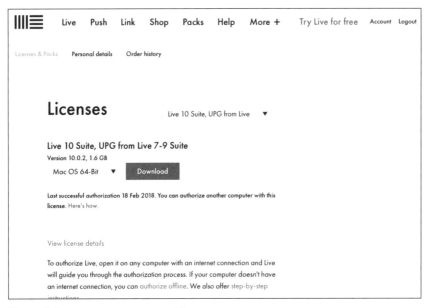

Figure 2.3 The Account page on Ableton.com

3. Generally, the most recent Ableton Live installer is shown by default. If necessary, you can click on the pop-up menu next to Licenses and choose an alternate version of Ableton Live.

Licenses

Live 10 Suite, UPG from Live   ▼

Live 10 Suite, UPG from Live 7-9 Suite
Version 10.0.2, 1.6 GB

Mac OS 64-Bit   ▼   Download

Figure 2.4 Viewing the available installers in your account

4.   Choose the appropriate operating system for your computer (Mac or Windows), and click on the **Download** button to download the installer.

Included Devices and Packs

Devices are special-purpose software components that provide additional signal processing and other functionality within Ableton Live. Ableton devices come in three varieties: instruments, audio effects, and MIDI effects.

 Other digital audio workstation software such as Pro Tools, Logic Pro X, and Cubase use the term *plug-in* for the processors used on a track. Ableton uses the term *device* to describe the built-in processors included with Live, and the term *plug-in* to describe optional third-party processors in VST or AU format.

Ableton Live Intro comes with a small set of Ableton devices. Ableton Live Standard adds an instrument and a variety of audio effects. Ableton Live Suite comes with the full complement of Ableton devices and also includes Max for Live.

Audio & MIDI Effects Devices

Ableton audio effects devices include a standard assortment of EQ, dynamics, reverb, delay, modulation, and harmonic effects, and many more specialized devices that can be used to create unique and exotic results. While Live Intro offers just the essentials, more than 46 audio effects are included in Ableton Suite!

Ableton MIDI effects devices are also quite varied and include arpeggiation, chord creation, velocity and pitch manipulation, and several more. The audio and MIDI effects devices installed with Ableton Live are described in Appendix A, "Ableton Live Audio and MIDI Effects."

Instrument Devices

Ableton instrument devices are a collection of virtual instruments that use a MIDI input to create sound. Live Intro offers a basic set of instruments, including percussion devices (Drum Rack and Impulse), a basic sampler (Simpler), and a device for organizing and controlling instruments (Instrument Rack). Live Standard offers the same set and adds the External Instrument device that can be used to integrate hardware synthesizers or drum machines into your setup.

Live Suite includes all of Ableton's instrument devices. In addition to those mentioned above, this set includes an analog synth (Analog), an FM and additive synth (Operator), a wavetable synth (Wavetable), a full-featured sampler (Sampler), and many more.

A description of the included instrument devices is provided in Appendix B, "Ableton Live Software Instruments."

Installing Additional Packs

Depending on the edition of Ableton Live that you have purchased, you may be entitled to additional devices and content that are not automatically installed. Ableton builds these additional items into "Packs" that can be installed manually or through the Ableton Live application (Ableton Live 10 and later only).

Installing Packs Manually

For all versions of Ableton Live, you can go to Ableton.com and download packs to manually install.

To access the installers for Ableton Live packs, do the following:

1.   Go to Ableton.com and log in to your account.

2.   Click on the **ACCOUNT** link in the upper right corner of the webpage.

3.   Scroll down past the Ableton Live application installers until you see Packs. Click the link to the right to see all available packs (**ALL**) or only the packs that you have not previously downloaded (**NOT YET DOWNLOADED**).

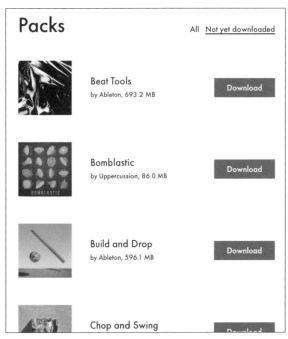

Figure 2.5 Viewing available packs in an Ableton user account

4.   Click on the **DOWNLOAD** link to download a specific pack.

5.   Once the pack has downloaded, double-click on the installer. The Ableton Live application will automatically install the pack on your computer.

Installing Packs in the Ableton Live Application

Users running Ableton Live 10 and later have the ability to download and install packs directly from inside of the Ableton Live application.

To download and install packs inside the Ableton Live application:

1. Verify that the Show Downloadable Packs preference is enabled:

    *   Choose **LIVE > PREFERENCES** (Mac) or **OPTIONS > PREFERENCES** (Windows) to open the Preferences window.

    *   Click on the **LIBRARY** tab on the left side of the window.

    *   Set Show Downloadable Packs to On by clicking on the toggle display.

2. Close the Preferences window.

3. Make sure that the Ableton Live Browser is displayed (**VIEW > SHOW BROWSER**).

  The Browser is discussed in detail in Chapter 5 of this book.

4. Click on **PACKS** under the Places section in the Browser sidebar. The display will switch to show the packs that are available to download and install.

5. Click the triangle next to Available Packs at the top of the content pane (the **NAME** column) to see the packs that are available in your account. (See Figure 2.6 on page 31.)

6. Click the download arrow next to the desired pack. The pack installer will begin downloading to your computer.

    Once the pack has downloaded, the **INSTALL** button will appear.

7. Click **INSTALL** to automatically install the pack on your computer.

Sidebar   Content Pane

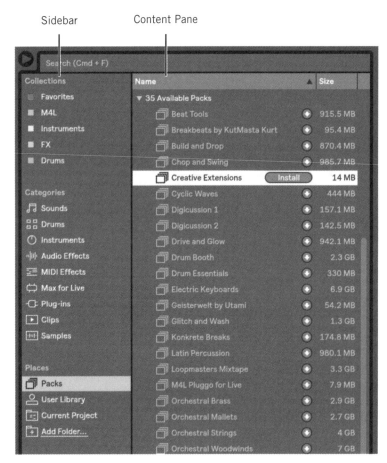

Figure 2.6 Viewing available packs in the Ableton Live application

Ableton Edition Comparison

As mentioned in Chapter 1, Ableton provides three separate *editions* of the Ableton Live application: Live Intro/Lite, Live Standard, and Live Suite. Each edition offers a different feature set, with the Intro edition offering a limited feature set, the Standard edition offering the full set of key features but a limited number of devices, and the Suite edition adding the full collection of Ableton devices, including Max for Live.

For most users, the major limitation of Ableton Live Intro will be its limit of 16 audio and MIDI tracks. The smaller collection of devices in Intro can also be a limiting factor, but many users will opt to purchase third-party plug-ins from manufacturers such as Native Instruments and others, so they may not require the Ableton devices. Note that Ableton Live Intro does support video import and export.

Both Ableton Live Standard and Ableton Live Suite support an unlimited number of audio and MIDI tracks. The major difference here is the number of included devices and access to Max for Live. The impact these additional features will have on your personal production workflow will depend on your collection of third-party plug-ins. Additionally, Ableton Live Standard and Suite can import movies in Apple QuickTime format (.mov) to be used as video clips, making these editions ideal for scoring and sound design for picture. Be sure to consider your long-term goals before committing to a particular edition of Ableton Live.

Table 2.1 below summarizes the features included in each edition of Live.

Table 2.1 Ableton Live Editions

Edition:	Intro/Lite	Standard	Suite
Key Features	Limited	Full	Full
Audio & MIDI Tracks	16	Unlimited	Unlimited
Send & Return Tracks	2	12	12
Software Instruments	4	5	15
Audio Effects	21 (Intro)/12 (Lite)	34	46
MIDI Effects	8	8	16
Mono Audio Inputs	8	256	256
Mono Audio Outputs	8	256	256
Sounds	5+ GB	10+ GB	70+ GB
Scenes	8	Unlimited	Unlimited
Video Support	No	Yes	Yes

Ableton Live File Structure

With all of the software components properly installed, you will likely be anxious to launch Ableton Live and get to work. But before you create your first Ableton Live document, or *Set*, it is helpful to understand how the software interacts with the various files that are related to the Set. Rather than storing a Set as a single file, Ableton Live stores various Set components separately and maintains a roadmap to the files it uses in a Set file. All of the files used for a project are grouped together in a *project folder*.

Additional information on creating Ableton Live Sets is provided in Chapter 4.

File Organization

When you create an Ableton Live Set, the system sets up a standard hierarchy for the Set and its associated files by automatically creating a top-level project folder. This folder contains the Ableton Live Set file (*filename.als*) as well as subfolders for various supplemental files used for the Set. (See Figure 2.7.) When you record, convert, import, or edit material, specific files will appear in each of these subfolders.

Ableton Project   Backup   My First Set.als   Samples
Info

Figure 2.7 *Ableton Live project folder hierarchy*

Ableton Live keeps related files together in this hierarchy to facilitate backups of Sets and transfers between computers.

Project Components

The types of files that Ableton Live generates and stores in each folder in the hierarchy are described in the following sections. Ableton Live creates many of these files automatically as you work on a project, although some are generated by export operations only.

Ableton Live Set

A *Set* is the document that Ableton Live creates when you start a new project. Ableton Live creates this file (along with various subfolders) inside a project folder of the same name. Set files created in Ableton Live are recognizable by their *.als* extensions.

The Set file contains a map of all the tracks, audio files, video files, settings, and edits associated with your project. Set documents can be saved and reopened, recalling a given project with all of its edit information, input/output assignments, and links to the associated media files. You can easily copy and rename Set documents, allowing you to save alternate versions of a project without changing the source audio.

Ableton Project Info Folder

Each Ableton Live Set you create will also have an associated *Ableton Project Info* folder created inside the project folder. This folder houses a configuration file that contains important project information and uses a *.cfg* extension. You will not need to modify this file when working with Ableton Live.

Backup Folder

Ableton Live will automatically create a Backup folder when you first save a Set. This folder will contain the 10 most recent prior saves of the Set.

 Backups are enabled in Ableton Live by default. There is no way to disable this feature or change the frequency or number of backups.

Samples Folder

The Samples folder is where imported and recorded audio clips are saved while working with Ableton Live. You may not see the Samples folder when you first create a new Set. This folder is created only when you record audio or you collect files for export.

When you record audio into an unsaved Ableton Live Set, each recording is initially stored in a Temp Project folder. Once the Set is saved, the files are moved from the temporary location to a folder inside the Samples folder titled Recorded.

 You can change the location of the Temp folder using the File/Folder tab of the Live Preferences window.

Ableton Live natively supports audio files in either the WAV or AIFF format. For compatibility purposes, WAV is typically the best choice on both Mac and Windows systems.

 Audio that you record in Ableton Live is saved *only* in the Samples/Recorded folder; it is not saved in the Set file (.als). When transferring projects between systems, be sure to copy over the entire top-level project folder in order to include all associated audio files and other material needed for the project.

When you import audio or video files into Ableton Live, the imported files are not automatically copied to the Samples folder. Instead, Ableton Live will simply play the files from their original location on your computer's hard drive. If you use the FILE > COLLECT ALL AND SAVE command, Ableton Live will create a folder inside the Samples folder titled Imported and will copy the imported files to that location.

 It's a good idea to use COLLECT ALL AND SAVE when you finish an Ableton Live project to ensure that all of the associated media files are in the project folder. This makes it easy to archive the project and open it again at a later date.

MIDI Files

MIDI data is normally stored within the Ableton Live Set; as such, no MIDI files will exist outside of the Set document. However, MIDI files can be exported from Ableton Live using the FILE > EXPORT MIDI CLIP command. Exported MIDI files can be recognized by their *.mid* extensions.

Starting Ableton Live

Because Ableton Live systems are often comprised of both hardware and software, preparing your system for use might involve more than simply turning on your computer and launching the Ableton Live application. The larger the system, the more important it becomes to follow a specific startup sequence.

Powering Up Your Hardware

When starting a computer–based audio system, it's important to power up the system components in the proper order. Starting components out of sequence could cause a component to not be recognized, prevent the software from launching, or cause unexpected behavior.

The recommended sequence for starting any computer–based audio system is as follows:

1. Start with all your equipment (including your computer) powered off.

2. Turn on any external hard drives that require external power and wait about 10 seconds for them to spin up to speed.

3. Turn on any MIDI interfaces and MIDI devices that require external power (including any MIDI control surfaces) as well as any synchronization peripherals, if used.

4. Turn on your audio interface (if not bus powered). Wait at least 15 seconds for the audio interface to initialize.

5. Start your computer and launch Ableton Live.

6. Turn on your audio monitoring system, if applicable.

> (i)   Many audio interfaces get their power from the computer (via a USB port or other connection); these interfaces do not need to be powered up in advance.

Launching Ableton Live

Ableton Live software can be launched by double-clicking on the application icon on the system's internal drive or by double-clicking on a shortcut to the application. On Windows systems, the Ableton Live application is typically installed under C:\Program Files\Ableton\Ableton Live\AbletonLive10.exe, and a shortcut is placed on the desktop. On the Mac, Ableton Live is typically placed under Applications\Ableton Live 10.app, and an application shortcut is placed in the dock.

Figure 2.8 The Ableton Live application icon

On Windows systems, Ableton Live may also be available from the Start menu at the lower-left corner of the display.

When you first launch Ableton Live, the application will prompt you for authorization.

Authorizing Live

Ableton Live software uses copy protection, as do many other software products and plug-ins. The Ableton Live license is intended for a single user. However, Ableton permit you to install the Live application on up to two computers belonging to the registered user.

The first time you launch Ableton Live, an authorization dialog box will appear (Figure 2.9). At this point, you must choose one of three options:

- Authorize with ableton.com

- No Internet on this computer

- Authorize later

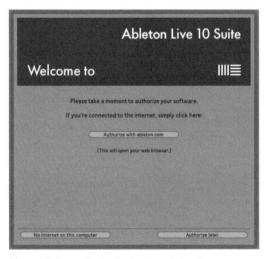

Figure 2.9 Live's Authorization dialog box

Authorize with Ableton.com

If your computer has Internet access, you can quickly authorize Ableton Live with Ableton.com.

To authorize Ableton Live with Ableton.com, do the following:

1. Choose **AUTHORIZE WITH ABLETON.COM** from the authorization dialog box; your computer will automatically open a browser and take you to the Ableton website.

2. Log into your Ableton.com account. You'll be asked to select the license that you would like to authorize.

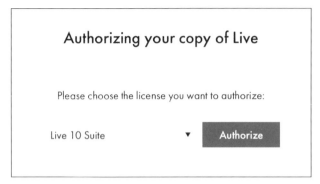

Figure 2.10 Selecting the license to authorize from your Ableton.com account

3. Assuming you have already registered Ableton Live using a registration code (see "Registering Your Software" earlier in this chapter), choose the appropriate license from the Licenses list and click the **AUTHORIZE** button. Ableton.com will send an authorization to your computer.

   This may take few seconds, during which time you will see a progress bar near the bottom of the authorization dialog box.

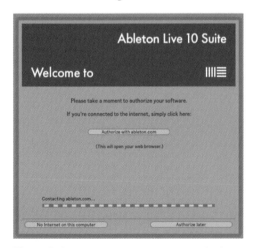

Figure 2.11 The progress bar in the Authorization dialog box

4. Once the authorization is complete, you will get a confirmation message. (See Figure 2.12.) Click **OK** to begin using Ableton Live!

Figure 2.12 The authorization confirmation message

Authorizing Offline

If you have no Internet access on your computer, or have difficulty authoring using the Authorize with albeton.com option, you can authorize offline.

To authorize Ableton Live offline, do the following:

1. Choose **NO INTERNET ON THIS COMPUTER** in the authorization dialog box. The offline authorization dialog box will appear.

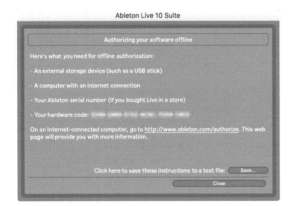

Figure 2.13 The offline authorization dialog box

2. Note the hardware code or save it to a text file by clicking the **SAVE** button.

3. On a computer with Internet access, log into your Ableton.com account.

4. Click the **ACCOUNT** link in the upper right corner of the website.

5. Select the appropriate license from the Licenses list and then click the **AUTHORIZE OFFLINE** link. This will take you to the Authorize Offline page.

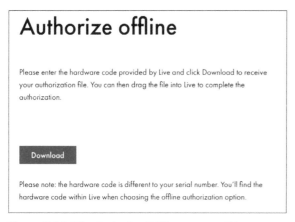

Figure 2.14 The Authorize Offline page on Ableton.com

6. Enter your hardware code and click the **DOWNLOAD** button. Ableton.com will generate an authorization file (.auz), and the file will download to your computer.

7. Transfer the .auz file to the computer that you wish to authorize.

8. Double-click the .auz file (or drag and drop it onto the Authorization dialog box) to complete the authorization process.

Authorize Later

If you choose the **AUTHORIZE LATER** option from the Authorization dialog box, Ableton Live will still launch, but saving and exporting will be disabled until you complete the authorization process.

Accessing Connected Audio Devices

When Ableton Live launches, it will generally be configured to use the default audio device on your computer. If no supported audio device is found, Ableton Live will launch with the audio engine turned off. You can immediately recognize that the audio engine is off because the **CPU LOAD METER** at the far right of the toolbar will turn red and display the word OFF.

Figure 2.15 The CPU Load Meter when the Audio Engine is off

To configure Ableton Live to use a specific audio device, such as a connected USB microphone or a separate audio interface, you will need to go to the **AUDIO** tab on the left side of the Live Preferences window (**LIVE > PREFERENCES** [Mac] or **OPTIONS > PREFERENCES** [Windows]).

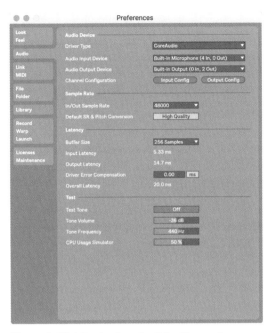

Figure 2.16 The Audio tab of the Live preferences

> If your supported audio interface is connected but not recognized by Ableton Live, you may need to install or update the device drivers. Check the manufacturer's website for the latest drivers for your interface.

Optimizing Ableton Live Performance

The **AUDIO** tab of the Live Preferences window is also used to optimize the performance of the software. Like most audio software, Ableton Live utilizes the computer's processing capacity to carry out operations such as recording, playback, mixing, and plug-in processing (virtual instruments and effects). You can monitor the current CPU usage at any time using the CPU Load Meter in the upper right corner of the toolbar.

Figure 2.16 The CPU Load Meter showing 7% usage

While the default system settings are adequate in some scenarios, Ableton Live lets you adjust a system's performance using the Sample Rate and Latency settings in the Audio tab of the Preferences window.

Sample Rate Settings

The Sample Rate setting will affect the quality of the audio that is going into or out of your system through a connected audio interface. The Sample Rate setting will also determine the sample rate of audio files that result from recording on an audio track.

A higher sample rate requires more processing power than a lower sample rate, and will reduce the number of tracks and plug-ins you can run on a particular computer. For this reason, many producers prefer to work with sample rates of 44,100 and 48,000. While high-definition sample rates (such as 88,200 and 96,000) will result in better fidelity in the studio, they don't necessarily translate to better quality in final mixes that are distributed as MP3 files or streamed on services such as SoundCloud or Spotify.

 Refer to the "Audio Basics: Waveform, Frequency, and Amplitude" section in Chapter 1 for details on how the sample rate affects audio quality.

Latency Settings

The Buffer Size setting in the Audio tab of the Preferences dialog box controls the size of the hardware buffer. This buffer handles processing tasks such as plug-in processing.

- Lower Buffer Size settings reduce monitoring latency when you are recording or monitoring an active input.

- Higher Buffer Size settings provide more processing power at the expense of greater monitoring latency.

As a general rule, the Buffer Size should be set as low as your project will allow, in order to minimize latency when monitoring an active input. You may need to change the setting later as your project becomes more complex.

Reducing Latency on Tracks with an Active Input

Ableton Live offers an additional option for reducing latency on tracks with an active input. By activating **Options > Reduced Latency when Monitoring**, any track with an input set to **In** or **Auto** will have the smallest possible amount of latency given the current configuration of the Audio Engine. However these tracks may be out of sync with other tracks in your set, such as Return tracks.

 Enabling this setting turns off delay compensation for input-monitored tracks.

Modifying Performance Settings

Adjustments to the Sample Rate and Latency settings can be made in the in the Audio tab of the Preferences window, as follows:

1. Choose **LIVE > PREFERENCES** (Mac) or **OPTIONS > PREFERENCES** (Windows).

2. Select the **AUDIO** tab.

3. From the Sample Rate section, click the **IN/OUT SAMPLE RATE** pop-up menu and choose the desired sample rate.

4. From the Latency section, click the **BUFFER SIZE** pop-up menu and select the buffer size in samples—lower the setting to reduce latency; raise it to increase processing power for plug-ins.

5. Click **OK**.

The Ableton Live Menu Structure

Before beginning to work on an Ableton Live Set, you should have some basic familiarity with the software interface, including the menu structure and views.

Among the first things you see upon launching Ableton Live is the menu system across the top of the screen. Learning how the menus are organized will save you a lot of time when you are trying to find a specific Ableton Live function. Following is a brief description of each menu.

File Menu

File menu commands let you create and maintain Ableton Live Sets and perform other file-based commands. The File menu includes options for opening, creating, and saving Sets; exporting audio, video, and MIDI; installing packs; and managing files.

Edit Menu

Edit menu commands allow you to edit and manipulate the media in your current selection. The Edit menu includes options for cutting, copying, and pasting; duplicating, deleting, and renaming; splitting, consolidating, freezing, and quantizing; and performing similar operations.

Create Menu

Create menu commands generally result in the creation of new tracks in Ableton Live. The Create menu includes options for inserting Audio, MIDI, and Return tracks; processing audio and MIDI data to new tracks; inserting scenes; and importing audio files.

View Menu

View menu commands affect the display within Ableton Live windows and tracks. Most View menu commands show or hide parts of the main Ableton Live windows. Selecting a command will display a component part of a window, and deselecting the command will hide it. Zoom commands are also included in the View menu.

Options Menu

The Options menu commands let you toggle several editing, recording, monitoring, playback, and display options on/off. From this menu, you can define MIDI and key mapping, enable delay compensation, adjust launch quantization, change the solo mode, set the time ruler format, and make other similar choices.

 The Options menu displays independent functions that toggle on or off. Menu items with a check mark next to them are currently on, or enabled; items without a check mark are off, or disabled. Selecting an item toggles its state on/off.

Help Menu

The Help menu allows you to show or hide the Help View and provides links to important documentation and online resources, including the Ableton Live Manual, the Ableton User Forum, and your Abeton.com account. You can also check for Ableton Live updates from this menu.

Ableton Live Views and Sections

Ableton Live software displays either one or two main windows, depending on your settings (**VIEW > SECOND WINDOW**). Within these windows are a number of available "views" and "sections" that are used to accomplish various tasks.

The primary components that you will need to be familiar with to begin working with Ableton Live include the following:

- The Control Bar at the top of the window(s)

- The two main views: the Session View and the Arrangement View

- The two optional displays: the Browser display and the Detail View.

In addition, the Detail View features two separate view options: the Device View and the Clip View.

 The Browser display and Detail View can be shown or hidden separately in the Session View and the Arrangement View.

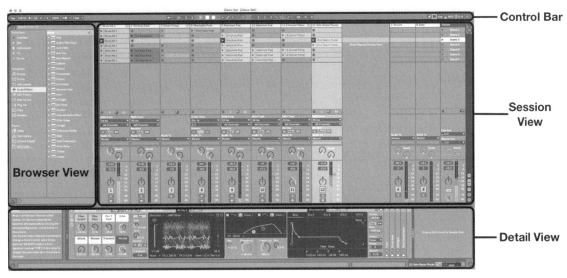

Figure 2.18 The Control Bar (top), Browser (left), Session View (right), and Detail View (bottom; Device View shown)

Session View

The Session View is the view that sets Ableton Live apart from most audio software. When the first version of Ableton Live was released in 2001, it was the Session View that caught the attention of music producers around the world. There was nothing else like it!

The Session View provides a number of controls grouped into sections. Several of these sections, such as the Clips Slots section and the Scenes section, are unique to the Session View. Other sections, such as the In/Out, Sends, and Mixer sections, can also be found in the Arrangement View.

Clip Slots Section

The Clips Slots section of the Session View offers a collection of slots into which audio and MIDI clips can be placed. When a clip is played (or "launched") from a Clip Slot, the signal from the audio clip or MIDI instrument plays through the signal path comprised of the track sections that follow it (see below).

1 Drum Kit 1	2 Oxi Bass Rack	3 Wavetable Pads	4 Sidechain Pad	5 Sidechain Pad	6 A Hornet Pillow	7 Velo-Rezzo Plucks
▶ Drum Kit 1		▶ Wavetable Pads				
▶ Drum Kit 1	▶ Oxi Bass Rack		▶ Sidechain Pad		▶ A Hornet Pillow	
▶ Drum Kit 1			▶ Sidechain Pad			▶ Velo-Rezzo Plucks
▶ Drum Kit 1			▶ Sidechain Pad			▶ Velo-Rezzo Plucks
▶ Drum Kit 1	▶ Oxi Bass Rack		▶ Sidechain Pad	▶ Sidechain Pad	▶ A Hornet Pillow	
▶ Drum Kit 1	▶ Oxi Bass Rack		▶ Sidechain Pad	▶ Sidechain Pad	▶ A Hornet Pillow	
▶ Drum Kit 1	▶ Oxi Bass Rack		▶ Sidechain Pad	▶ Sidechain Pad		

Figure 2.19 Clip Slots section of the Session View

Scenes Section

The Scenes section of the Session View is displayed on the Master track and allows you to launch an entire row of clips (a "scene") all at once. Scenes are typically used to navigate through sections of a single song (verse, chorus, etc.) during production, or to move between complete songs during performance.

Figure 2.20 Scenes section of the Session View

In/Out Section

The top portion of each channel strip in the Session View provides controls for routing signals for the track. Depending on the type of track, these controls may include Audio Input and Output selectors, MIDI Input and Output selectors, and Monitor controls.

Audio Input and Output selectors are used to route input and output signals from your audio interface for recording or playback. MIDI Input and Output selectors are used to route MIDI data from MIDI controllers to either instrument plug-ins or external MIDI hardware. The Monitor controls determine whether you will hear the live track input or playback of an existing clip on a given track. The Monitor controls can generally be left on the **AUTO** setting, which will automatically switch from monitoring live input when a track is recording (or record-armed in stop) to monitoring clip playback when the track is in play.

Figure 2.21 The In/Out section of the Session View

Mixer Section

The Mixer section of the Session View provides a mixer-like environment for working with tracks. In the Mixer section, tracks appear as mixer strips (also called *channel strips*). Each track displayed in the Mixer section has controls for panning and volume. The Mixer section also provides buttons for enabling record, activating/deactivating tracks, and toggling solo on and off.

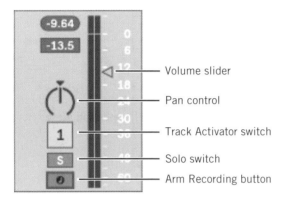

Volume slider

Pan control

Track Activator switch

Solo switch

Arm Recording button

Figure 2.22 The Mixer section of the Session View

The Pan controls can be used to position the output of a track within a stereo field. The Track Activator, Solo, and Arm Recording buttons can be used for mute, solo, and record arm functions, respectively, during record and playback. The Volume slider can be used to adjust the playback/monitoring level of a track.

  The Volume slider in the Mixer Section does not affect the input gain (record level) of a signal being recorded. The signal level must be set appropriately at the source or adjusted using a preamp or gain-equipped audio interface.

Additional Session View Sections

Other Session View sections include the Sends Section, Returns Section, Delay Section, and X-Fade Section. These are discussed in more detail in later chapters.

Arrangement View

The Arrangement View provides a timeline display of audio, MIDI data, video, and mixer automation for recording, editing, and arranging tracks. This view displays waveforms for audio clips and MIDI note data for MIDI clips.

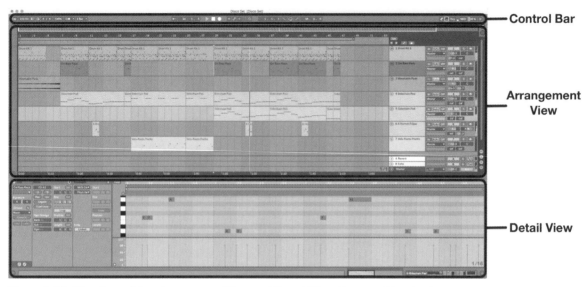

Figure 2.23 The Control Bar, Arrangement View, and Detail View (showing Clip View)

Each Audio and MIDI track in the Arrangement View features some of the same track sections as the Session View, including the In/Out section and Mixer section.

You can toggle between the Session View and Arrangement View at any time by pressing the TAB key.

The Browser

The Browser can be displayed on the left–hand side of the main window. It can be accessed when either the Session View or Arrangement View is active.

The Browser is used to locate clips, samples, instruments, audio and MIDI effects, plug-ins, and Max for Live devices. The Browser is also used to access and install Ableton Packs (in Ableton Live 10 or later), to browse through user settings and current project files, and to quickly access folders located anywhere on your computer.

To display the Browser, choose VIEW > SHOW BROWSER in either the Session View or the Arrangement View.

The Browser display is divided into two sections, with the sidebar on the left and the content pane on the right. You can resize the sections by dragging the divider line horizontally.

Figure 2.24 The Ableton Live Browser display showing the sidebar (left) and content pane (right)

Detail View

The Detail View section can be displayed at the bottom of the main window. Like the Browser, the Detail View is accessible regardless of whether the Session View or Arrangement View is currently active. The Detail View section is always operating in one of two modes: Device View or Clip View.

 To toggle the Detail View section between Device View and Clip View, press
SHIFT+TAB.

Device View

When the Detail View section is set to Device View (Figure 2.25), it will display any devices inserted onto the currently selected track. These devices can include instruments, audio effects and MIDI effects, as well as Max for Live devices.

Figure 2.25 The Device View

Clip View

When the Detail View section is set to Clip View, it will display the currently selected audio clip's waveform in the Sample Editor, or the currently selected MIDI clip's data in the MIDI Note Editor. The Clip View also features several property boxes that can be used to modify various aspects of a clip.

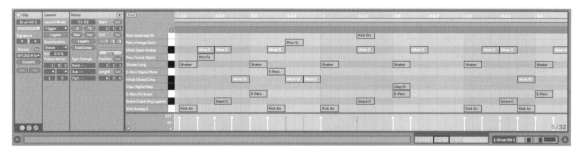

Figure 2.26 The Clip View

Info View

The Info View is an additional display that is available as part of the Detail View. When active, the Info View appears at the far left side of the Detail View. The Info View provides a brief description of any element that you position the mouse over within the Ableton Live user interface.

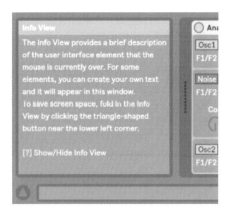

Figure 2.27 The Info View

Control Bar

Ableton Live provides a variety of controls in the Control Bar area at the top of the main window. These controls cover a wide range including tempo, time signature, and quantization settings; transport and looping controls; edit settings; keyboard and MIDI mapping; and performance indicators.

Figure 2.28 The Control Bar

Overview (Arrangement View only)

The Overview section appears just below the Control Bar in the Arrangement View. It appears as a miniature representation of all of the clips that are currently on tracks in the Arrangement View. You can click in the Overview to quickly navigate to a new position in the Set. You can also click and drag within the Overview to change the horizontal or vertical zoom level.

Figure 2.30 The Overview Arrangement View

 For details on zooming with the Overview, see "Zooming in Arrangement View" in Chapter 3 of this book.

Rulers and Scrub Area (Arrangement View only)

Rulers are horizontal strips that appear in the Arrangement View, just above and below the Track Display area. Rulers provide measurement indicators to help you identify specific locations in your Set's timeline.

Figure 2.30 The beat-time ruler and Scrub Area in the Arrangement View

- **Beat-Time Ruler.** This ruler appears above the Track Display. It will display bar numbers when zoomed out, but will also show beats and sub-beats as you zoom in.

- **Scrub Area.** The Scrub Area sits just below the beat-time ruler and performs a number of functions. You can click in the Scrub Area to start playback from a specific location. You can also set loop start and end points by dragging the left or right side of the loop brace (or by entering values into the Loop Start and Loop Length fields in the Control Bar). In addition, you can right-click in the Scrub Area to insert a time signature change or to add a Locator.

- **Time Ruler.** The Time Ruler is a secondary ruler that appears at the bottom of the Arrangement View. The user can configure this ruler to show Time (minutes:seconds), or film and video frame positions at a variety of frame rates, including 24 fps (film), 25 fps (PAL), and 29.97 fps (NTSC). This can be helpful when working with imported video clips.

Adjusting the Display of Views and Sections

Ableton Live lets you customize the display of the windows to accommodate your needs at any given point in your project.

 Either the Session View or Arrangement View must be visible at all times.

Showing/Hiding Views

You can toggle the display between Session View and Arrangement View at any time by pressing the **TAB** key. If you are displaying a second main window (**VIEW > SECOND WINDOW**), pressing Tab will swap the views in the two windows.

The secondary Ableton Live views (the Browser, Detail View, and Info View) can be shown or hidden in one of two ways.

To show or hide views, do one of the following:

- Go to the **VIEW** menu and select a view to show or and hide.

  Or

- Click the triangular Show/Hide button corresponding to the view you wish to show or hide.

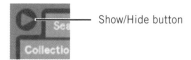 ——— Show/Hide button

Figure 2.31 The triangular Show/Hide Button for the Browser display

Showing/Hiding Sections

Sections in both Session View and Arrangement View (such as the In/Out Section and the Mixer Section) can be shown or hidden in one of two ways.

To show or hide sections, do one of the following:

- Go to the **VIEW** menu and select the section to show or hide.

■ Click the Show/Hide section buttons located in the bottom right corner of the Session View and Arrangement View.

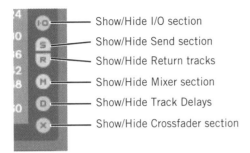

Show/Hide I/O section

Show/Hide Send section

Show/Hide Return tracks

Show/Hide Mixer section

Show/Hide Track Delays

Show/Hide Crossfader section

Figure 2.32 The Show/Hide Buttons for the sections in the Session View

Resizing Views

Several of the Ableton Live views can be resized to accommodate a particular task. These include the Browser display and the Detail View section.

To adjust the width or height of a view, follow these steps:

1. Position the mouse over the view separator where the cursor changes into a double-headed arrow.

2. Click and drag on the view separator to adjust its position as needed.

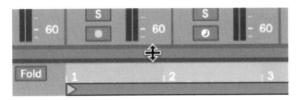

Figure 2.33 Clicking on the view separator to resize the Detail View section at the bottom of the Arrangement view

Review/Discussion Questions

1. What are some of the differences between Ableton Live editions? Which editions offer support for video playback? (See "Ableton Edition Comparison" beginning on page 30.)

2. Name some of the folders and files that Ableton Live creates as part of the project hierarchy. Where is the Live Set file (.als) stored? (See "Project Components" beginning on page 32.)

3. Where are imported and recorded audio files stored in the project hierarchy? (See "Project Components" beginning on page 32.)

4. Where are Ableton Live's MIDI files normally stored? (See "Project Components" beginning on page 32.)

5. Which component should you turn on first when powering up an Ableton Live system? Which component should you turn on last? (See "Powering Up Your Hardware" beginning on page 34.)

6. What type of processing does the Buffer Size preference affect? (See "Latency Settings" beginning on page 40.)

7. What Buffer Size setting should you choose when recording audio or MIDI? (See "Latency Settings" beginning on page 40.)

8. What kinds of commands can be found under the Ableton Live Create menu? (See "The Ableton Live Menu Structure" beginning on page 41.)

9. What kinds of commands can be found under the Ableton Live Options menu? (See "The Ableton Live Menu Structure" beginning on page 41.)

10. Which Ableton Live View provides access to the Clips Slots section for launching clips? (See "Ableton Live Views and Sections" beginning on page 42.)

11. Which main Ableton Live View provides a timeline display of audio waveforms and MIDI data on horizontal tracks? (See "Ableton Live Views and Sections" beginning on page 42.)

12. Is it possible to see Pan and Volume controls for each track in both the Session View and the Arrangement View? (See "Ableton Live Views and Sections" beginning on page 42.)

 To review additional material from this chapter and prepare for certification, see the Ableton Live 101 Study Guide module available through the Elements|ED online learning platform at ElementsED.com.

Identifying Ableton Live Views

🎧 Activity

In this exercise worksheet, you will identify the main views in Ableton Live and their component sections. The information referenced in these questions is covered in Chapter 2.

🕐 Duration

This exercise should take approximately 10 minutes to complete.

⊕ Goals/Targets

- Identify the main views in Ableton Live

- Recognize the component sections of the main Views

- Identify the two options for viewing clips in the Detail view

Instructions

Answer the questions in this exercise by filling in the blanks on the following pages or by listing your answers on a separate sheet of paper or worksheet. Be sure to use the terminology referenced in Chapter 2 as you complete this exercise.

Components of the View that Shows Clip Slots

Refer to Figure 2.34 when answering the questions below. Refer to the section on "The Ableton Live Software Interface" in Chapter 2 for assistance.

Questions 1 through 4 refer to Figure 2.34.

1. The view shown in Figure 2.34 is called the _____ view.

2. The area labeled **A** across the top of the window is called the _____.

3. The area labeled **B** on the left side of the window is called the _____.

4. The area labeled **C** is currently showing the _____ view.

Figure 2.34 The Ableton Live View that displays the Clip Slots Section

Components of the View that Shows the Timeline

Refer to Figure 2.35 when answering the questions below. Refer to the section on "The Ableton Live Software Interface" in Chapter 2 for assistance.

Questions 5 through 10 refer to Figure 2.35.

5.   The view shown in Figure 2.35 is called the _____ view.

6.   The area labeled **A** at the top of the window is called the _____.

7.   The area labeled **B** is currently showing the _____ view.

8.   The clip displayed in the area labeled B is a/an _____ clip.

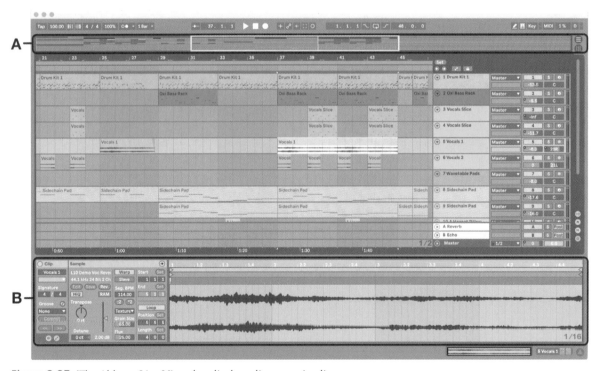

Figure 2.35 The Ableton Live View that displays clips on a timeline

Chapter 3

Ableton Live Basic Controls

This chapter provides an overview of the edit functions, zoom options, and MIDI controls used in Ableton Live's Arrangement View. It also discusses the Edit Grid available in Ableton Live, how to set the Edit Grid Value, and how to work with Rulers.

 Learning Targets for This Chapter

■ Understand how to activate playback in the Arrangement View

■ Perform typical clip editing and zooming functions in the Arrangement View

■ Configure the Edit Grid

■ Work with Rulers and the Scrub Area

■ Recognize the available performance controls

■ Understand the difference between Edit Mode and Draw Mode in the MIDI Note Editor

 Key topics from this chapter are illustrated in the Ableton Live 101 Study Guide module available through the Elements|ED online learning platform. Sign up for free at ElementsED.com.

This chapter provides an overview of the playback functions, editing controls, display options, and rulers available in the Ableton Live Arrangement View. These primary controls are used day-in and day-out in Ableton Live for recording, playback, and basic editing of audio and MIDI material. Establishing some familiarity with the available tools, operational modes, and performance control functions early on will help you in all aspects of the work you do in Ableton Live.

Playback in Arrangement View

When you first create an Ableton Live set, the Play function in the Control Bar will serve to activate playback of the state stored in the Arrangement View. However, if you activate playback of a Clip Slot or Scene in Session View for the Set, the Play function will generally switch to activate playback of the current state of the Session View instead. This may cause the media on tracks in the Arrangement View to appear dimmed (grayed out) and to not play back as expected.

When this happens, the **BACK TO ARRANGEMENT** button will light in red to indicate that one or more tracks are currently not playing the Arrangement, but are playing a clip from the Session View instead. This button is available in both the Session View and the Arrangement View.

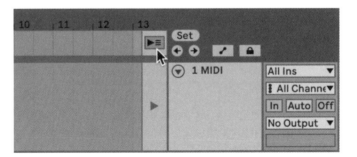

Figure 3.1 The Back to Arrangement button in the Session View (left) and in the Arrangement View (right)

To reactivate playback for the Arrangement View, click the lit **BACK TO ARRANGEMENT** button in either the Session View or the Arrangement View so that it becomes unlit (Session View) or disappears (Arrangement View).

You can also press function key F10 to activate the Back to Arrangement function for the Transport.

Clip Editing in Arrangement View

Unlike most other audio applications that require users to change tools to perform clip-editing tasks, Ableton Live has a single tool that is used for clip editing. This unified tool provides instant access for selecting, moving, and resizing clips. This tool can also be used to create fade-ins, fade-outs, and crossfades.

 Clip editing in the Session View is discussed in Chapter 6 (for MIDI clips) and Chapter 7 (for Audio clips).

Selecting a Clip

Ableton Live allows you to select an entire clip or just a portion of a clip without changing tools.

To select an entire clip:

■ Click once in the upper half of the clip, where the hand icon appears.

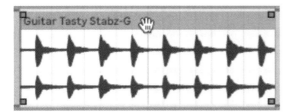

Figure 3.2 Selecting an entire clip by clicking in the upper half

To select time within a clip:

■ Click and drag (forwards or backwards) in the lower half of the clip, where the pointer icon appears.

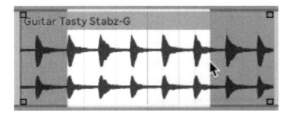

Figure 3.3 Selecting time within a clip by clicking and dragging in the lower half

Moving a Clip

As with selecting, Ableton Live allows you to move an entire clip or a selected portion of a clip without changing tools.

To move an entire clip:

- Click in the upper half of the clip and, without releasing the mouse button, drag the clip to the left or right.

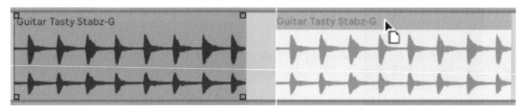

Figure 3.4 Moving an entire clip by clicking and dragging in the upper half

To move a time selection within a clip:

1. Make a time selection by clicking and dragging (forwards or backwards) in the lower half of the clip.

2. Release the mouse button.

3. Click in the upper half of the clip within the existing time selection and, without releasing the mouse button, drag the selected portion of the clip to the left or right. The selected audio will be removed from the original clip, creating a new, independent clip.

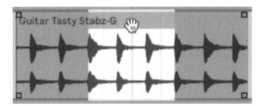

Figure 3.5 Clicking in the upper half of an existing time selection within the clip

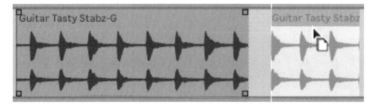

Figure 3.6 Moving the time selection

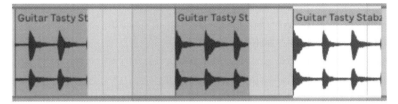

Figure 3.7 The result of moving the time selection after releasing the mouse

Dragging a clip vertically (up or down) will move the clip to another compatible track in your Set.

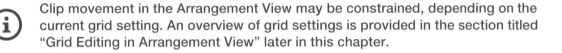

Clip movement in the Arrangement View may be constrained, depending on the current grid setting. An overview of grid settings is provided in the section titled "Grid Editing in Arrangement View" later in this chapter.

Resizing a Clip

Ableton Live offers a clip–resizing feature that can be used to adjust the clip boundaries to hide or expose underlying material. This feature can be used on audio, MIDI, and video clips. Like all clip editing in Ableton Live, resizing a clip is *nondestructive*, meaning it will leave the underlying source media file unchanged.

To resize a clip:

■ Click and drag in the upper half of the clip near the clip boundary (beginning or end), where the bracket icon appears.

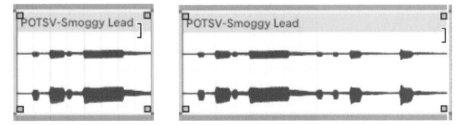

Figure 3.8 Extending the end of a clip to expose underlying material from the source file: before (left) and after (right)

Note that extending the length of a clip earlier or later can create two different outcomes:

■ If the clip has underlying material available in the source media file, the clip will extend normally.

■ If there is not sufficient additional material available, and the Loop switch is active for the clip, Ableton Live will automatically loop the clip to create the desired extension.

The Loop switch for a clip is available in the Sample box in Clip View, as discussed in Chapters 4 and 9 of this book.

Creating Fades

A *fade* is a steady volume ramp that you create on a clip boundary. Fades have many different applications, from smoothing out an edit, to creating seamless clip overlaps, to building volume fade-ins and fade-outs for music and sound effects. This section covers the process of creating simple fade-ins, fades-outs, and crossfades.

It's very easy to add fades to audio clips in Ableton Live. When you hover the cursor over an audio clip, fade controls will appear as handles in all four corners of the clip. These handles can be used to create a fade in, fade out, or crossfade.

 Fade handles may not appear at small track heights. If needed, you can adjust a track's height by clicking and dragging on its lower boundary.

As an alternative, you can also apply a fade based on an existing selection.

Applying Fades using Fade Handles

A quick way to apply fades is to use the fade handles that appear in the upper corners of audio clips.

To create a fade in or fade out using fade handles:

■ Click and drag inward on the fade handle in the upper corner of the clip. Use the fade handle at the start of the clip to create a fade-in; use the fade handle at the end of the clip to create a fade-out.

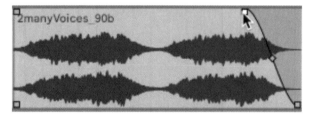

Figure 3.9 Adding a fade out to an audio clip

Applying Fades using Selections

Fade-in and fade-out effects can also be created at the beginning or ending of any audio clip using a selection that touches or crosses the clip boundary.

To create a fade from a selection, do the following:

1. Select across the beginning or ending of a clip.

2. Choose CREATE > CREATE FADE IN/OUT or press OPTION+COMMAND+F (Mac) or CTRL+ALT+F (Windows).

   The corresponding fade-in or fade-out will be created and will appear at the head or tail of the clip.

Following are some basic guidelines for creating fades using selections:

- Make your selection to match the desired fade length.

- Make a selection that touches or crosses an open clip boundary (not adjacent to another clip); selecting across adjacent clips will create a crossfade. (See "Applying Crossfades" below.)

- To create a fade-in, select from the start of the clip or before the start of the clip; to create a fade-out, select up to or across the end of the clip.

- Fade-ins always begin at the head boundary, and fade-outs always end at the tail boundary. Extending a selection into the blank area beyond a clip's boundaries will not change the clip length when the fade is applied.

Applying Crossfades

Ableton Live allows you to create crossfades between any two adjacent audio clips that have sufficient underlying audio in their parent audio files. *Crossfading* is essentially the process of overlapping two audio sources and fading out the first source while simultaneously fading in the second source. Ableton Live achieves this effect using the underlying audio on either side of the boundary between adjacent trimmed clips.

 If insufficient audio exists in the underlying clips, and the Loop switch is active for one or both clips, Ableton Live will loop the clips to extend their audio as needed to accommodate the crossfade.

To create a crossfade, do one of the following:

- Click a fade in or fade out handle and drag it across an adjacent clip's edge.

- Select a range of time that includes the boundary between two adjacent clips and choose CREATE > CREATE CROSSFADE or press OPTION+COMMAND+F (Mac) or CTRL+ALT+F (Windows) .

Fade Settings

The curve shapes determine how the amplitude of the clip's audio will change over the course of the fade.

Once a fade has been created, you can adjust the slope of the fade.

To adjust the slope of an existing fade:

■   Click and drag the slope handle that appears in the middle of the fade.

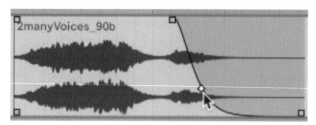

Figure 3.10 Adjusting the slope of a fade

Selecting an Area for Playback or Editing

You can use the mouse to position the insert marker or to select an area on a track for playback or editing.

To position the insert marker, click at the point where you want playback to begin. To select an area for playback or editing, click and drag across any area on one or more tracks.

You can select both horizontally and vertically, allowing you to create selections across multiple tracks in a single operation. Selected areas are represented with a white highlight in the Arrangement View. The selection range is also indicated by two small markers along the bottom of the Scrub Area, just above the Arrangement View.

Figure 3.11 Selection across multiple tracks

You can use the mouse with the Shift key to quickly make a selection, as follows:

1. Click to position the insert marker where you want the selection to start.

2. Scroll to the desired endpoint.

3. Shift-click at the desired endpoint to complete the selection.

Zooming in Arrangement View

You can use Ableton Live's zoom features to zoom into and out of a particular area within the set. Zooming in is often helpful when you need to examine a clip or waveform closely.

Figure 3.12 The beat-time ruler (bottom) and Overview area (with white highlight) of the Arrangement View

The Arrangement View provides several different ways to zoom, including using the magnifying glass icon, using the Arrangement Overview, and using keyboard shortcuts.

Zooming with the Magnifying Glass Icon

The most common technique for zooming in the Arrangement View is to use the magnifying glass icon in the beat-time ruler or the Arrangement Overview.

To zoom using the magnifying glass icon:

1. Position the mouse cursor over the beat-time ruler or the Arrangement Overview, where the magnifying glass icon appears.

2. Click and drag vertically to change the zoom level: drag down to zoom in; drag up to zoom out.

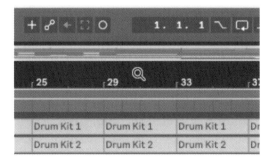

Figure 3.13 Zooming with the magnifying glass icon in the beat-time ruler

Zooming with the Arrangement Overview

The Arrangement Overview is like a "bird's eye" view of your entire set. It always shows the complete song in a miniature form. The current zoom level is indicated by a black or white box in the Arrangement Overview (depending on your chosen color theme).

To change the zoom level using the Arrangement Overview, do the following:

1. Position the mouse cursor along the left or right border of the Arrangement Overview's rectangular outline, where the bracket icon appears.

2. Click and drag the border of the outline to extend or shrink the currently visible area.

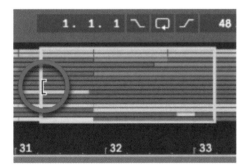

Figure 3.14 Zooming with the Arrangement Overview by dragging the start of the outline with the bracket icon

Zooming with Keyboard Shortcuts

More experienced users generally prefer to use keyboard shortcuts to zoom in the Arrangement View. Each key press zooms all tracks in by one level, with the Arrangement View centered on the insert marker.

To zoom using keyboard shortcuts:

■   Press the **+** (plus) or **−** (minus) keys on your computer's keyboard.

   Press Z to zoom the current Arrangement Time Selection to fill the screen. Press X to return to the previous zoom; press X a second time to zoom all the way out and see the complete Arrangement.

Grid Editing in Arrangement View

Ableton Live's Arrangement View features a flexible Edit Grid to assist in a number of common editing tasks. With the Edit Grid enabled, the cursor will snap to grid lines that represent a subdivision of the current song tempo. Selections, clip movements, and clip resizing operations are all constrained to the grid.

Moving and Placing Clips

Clips and MIDI notes that are moved with the Edit Grid enabled will snap to the nearest time increment using the current Edit Grid Value. The current Edit Grid Value is displayed in the lower right corner of the Arrangement View.

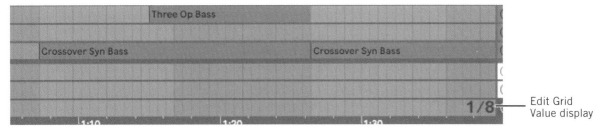

Figure 3.15 The current edit grid value (1/8 note) is visible in the bottom right corner of the Arrangement View

Regardless of the Edit Grid Value, clips can be placed anywhere on a track, so long as they start on a grid line. Clips can be positioned to overlap or cover other clips. Any underlying clips will be resized or obscured by overlapping clips.

Editing Clips

Editing Clips in the Arrangement View does not affect the timing of other clips on the same track. Deleting a clip or partial clip will leave empty space at the edit location. Pasted or duplicated material will overlap any other clips within the edit range.

Resizing a clip will trim the start or end of the clip to the nearest grid line or increment.

You can use the Edit Grid for making precise edits and aligning clips and selections using precise time intervals based on the Edit Grid Value. This is especially useful when using the Edit Grid for editing musical material that is aligned to the Set tempo.

Edit Grid Modes

Ableton Live's editing grid can be set to one of two modes: fixed grid and zoom-adaptive grid.

Fixed Grid

In fixed grid mode, selections, clip movements, and resizing operations are constrained to a specific grid value that does not change regardless of the zoom level.

Zoom-Adaptive Grid

In zoom-adaptive grid mode, selections, clip movements, and resizing operations are constrained to a grid value that changes based on the zoom level. Zooming in causes the Edit Grid to switch to progressively smaller values.

Setting the Edit Grid Mode and Value

To switch between edit grid modes and values, do one of the following:

- With no clip selected, **Right-click** in the Arrangement View and select the desired edit grid mode and value from the context menu:

  - Select an Adaptive Grid option, from Widest to Narrowest, to enable zoom-adaptive grid mode.

    The Widest setting uses grid values starting a 16 bars when fully zoomed out; the Narrowest setting uses grid values starting at 1/2 note when fully zoomed out.

  - Select a Fixed Grid option, from 8 Bars to 1/32 note, to enable fixed grid mode.

  - Select Off under Fixed Grid to disable the Edit Grid.

   Disabling the Edit Grid allows you to position clips freely anywhere within the Arrangement view, without being constrained to grid lines.

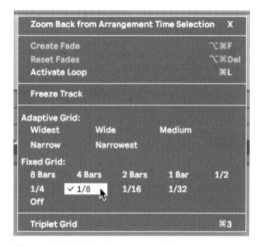

Figure 3.16 The Arrangement View context menu showing Edit Grid options

- Press **Command+5** (Mac) or **Ctrl+5** (Windows) to toggle between fixed and zoom-adaptive grid modes.

 Edit Grid settings can also be modified under the Options menu.

With the Edit Grid active, you can hold Command (Mac) or Alt (Windows) when performing editing tasks to temporarily suspend snapping to grid lines.

Time Scales and Rulers in Arrangement View

Both the Session View and Arrangement View always display the current playback position and loop/punch start and length values in dedicated fields in the Control Bar. These values are always displayed in a bars.beats.sixteenths format.

Arrangement Position

The current playback position is displayed in the Arrangement Position field. Arrangement Position locations are represented in bars, beats, and sub-beats relative to the start point of the Set.

Figure 3.17 The Arrangement Position display in the Control Bar (highlighted in red)

Loop and Punch-In Start and Length

If you're planning to loop a section of a song or to punch in for a record pass, you'll need to enter the starting position in the **LOOP START/PUNCH-IN POINT** field. You then have the option to set the loop length or the length of the punched record take using the **LOOP/PUNCH-IN REGION LENGTH** field.

Figure 3.18 The Loop/Punch Start display (left) and Length display (right) in the Control Bar

Rulers

Every Ableton Live Set features two rulers: the beat-time ruler and the time ruler.

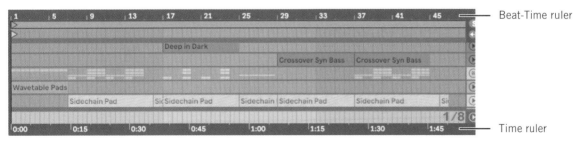

Figure 3.19 The beat-time ruler (top) and the time ruler (bottom) in the Arrangement View

Beat-Time Ruler

The beat-time ruler appears at the top of the Arrangement View and displays in a bars.beats.sixteenths format (depending on the current zoom level). This ruler is used for all transport functions including Arrangement Position, Loop and Punch-In Start and Length, and Edit Grid values.

Time Ruler

The time ruler provides additional timing reference and appears at the bottom of the Arrangement View. The time ruler can display one of several time formats:

To choose the time ruler format:

1. Right-click on the time ruler.

2. Choose the desired format from the context menu. (See Figure 3.20.)

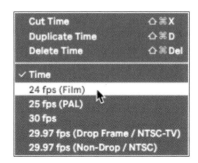

Figure 3.20 Setting the format from the time ruler's context menu

Time Ruler Display Options

Unlike the beat-time ruler, which always displays bars and beats, the time ruler format can be changed and set as needed. This can be useful for measuring the Set length in minutes and seconds, and also for referencing frame locations when producing music for film or TV. Ableton Live provides options for common film and video frame rates in frames per second (fps).

The available time ruler formats include the following:

*   Time (minutes:seconds:milliseconds)

*   24 fps (Film)

*   25 fps (PAL)

*   30 fps

*   29.97 fps (Drop Frame/NTSC TV)

*   29.97 (Non-Drop/NTSC)

> (i) A discussion of frame rates is beyond the scope of this book. However, the most important consideration here is to select the frame rate that matches the video you are using in your Set.

The Scrub Area in Arrangement View

The Scrub Area appears just below the beat-time ruler in the Arrangement View. Clicking in the Scrub Area will make playback jump to that specific location in the Set. The playback point will be quantized based on the global launch quantization value. To continuously scrub through the Set, set the global launch quantization value to **NONE** in the Quantization Menu (see "Quantization Menu" later in this chapter).

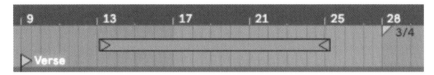

Figure 3.21 The Scrub Area with locator (left), loop brace (center), and time signature change (right).

 Although the Scrub Area appears by default, it can be disabled using the Permanent Scrub Area option in the LOOK/FEEL tab of the Ableton Live Preferences window.

 You can also jump to a playback position by holding the SHIFT key and clicking on the beat-time ruler.

Adjusting the Loop Start/Punch-In Point and Length

The Scrub Area displays a loop brace that can be used to view and modify the Loop Start/Punch-In Point and Length values.

To move the loop to a new location:

■ Click and drag the center of the loop brace, where the double-headed arrow icon appears.

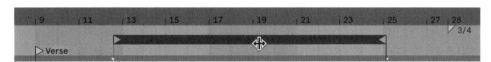

Figure 3.22 Moving the loop brace

To adjust the loop/punch start/end and length:

■ Click and drag on the left or right edge of the loop brace, where the bracket icon appears.

Figure 3.23 Adjusting the length of the loop brace

Changing the Time Signature

The Scrub Area can also be used to add and edit Time Signature changes.

To create a Time Signature Change:

1. Right-click in the Scrub Area and select **INSERT TIME SIGNATURE CHANGE** from the context menu.

2. Type in a value for the time signature, such as 3/4 or 7/8.

To delete a Time Signature Change, do one of the following:

■ Right-click anywhere in the Scrub Area and select **DELETE ALL TIME SIGNATURE CHANGES** from the context menu.

■ Right-click directly on a Time Signature Marker and select **DELETE** from the context menu.

To reposition a Time Signature Change:

■ Click directly on a Time Signature Marker and drag it to a new position.

Figure 3.24 Moving a Time Signature Marker

Using Locators

Locators provide a great way to navigate to specific locations in your set. Locators are created in the Scrub Area of the Arrangement View.

To create a locator:

1. Do one of the following:

    • Right-click in the Scrub Area and select **ADD LOCATOR** from the context menu.

    • Position the insert marker on a track at the desired location and choose **CREATE > ADD LOCATOR**.

    A new locator icon will appear in the Scrub Area, with its name field active.

2. Type a name of the locator and press **RETURN** (Mac) or **ENTER** (Windows).

To begin playback using a locator:

■ Double-click on the locator with the transport stopped.

To rename a locator:

1. Right-click on the locator and select **RENAME** from the context menu.

2. Type a new name and press **RETURN** (Mac) or **ENTER** (Windows).

To delete a locator, do one of the following:

■ Click on the locator and press the **DELETE** key.

■ Right-click on the locator and select **DELETE** from the context menu.

To reposition a locator:

■ Click on the locator and drag it to a new position.

 For information on triggering locators using the Next and Previous functions, see Chapter 8 in this book.

Performance Control Features

The Ableton Live toolbar provides access to various additional controls and options that affect playback and recording operations for the performance in your Set. Some of the available functions include the Tap Tempo button, the Tempo field, the Meter display, the Metronome button, the Metronome Settings selector, and the Quantization Menu.

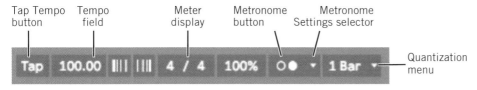

Figure 3.25 The performance controls on the left side of the toolbar

Tap Tempo Button

To set the tempo by tapping along with a performance, you can use the Tap Tempo button (labeled **TAP** in the Playback Controls). Click the mouse using successive clicks at the desired tempo. Ableton Live will display the tempo (BPM value) in the adjacent field (see below) based on your tap speed.

Tempo Field

The Tempo field displays the Set's current tempo based on the play location. You can set this value by using Tap Tempo or by entering a BPM value directly.

 The tempo of the Set affects playback speed of audio and MIDI performances as well as the spacing of bars and beats on the beat-time ruler and edit grid.

 See the section on "Setting the Tempo and Time Signature" in Chapter 6 for more information on adding tempo changes to a Set.

Meter Display

The Meter display field indicates the Set's current meter based on the play location. You can enter a meter change value directly into this field to change the Time Signature for the current section (starting at any existing Time Signature Change within the section and ending at the next Time Signature Change). This will not affect Time Signature Changes that you've added before or after the current section.

The meter determines how many beats are included in each measure on the beat-time ruler. It also affects the playback of the click sound—see "Metronome Button" below. (The click places emphasis on the first beat of every measure.)

Metronome Button

The Metronome button controls whether or not the metronome click will be audible. When the Metronome button is enabled (highlighted in orange), a metronome click will sound during playback and recording, as specified by the metronome settings.

Metronome Settings Selector

Next to the Metronome button is a down-pointing arrow button called the Metronome Settings selector. You can use this selector to set the Count-In duration and other attributes that affect the metronome click.

To modify the metronome settings:

- Click on the Metronome Settings selector and choose the desired settings from the Metronome menu.

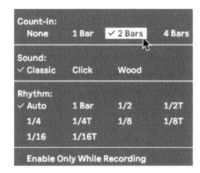

Figure 3.26 The Metronome menu

The Count-In setting determines if a click will play before playback or recording begins. You can also specify the number of bars that will be used for the count-in.

Quantization Menu

The Quantization menu to the right of the metronome controls on the toolbar is used to choose the global launch quantization setting for your Set. This sets the interval used to begin playback at a new position, such as when clicking in the Scrub Area or triggering a locator during playback.

To set the global launch quantization, do the following:

1. Click on the Quantization menu.

2. Select a quantization value from the pop-up menu, or select **NONE** from the top of the menu to disable launch quantization.

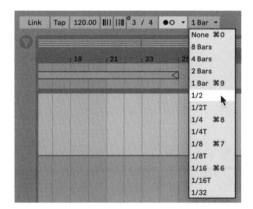

Figure 3.27 Options available in the Quantization menu

Modifying Devices and Clips

As mentioned in Chapter 2, the Detail View area is an optional display that can be shown at the bottom of the Session or Arrangement View. This area features two separate display options: the Device View and the Clip View.

Accessing Devices in Device View

When Device View is active in the Detail View area, clicking on a track's title bar will display the track's device chain at the bottom of the Session View or Arrangement View. Devices displayed here can include Live's built-in audio effects, MIDI effects, and instruments, as well as third-party plug-in devices in VST and AU format.

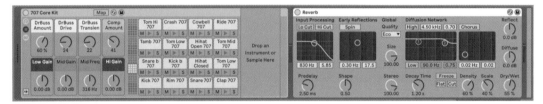

Figure 3.28 Device View shown in the Detail View area

 If Device View is not active, double-click on a track's title bar to display the Device View with the track's device chain shown.

Ableton Live's devices and third-party plug-ins are available from the Browser and can be added to tracks by dragging them from the Browser into the Device View. The Device View allows you to add, view, and delete devices and plug-ins for the selected track. This is also where you can see and adjust parameters for the devices and plug-ins used on a track.

 Additional details on devices and plug-ins are provided in Chapter 10 of this book.

Accessing Clips in Clip View

When Clip View is active in the Detail View area, selecting a clip on a track in Arrangement View or in a Clip Slot in Session View will display the clip's waveform or MIDI note arrangement in the Clip View area. The Clip View also displays the properties of the selected clip and allows you to modify clip properties.

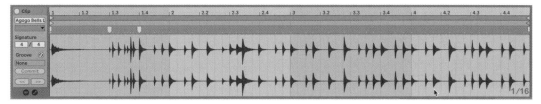

Figure 3.29 Clip View shown in the Detail View area (with an audio clip selected)

 If Clip View is not active, double-click on a clip to display the Clip View with the clip's waveform or MIDI performance shown.

MIDI clips and audio clips in Live have somewhat different Clip View controls. However, the Clip View has the following items in common for both audio and MIDI clips:

- The Clip box, which is used to adjust basic clip settings.

- The Launch box, which is used to control clip launch behavior in the Session View (available for Session View clips only).

- The Envelopes box, which is used to modulate clip, mixer, and device parameters within each clip.

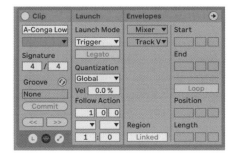

Figure 3.30 The Clip box (left), Launch box (middle), and Envelopes box (right) in the Clip View

Audio clips have some unique Clip View controls, including the following:

- The Sample box, which is used to modify the sample playback, looping, and warping behavior.

- The Sample Editor, which shows an overview of the sample and allows you to adjust Transient and Warp Marker positions.

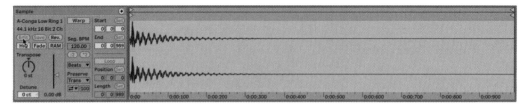

Figure 3.31 The Sample box (left) and Sample Editor (right) in the Clip View

MIDI clips also have some unique Clip View controls, including the following:

- The Notes box, which is used to modify the note arrangement and playback behavior for the clip.

- The MIDI Note Editor, which is used to edit individual MIDI notes within the clip.

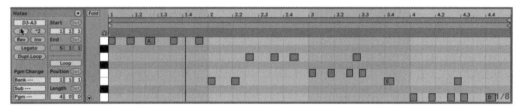

Figure 3.32 The Clip box (left) and the MIDI Note Editor (right) in the Clip View

Edit Mode Versus Draw Mode

The Ableton Live Clip View operates in Edit Mode by default; however, you can switch to Draw Mode at any time. Edit Mode is used to adjust Transient and Warp Marker positions for audio clips and to edit notes by clicking and dragging for MIDI clips. In this mode, MIDI notes can also be added or deleted by double-clicking in the MIDI Note Editor.

Draw Mode offers alternate functionality for editing MIDI notes and automation data. With Draw Mode active, you can "draw" notes in the MIDI Note Editor by clicking with the Pencil tool; you can also click and drag to draw multiple notes in succession. When working with automation, Draw Mode allows you to click and drag to draw envelope curves.

To toggle Draw Mode on/off, do one of the following:

- Click the **DRAW MODE** button in the Control Bar.

- Press the **B** key.

The Draw Mode button will be highlighted in yellow when enabled.

Figure 3.33 The Draw Mode button (yellow) in the Control Bar

Using Draw Mode to create MIDI notes or automation will create items that adhere to the current Edit Grid value.

Using the Info View

As discussed briefly in Chapter 2, the Info View is an additional display that is available within the Detail View area. It is visible in both the Session View and Arrangement View. When displayed, the Info View appears at the far left side of the Detail View. When you position the mouse pointer above an element of the Ableton Live user interface, the Detail View will display a short description of that element.

The Info View is extremely helpful for learning various aspects of the Ableton Live interface. It not only helps you to understand what a particular knob or button can do, but also helps you to learn the correct terminology for the software.

To show or hide the Info View, do one of the following:

■ Click the **SHOW/HIDE INFO VIEW** button (triangle actuator) in the bottom left corner of the Session View or Arrangement View.

■ Select **VIEW > INFO** from the main menus.

■ Press **SHIFT+?** (question mark) on your computer keyboard.

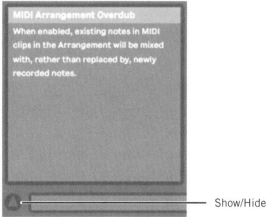

Show/Hide Info View button

Figure 3.34 The Info View with the Show/Hide button visible at the bottom left

Review/Discussion Questions

1. Which part of a clip must be clicked to select the entire clip? Which part of a clip must be clicked to select a portion of a clip? (See "Selecting a Clip" beginning on page 59.)

2. How can you move a portion of a clip, separating it from the underlying clip? (See "Moving a Clip" beginning on page 59.)

3. Where must you click in a clip to resize the clip beginning or end? (See "Resizing a Clip" beginning on page 61.)

4. What are the two ways that fades can be applied at the beginning or end of a clip? (See "Creating Fades" beginning on page 62.)

5. How can you adjust the slope of a fade or crossfade? (See "Fade Settings" beginning on page 63.)

6. Which key on the computer keyboard can be used to quickly make a lengthy selection for playback or editing? (See "Selecting an Area for Playback or Editing" beginning on page 64.)

7. What are some ways that you can zoom in the Arrangement View? (See "Zooming in Arrangement View" beginning on page 65.)

8. Will editing clips on a track in the Arrangement View affect the other clips on the track? (See "Editing Clips" beginning on page 67.)

9. What are the two Edit Grid Modes in Ableton Live? How can you set the Edit Grid Mode and Value? (See "Edit Grid Modes" beginning on page 67.)

10. What two rulers are available in the Arrangement View? Is it possible to change the time format for both rulers? (See "Rulers" beginning on page 69.)

11. What happens when you click in the Scrub Area at the top of the Arrangement View? (See "The Scrub Area in Arrangement" beginning on page 71.)

12. What are some ways to set the Tempo of your Set? (See "Performance Control Features" beginning on page 73.)

 To review additional material from this chapter and prepare for certification, see the Ableton Live 101 Study Guide module available through the Elements|ED online learning platform at ElementsED.com.

Identifying Primary Tools and Controls

🎧 Activity

In this exercise worksheet, you will identify various Ableton Live controls. The information referenced in these questions is covered in Chapter 3.

🕐 Duration

This exercise should take approximately 10 minutes to complete.

⊕ Goals/Targets

- Identify components of the Control Bar
- Identify proper names for performance control options

Instructions

Answer the questions in this exercise by filling in the blanks on the following pages or by listing your answers on a separate sheet of paper or worksheet. Be sure to use the terminology referenced in Chapter 3 as you complete this exercise.

Control Bar Fields

See the section on "Time Scales and Rulers in Arrangement View" in Chapter 3 for assistance with the questions below.

Question 1 refers to Figure 3.35.

1.   The item labeled **A** in Figure 3.35 is called the _____ field.

Figure 3.35 Fields available in the Control Bar

Questions 2 and 3 refer to Figure 3.36.

2.   The item labeled **A** in Figure 3.36 is called the _____ field.

3.   The item labeled **B** in Figure 3.36 is called the _____ field.

Figure 3.36 The Looping Controls in the Control Bar

Performance Controls

Refer to the section on "Performance Control Features" in Chapter 3 for assistance with the questions below.

Questions 4 through 7 refer to Figure 3.37.

4.   The item labeled **A** in Figure 3.37 is called the _____ button.

5.   The item labeled **B** in Figure 3.37 is called the _____ field.

6.   The item labeled **C** in Figure 3.37 is called the _____ field.

7.   The item labeled **D** in Figure 3.37 is called the _____ button.

Figure 3.37 The performance controls in the Control Bar

Chapter 4

Creating Your First Live Set

This chapter covers the basics of working with Ableton Live. It introduces configuration options, playback and navigation controls, and project saving and opening operations.

⊕ Learning Targets for This Chapter

- Choose appropriate preferences for Live

- Create a new Live Set

- Create and name Audio and MIDI tracks

- Navigate your Live Set for playback and editing

- Save, locate, and open Live Sets

- Recognize the difference between a Live Set and a Live project

 Key topics from this chapter are illustrated in the Ableton Live 101 Study Guide module available through the Elements|ED online learning platform. Sign up for free at ElementsED.com.

Before you can begin working with audio or MIDI in Ableton Live, you need to have a Live Set open. This chapter covers the basics of creating Live Sets and Live projects, adding tracks to your Live Set, using basic navigation for your tracks, and saving and re-opening your work.

Creating and Configuring a Live Set

The first time you open Ableton Live, you are greeted with a pre-created Live Set that demonstrates some of the software's capabilities and features. While you are welcome to explore and edit the demo project, this chapter will guide you through creating a new blank Live Set, which will serve as a fresh starting point for expressing your creativity.

To create a new Live Set, do one of the following:

■ Launch Ableton Live, if it's not already running. Live will open a new untitled Set whenever the software launches.

■ Choose FILE > NEW LIVE SET, if Ableton Live is already running with another Set open.

Configuring Live's Audio Preferences

Before you start creating in your new Live Set, it is recommended that you configure several important Ableton Live preference settings. These settings include selecting the audio device you will use with Live and choosing the sample rate, file format, and bit depth for your audio. Audio preferences apply to Ableton Live as a whole: once you have configured your audio preferences, Live will use them for any and all projects you create or open in the future. If your audio needs or hardware devices change, you can modify your preference settings at that point.

To view Ableton Live preferences, do one of the following:

■ Choose LIVE > PREFERENCES (Mac) or OPTIONS > PREFERENCES (Windows).

■ Press COMMAND+, (comma) on Mac or CTRL+, (comma) on Windows.

The Live Preferences window will display. (See Figure 4.1.)

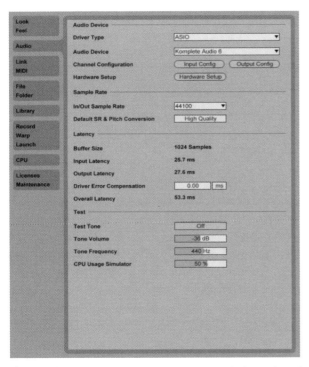

Figure 4.1 The Live Preferences window, with the Audio tab selected

Audio Device and Sample Rate Settings

The **AUDIO** tab in the Preferences window allows you to select an audio device, whether it's a dedicated hardware device or your computer's built-in audio driver, to use in conjunction with Live. You can also use this tab to set the sample rate to use for your Live Sets.

Selecting an Audio Device

To get started recording and playing back through an audio interface, you'll need to select a **DRIVER TYPE**, which allows Ableton Live to recognize and communicate with the interface. The options available to you will depend on the audio hardware drivers installed on your system. On Mac-based systems, you can select **CORE AUDIO** to use the built-in audio capabilities of your computer. Many audio interface options from third-party manufacturers are also Core Audio-compliant. Other interfaces may require that you download and install a specific driver.

 Consult your audio device manual or the manufacturer's website for information on the required drivers.

If you have a compatible audio interface connected to your computer, you can select it from the **AUDIO INPUT DEVICE** and **AUDIO OUTPUT DEVICE** dropdown menus. Once you've selected your device, you can use the **INPUT CONFIG** and **OUTPUT CONFIG** buttons to choose the hardware inputs and outputs that will be available for use in Ableton Live tracks. Click the **HARDWARE SETUP** button, if available, to launch the native configuration software for your connected audio device.

Use the Ableton Live Help View

If you're not familiar with audio devices and their configuration, you can access onscreen help from within the application to assist you during setup. Ableton Live features a "Setting up Audio I/O" help lesson, which walks you through the setup and optimization process.

To access the help lesson, click **HELP > HELP VIEW** from the menu bar, and then click **AUDIO I/O**.

Setting the Sample Rate

After selecting an audio device, you can choose from its available sample rates. Live supports sample rates up to 192 kHz, when used with a compatible audio interface. To optimize the file sizes in your Set, choose the lowest sample rate that meets the needs of your project.

A sample rate of 44.1 kHz is often adequate for home– and project–studio recordings. Higher sample rates can be chosen for demanding projects, to capture a greater frequency response from the source audio, and to minimize sound degradation throughout the project lifecycle. However, with higher sample rates come greater disk space requirements for your Set. (See Table 4.1 in the "File Size Considerations" section later in this chapter.)

You can change the sample rate in Ableton Live at any time. Audio clips with different sample rates can be used together in a Live Set because Live performs real-time sample rate conversion during playback.

For more details on sample rates, see "The Importance of Sample Rate" in Chapter 1 of this book.

File Type and Bit Depth Settings

Within the **PREFERENCES** window, the **RECORD/WARP/LAUNCH** tab allows you to select the audio file format and the bit depth to use with Ableton Live. While you can mix and match audio files of varying formats and bit depths in your Live Set, these preferences determine the format and bit depth of audio that you record or generate (through Freezing or Resampling, for example) within your Live Set.

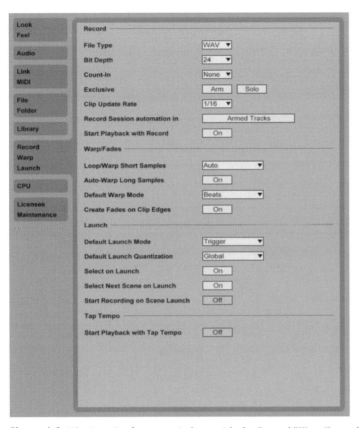

Figure 4.2 The Live Preferences window, with the Record/Warp/Launch tab selected

File Type

Live stores audio as WAV or AIFF files. WAV is the default file type on Windows computers, while AIFF is the default on Macs. Use the default format unless you intend to use your files for another purpose that requires the alternative format.

Bit Depth

Live works with files in 16-bit, 24-bit, or 32-bit floating-point audio resolution. The 16-bit option generates smaller files and is typically adequate for basic recording projects. The 24-bit and 32-bit options provide greater dynamic range in your recorded audio and also help lower the noise floor.

 For more details on bit depth, see "The Importance of Bit Depth" in Chapter 1 of this book.

Higher bit-depth options should be used for high-end recordings, especially recordings that include very quiet passages (such as a classical orchestra), recordings that require intensive processing, and recordings intended for media that support high resolution audio, such as DVD and Blu-ray disc.

For the highest quality audio, record at 24-bit or 32-bit floating point and properly dither down, if needed, during the final mix. Dithering is covered in Lesson 10.

File Size Considerations

A tradeoff of choosing higher sample rates and bit depths is an increase in the amount of disk space required to store your audio files and the amount of processing power required to manipulate them. Table 4.1 shows the relationship between sample rate, bit depth, and disk space consumption for the standard configurations supported in Ableton Live.

Table 4.1 Audio Recording Storage Requirements (Approximate)

Sample Rate	Bit Depth	Megabytes/Track Minute (Mono)	Megabytes/Track Minute (Stereo)
44.1 kHz	16-bit	5 MB	10 MB
44.1 kHz	24-bit	7.5 MB	15 MB
44.1 kHz	32-bit	10 MB	20 MB
48 kHz	16-bit	5.5 MB	11 MB
48 kHz	24-bit	8.2 MB	16.4 MB
48 kHz	32-bit	11 MB	22 MB
88.2 kHz	16-bit	10 MB	20 MB
88.2 kHz	24-bit	15 MB	30 MB
88.2 kHz	32-bit	20 MB	40 MB
96 kHz	16-bit	11 MB	22 MB
96 kHz	24-bit	16.5 MB	33 MB
96 kHz	32-bit	22 MB	44 MB
176.4 kHz	16-bit	20 MB	40 MB
176.4 kHz	24-bit	30 MB	60 MB
176.4 kHz	32-bit	40 MB	80 MB
192 kHz	16-bit	22 MB	44 MB
192 kHz	24-bit	33 MB	66 MB
192 kHz	32-bit	44 MB	88 MB

Working with Tracks

Once you've created a new Live Set, you will have a project with two MIDI tracks and two audio tracks, along with two return tracks and a Master track (provided you haven't changed the default Live Set template).

In Ableton Live, tracks are where audio, MIDI, and automation data are recorded and edited. Audio and MIDI data is stored in clips, which you can edit, arrange, and trigger in any order you choose to create patterns and songs.

Supported Track Types

Like most audio applications, Ableton Live supports a variety of track types that can be used for different purposes.

The basic track types supported in Live include the following:

- Audio tracks

- MIDI tracks

- Return tracks

- Master tracks

Ableton Live also includes a feature known as a Group Track. While not a track type in the traditional sense, a Group Track provides a summing container for submixing audio or MIDI tracks, or for nesting other existing Group Tracks.

> ### The Function of Group Tracks
>
> Group Tracks are unique in that they do not contain any audio or MIDI clips. Instead, they function as a *container* for other audio and MIDI tracks. They have mix controls and can host audio effects, making them a useful way of creating submixes within your Live Set.
>
> To create a Group Track, select the tracks you'd like to include in the group and choose **EDIT > GROUP TRACKS**. (You can also you can press **COMMAND+G** [Mac] or **CTRL+G** [Windows] to create a new Group Track.)
>
> Once created, you can add and remove audio and MIDI tracks from a Group Track by dragging them in and out of the Group.

Any combination of track types can be added to your Live Set, with the exception of the Master track, which is limited to one and is included in all Live Sets by default.

Audio Tracks

Audio tracks allow you to import, record, and edit audio signals as waveforms within clips. Live supports mono (one-channel) or stereo (two-channel) audio.

There is no limit to the number of audio tracks you can insert into a Live Set if you're running the Standard or Suite edition of Ableton Live. (Ableton Live Intro is capped at 16 audio and/or MIDI tracks.) However, the Set sample rate, the system hardware, and the continuity of audio all impact how many tracks can actually play back and record simultaneously.

 Live uses the computer's CPU to mix and process audio tracks. Computers with faster clock speeds and greater processor counts will support more tracks and audio effects than computers with slower CPUs or fewer processors.

MIDI Tracks

MIDI tracks store MIDI note and controller data within MIDI clips. Live's MIDI sequencer lets you import, record, and edit MIDI data in much the same way that you work with audio. However, MIDI on its own does not generate sound; it is data that is sent to software instruments, which output sound in response. MIDI and audio tracks can coexist in one Live Set.

As is the case with audio tracks, there is no limit to the number of MIDI tracks you can add to a Live Set (when running the Standard or Suite edition of Ableton Live). The capabilities of your system and your Ableton Live preference settings will determine how many MIDI tracks can play back or record simultaneously.

Return Tracks

Return tracks do not contain any audio or MIDI clips; instead, they host audio effects. A return track can process audio sent to it from any number of other tracks within the Live Set.

This is particularly useful for applying the same audio effect to multiple tracks. For instance, you could set up a delay effect on a return track and send signals to it from multiple audio and MIDI tracks, thereby saving system resources and setup time.

Master Track

The Master track serves to control the overall level of the audio output for your Set. A Master track is included by default in all Live Sets. It can host audio effects, and its Master Volume slider will control the level of Ableton Live's final output.

Adding Tracks to Ableton Live

To add audio or MIDI tracks to your Set, choose CREATE > INSERT AUDIO TRACK or CREATE > INSERT MIDI TRACK from the menu bar. You can also add new return tracks under the CREATE menu.

Shortcuts for Creating Tracks

Shortcuts exist to speed up the process of creating new MIDI, audio, and return tracks.

Use **COMMAND+T** (Mac) or **CTRL+T** (Windows) to create a new audio track.

Use **COMMAND+SHIFT+T** (Mac) or **CTRL+SHIFT+T** (Windows) to create a new MIDI track.

Use **COMMAND+OPTION+T** (Mac) or **CTRL+ALT+T** (Windows) to insert a new return track.

 Regardless of the method you use to create a new track, new MIDI and audio tracks will be inserted below or to the right of the currently selected track (in Arrangement View and Session View, respectively). To rearrange MIDI and audio tracks, click on the track name and drag the track to a new position.

Naming Tracks

When you create tracks in Ableton Live, they are added to the Live Set using generic names, such as 1 Audio, 2 Audio, 1 MIDI, and so on. Fortunately, you can easily change the generic track names to something more meaningful.

To change a track name, do one of the following:

- Right-click the track name and select **RENAME** from the pop-up menu.

- Click the track name and press **COMMAND+R** (Mac) or **CTRL+R** (Windows).

 To retain automatic track numbering at the start of a track name, include the "#" symbol as the first character. To number tracks using multiple digits (such as 01, 02, 03, etc.), use multiple "#" characters when renaming.

 Press TAB or SHIFT+TAB when renaming a track to cycle forward or backward through your tracks and rename each without leaving the keyboard.

Deleting Tracks

You can delete a track from your Live Set at any time. When you delete tracks, the audio or MIDI clips associated with the track will be lost. If you inadvertently delete a track or tracks, you can undo the operation by choosing **EDIT > UNDO DELETE TRACK(S)**.

To delete a single track:

1.   Click the track name to select the track.

2.   Choose **EDIT > DELETE** or press the **DELETE** key on the computer keyboard.

To delete a continuous range of tracks simultaneously:

1.   Click the track name of the first track you'd like to delete.

2.   **SHIFT-CLICK** on the track name of the last track you'd like to delete.

3.   Choose **EDIT > DELETE** or press the **DELETE** key on the computer keyboard.

To delete a discontinuous collection of tracks simultaneously:

1.   Click the track name of the first track you'd like to delete.

2.   **COMMAND-CLICK** (Mac) or **CTRL-CLICK** (Windows) on the track name of each additional track you'd like to delete.

3.   Choose **EDIT > DELETE** or press the **DELETE** key on the computer keyboard.

 You can also right-click on a track name and choose DELETE from the pop-up menu to remove all selected tracks.

Adding Audio to Tracks

Once you have created one or more audio tracks in your Set, you can begin adding audio clips, either by recording to your track(s) or by importing existing audio files (or *samples*) from a hard drive. Audio clips can be added to timeline locations on tracks in the Arrangement View (where they can be played sequentially) or to Clip Slots in the Session View (where they can be launched in non-sequential order).

 Importing audio files is covered in Chapter 5; audio recording is covered in Chapter 7.

Adding MIDI to Tracks

Once you have created one or more MIDI tracks in your Set, you can create MIDI clips and write MIDI data with the pencil tool by activating Draw Mode. You can also add MIDI to a track by recording a performance from a MIDI controller or by importing a MIDI file from a hard drive. Like audio, MIDI clips can be added to timeline locations on tracks in Arrangement View or to Clip Slots in Session View.

The various methods of importing, recording, editing, and working with MIDI data are covered in Chapters 5 and 6 of this book.

Controlling Playback

How you go about playing your Live Set is dependent on the current view mode you are using. You can choose between the Arrangement View and the Session View.

Playback in Arrangement View

When viewing a Live Set in the Arrangement View, the main Track Display window shows a horizontal timeline of the clips in your project. Playback starts from the location of the Arrangement Insert Marker (or playhead), which is a cursor indicated by a solid, blinking line that runs through one or more tracks, and an arrow that appears both in the lane above the Track Display (below the beat-time ruler) and in the area below the Track Display (in the time ruler). The playhead's location is reflected in the Arrangement Location counter at the top of the Live Set.

Click the **PLAY** button (or press the **SPACEBAR**) to begin playback based on the location of the playhead.

Selections

You can also click and drag within the Track Display window to select a period of time. The selection is indicated by a highlighted zone that can span one or more tracks, with markers on each end shown in the lane above the Track Display and in the time ruler below the Track Display. By making a selection on a track, you define an area for Ableton Live to perform a desired editing task, such as deleting, duplicating, or muting, among others.

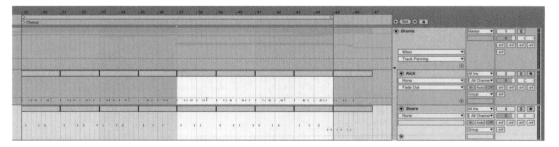

Figure 4.3 Selection from Bar 37 to Bar 45

Click the **PLAY** button (or press the **SPACEBAR**) to begin playback based on the start of the selection. Playback will continue until you click the **STOP** button (or press the **SPACEBAR** a second time).

Press OPTION+SPACEBAR (Mac) or ALT+SPACEBAR (Windows) to play *only* the selection, stopping at the selection end.

Be aware that you cannot make a selection by clicking and dragging an audio or MIDI clip, as that will move the clip. To make a selection, click and drag across empty space or, with a track expanded, click and drag in the bottom part of a clip to avoid selecting the clip itself.

Alternatively, you can click on an Audio or MIDI clip to create a selection. With the clip selected, playback will begin from the clip start.

The Arrangement Loop

As an alternative to the linear playback that is typical of the Arrangement View, you can activate the Arrangement loop, causing playback to loop repeatedly whenever playback starts within or crosses into the loop area. The loop span is demarcated in the Scrub Area by the Arrangement loop brace: a horizontal strip with triangle markers at either end.

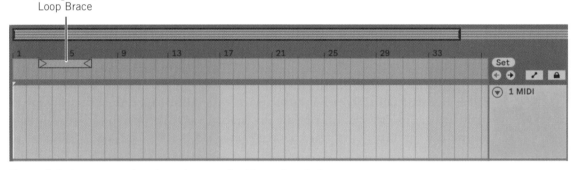

Figure 4.4 Arrangement loop brace in a new Set (shown inactive)

To activate the Arrangement loop, do one of the following:

■   Click the **LOOP** switch in the Control Bar so that it becomes highlighted.

Figure 4.5 The Loop switch enabled in the Control Bar

■   Choose **EDIT > ACTIVATE LOOP**.

■   Press **COMMAND+L** (Mac) or **CTRL+L** (Windows).

When active, the Arrangement loop brace will become highlighted in the Scrub Area.

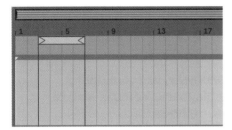

Figure 4.6 The Arrangement loop brace when the loop is active

 For more information on the Arrangement loop, see Chapter 9 in this book.

Starting and Stopping Playback

You can set the playback point by clicking directly on a track to position the Arrangement Insert Marker. You can then start and stop playback by clicking the Transport controls in the Control Bar or by pressing the SPACEBAR.

To play back a portion of your Live Set, follow these steps:

1. Click anywhere within an existing track (avoiding clicking in the top of a clip).

2. Press the SPACEBAR to begin playback from this point.

3. To stop playback, press the SPACEBAR again.

To move to a different playback point in the track, click a new position and press the SPACEBAR again.

Toggling the Scrolling Mode

Live includes a scrolling option called FOLLOW mode that causes the display to scroll during playback, keeping the playhead visible in the Track Display window. As the Live Set plays, the Track Display will scroll, either page-by-page or continuously, depending on the Follow behavior that is set in Preferences.

To enable/disable Follow mode, do one of the following:

- Choose OPTIONS > FOLLOW.

- Press COMMAND+SHIFT+F (Mac) or CTRL+SHIFT+F (Windows).

- Click the FOLLOW button in the Control Bar. The button will be highlighted in a yellow/orange color when Follow mode is active.

Figure 4.7 The Follow button in the Control Bar (shown active)

 Follow mode will pause if you make an edit, scroll horizontally, or zoom during playback. Follow will resume when you stop or restart playback. You can also re-engage Follow mode on-the-fly using any of the above methods.

 For detailed information on Follow behavior and the associated settings in Preferences, see Chapter 9 of this book.

Locating the Playhead

At times, the playhead might be off screen. For example, when **FOLLOW** mode is disabled as described above, the cursor will move off screen after reaching the edge of the Track Display window in the Arrangement View.

Ableton Live displays the playhead cursor as a single vertical line in the Clip Overview at the top of the window in Arrangement View. To jump to the playhead, you can click on the cursor line in the Overview, using the magnifying glass icon. The Overview will scroll to that area of the Set.

Alternatively, you can zoom out by pressing the – (minus) key until the playhead comes into view.

Playback in Session View

While the Arrangement View displays your Live Set along a fixed timeline, the Session View displays a grid of tracks and clips that you can play at any time and in any order. The Session View is designed for improvisation and dynamic, non-sequential playback, so the layout of tracks and clips does not predetermine their playback order.

Getting to Know Session View

The Session View is the feature that truly sets Ableton Live apart from the linear production focus of most DAWs. In the Session View, clips can be placed in a track's clip slots and triggered to play or stop independently. Each clip on a given track plays through the devices inserted on that track, so that the same instrument and/or signal processing is used by all clips on the track. You can also trigger an entire row of clips across all tracks simultaneously by launching a Scene.

Ableton Live Intro permits up to eight clip slots per track and scenes. Ableton Live Standard and Suite support an unlimited number of clips slots per track and scenes.

Because Session View features non-sequential playback, it can be useful for sketching out songs and performing them into the Arrangement View. This is a classic Ableton Live studio production workflow. The Session View is also a powerful live performance tool. It can be used to play backing tracks for a live band, to perform DJ sets that are free-flowing yet tightly synchronized, or to fire off music cues and sound effects for a theatrical performance.

Starting and Stopping Playback

Each clip that you load in the Session View has a triangular **CLIP LAUNCH** button (Play button) at its left edge. Clicking this button will launch playback for the clip at any time. Launching a clip will also activate playback of the Arrangement, if it is not already in progress.

Figure 4.8 The triangular Clip Launch button

To stop a clip from playing, click the **CLIP STOP** button on any Clip Slot in the track or in the Track Status Display.

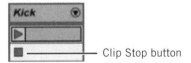

Figure 4.9 Click the square Clip Stop Button below an active clip to stop it from playing.

When you stop playback for a specific clip in the Session View, the Play button in the Control Bar will remain engaged and the Arrangement Position fields will continue running. These fields maintain a continuous flow of musical time so that you always know your position in song-time during a live performance or while recording clips into an arrangement.

You can stop playback by pressing the **STOP** button in the Control Bar or by pressing the **SPACEBAR**. Pressing the **STOP** button a second time (or anytime while playback is stopped) will return your Arrangement Insert Marker to the start of the entire Live Set.

Figure 4.10 The Control Bar, including Play and Stop buttons, as well as the Arrangement Position counter

Enabling Clip Looping

In addition to Ableton Live's Arrangement Loop feature (discussed earlier in this chapter), Live also provides the ability to enable looping for individual clips. Enabling Loop functionality for a clip will allow that clip to loop indefinitely when launched in the Session View. When used the Arrangement View, a Loop-enabled clip can be resized beyond the length of its original media, with Ableton Live automatically adding successive iterations (repetitions) of the clip contents to achieve the desired length.

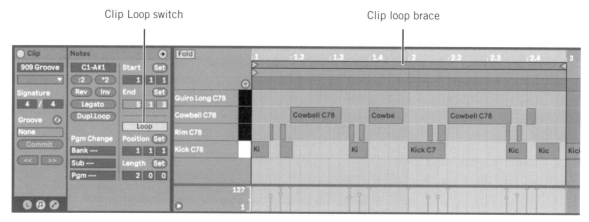

Figure 4.11   The Clip View, showing the Loop switch and loop brace for a MIDI clip

   The Warp switch must be activated to loop an audio clip. Unwarped audio clips cannot be looped.

To enable clip looping:

1.   Double-click on the target clip to open it in the Clip View.

2.   If necessary, enable warping for the clip (required for audio clips).

   For information on enabling and using Warping for audio clips, see "Audio, MIDI, and Tempo Changes" in Chapter 5.

3.   Click the **LOOP** switch in the Notes box (for MIDI clips) or in the Sample box (for audio clips).

To modify the length of the loop, do one of the following:

■   Click and drag the triangle markers at either end of the loop brace to change its position and length.

■   Type in exact position and length values in the Notes box (for MIDI clips) or the Sample box (for audio clips).

Saving, Locating, and Opening Live Sets and Projects

As with most software applications, Live provides commands for saving and opening your files under the FILE menu. The following sections describe the options for saving, locating, and opening your Live Sets and other files related to your Live Projects.

Live Sets and Live Projects

The type of document that you create and edit in Ableton Live is called a Live Set. Live Sets are contained within a Live Project, which is the top-level folder containing Ableton Live-related files, such as audio files that belong to the Live Set.

When you save an existing Live Set under a new name and folder location, Ableton Live will create a new project folder and store the Live Set within that folder.

Saving a Live Set

While working in Ableton Live, it is important to save your work often. Note that when you save your progress in Live, you are saving only the Live Set document, not its associated files. (Audio clips in a Set either reference existing files on disk or are recorded directly to disk within the project folder, so you don't have to save them independently.) This means even very large Live Sets can be saved quickly.

Save Live Set Command

Saving can be done manually by choosing the SAVE LIVE SET command from the FILE menu. This saves the changes you have made since the last time you saved and writes the Live Set in its current form over the old version. You cannot undo the Save command.

 If you need to return to an earlier state after completing a Save command, you can use the Undo command to work backwards through previous actions.

Save Live Set As Command

The SAVE LIVE SET AS command is useful for saving a copy of a Set under a different name or in a different drive location. Because this command leaves the original Set unchanged and allows you to continue working on the renamed copy, it is particularly useful for experimenting and saving successive stages of your work. You can save each stage under a different name, such as "Edit Session-Day 1," "Edit Session-Day 2," and so on. By working this way, you can always retrace your steps if you should want to go back to an earlier stage of the project.

To use the Save Live Set As feature, follow these steps:

1. From within an open Set, choose FILE > SAVE LIVE SET AS. The associated dialog box will appear.

2. Type a new name for the Set in the dialog box.

3. Optionally, navigate to a new drive location.

4. Click **SAVE**.

The renamed, newly saved Set will remain open for you to continue your work.

 The Save Live Set As command should not be used to transfer a Live project to a portable drive. Doing so will copy the Live Set document file only, without including the associated audio files.

Save a Copy Command

The **SAVE A COPY** command simply saves a copy of the current Live Set with a different name or within a different directory location without affecting the currently open Set. After saving a copy, the original version of the project—not the copy—will remain open for you to continue your work.

To use the Save a Copy feature, follow these steps:

1. From within an open project, choose **FILE > SAVE A COPY**. The Save a Copy dialog box will appear.

2. Type a new name for the project version in the dialog box.

3. Optionally, navigate to a new drive location.

4. Click **OK**.

Collect All and Save Command

The **COLLECT ALL AND SAVE** command simultaneously saves your current Live Set and packages all of the associated audio files into the Live Project folder structure. This is useful when you are saving a project for an archive or for use on another computer, or when you are sending the Live Set to a collaborator who doesn't already have all of the source audio files.

To use the Collect All and Save feature, follow these steps:

1. From within an open project, choose **FILE > COLLECT ALL AND SAVE**. The Collect All and Save dialog box will appear.

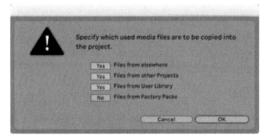

Figure 4.12 The Collect All and Save dialog box

2. Choose the types of audio files you want to save into the Live Project folder.

3. Click **OK** to complete the save. If you haven't previously saved the Live project, you'll be prompted to provide a new name for the project in a Save Live Set As dialog box.

The Collect All and Save command can be used when first saving a Live Set, or at any time while working on an existing Live project. If you use the Collect All and Save feature multiple times, Live will only collect audio files that have been added since the previous Collect All and Save command.

 For information on using Collect All and Save to create a self-contained backup or archive of a Set, see Chapter 10 in this book.

Locating and Opening a Live Set

If you know the location of a Live Set file you want to open, you can open it directly from the File menu. In addition, Ableton Live makes it very easy to open a recently used Live Set regardless of the location.

To open a Live Set, do one the following:

■   Choose FILE > OPEN LIVE SET.

■   Press COMMAND+O (Mac) or CTRL+O (Windows).

To open a recently used Live Set, do the following:

■   Choose FILE > OPEN RECENT SET and select the file that you wish to open from the submenu.

 You can also open Live Sets from the computer's hard drive by double-clicking on the Live Set file in an Explorer or Finder window.

Regardless of which method you choose, the Live Set will open with all tracks and clips appearing exactly as they were when last saved.

Ableton Live can have only one Live Set open at a time. If you attempt to open a Live Set while another is open, Live will prompt you to save the current Live Set and close it before opening the new one.

Review/Discussion Questions

1. What is the maximum sample rate supported in Live? (See "Audio Device and Sample Rate Settings" beginning on page 87.)

2. What audio file types are supported in Ableton Live? What is the default file type on Mac and Windows? (See "File Type and Bit Depth Settings" beginning on page 88.)

3. What is the maximum bit depth supported in Live? (See "File Type and Bit Depth Settings" beginning on page 88.)

4. What are the four basic track types supported in Live? What are Group Tracks? (See "Adding Tracks to Ableton Live" beginning on page 92.)

5. What menu command lets you add audio tracks to your Live Set? What menu command lets you add MIDI tracks to your Live Set? (See "Adding Tracks to Ableton Live" beginning on page 92.)

6. Why might Audio and MIDI tracks respond differently to changes in the tempo of a Live Set? What setting affects this behavior? (See "Audio, MIDI, and Tempo Changes" beginning on page 123.)

7. What happens to the audio and MIDI clips on a track when the track gets deleted from your Live Set? Can the delete command be undone? (See "Deleting Tracks" beginning on page 93.)

8. What are the two different views you can use to interact with a Live Set? (See "Controlling Playback" beginning on page 95.)

9. In Arrangement View, what is the Arrangement Insert Marker? How does it appear in the Live Set? (See "Playback in Arrangement View" beginning on page 95.)

10. How does playback differ between the Arrangement and Session views? (See "Playback in Session View" beginning on page 98.)

11. What is the purpose of the Save Live Set As command? Which Set will be open after completing the Save Live Set As command—the original or the renamed copy? (See "Save Live Set As Command" beginning on page 101.)

12. How does the Collect All and Save command differ from the normal Save or Save Live Set As commands? (See "Collect All and Save" beginning on page 102.)

13. What are some ways you can open a Set from within Live? (See "Locating and Opening a Live Set" beginning on page 103.)

To review additional material from this chapter and prepare for certification, see the Ableton Live 101 Study Guide module available through the Elements|ED online learning platform at ElementsED.com.

Creating a Live Set

🎧 Activity

In this exercise tutorial, you will create a new Live Set, configure your Ableton Live preferences, add and remove tracks for the Live Set, name each of the tracks you are keeping, and save the Live Set as an Ableton Live project for use in subsequent exercises.

🕐 Duration

This exercise should take approximately 10 to 15 minutes to complete.

⊕ Goals/Targets

- Create a new Live Set

- Configure audio device and sample rate

- Choose an appropriate file type and bit depth

- Add and rename Audio and MIDI Tracks

Downloading the Media Files

To complete the exercises in this book, you will need to use various media files included in the **Media Files 2019-Live101** folder. If you haven't done so already, you can download the media files now. Be sure to save the files to a location that you will have ongoing access to as you complete the exercises and projects in this book.

To download the media files, point your browser to www.halleonard.com/mylibrary and enter your access code (printed on the opening page of this book). Next, click the **Download** link for the **Media Files 2019-Live101** listing in your **My Library** page. The Media Files folder will begin transferring to your Downloads folder.

Getting Started

To get started, you will need to open Ableton Live, create a new Live Set, and configure its audio settings (audio device, sample rate, bit depth, and file format) to suit your needs.

Launch Live and create a new Live Set:

1. Power up your computer and any connected hardware.

2. Do one of the following to launch Ableton Live:

    *   Double-click on the Ableton Live shortcut icon on the desktop.

    *   Click the Ableton Live icon in the Dock (Mac).

    *   Click **START > ABLETON LIVE** (Windows).

3. Once Ableton Live has launched, click **FILE > NEW LIVE SET** from the menu bar. A new untitled Set will be created.

Configure Live's audio device and Sample Rate:

1. Open the Preferences window by selecting **LIVE > PREFERENCES** (Mac) or **OPTIONS > PREFERENCES** (Windows).

2. Under the **AUDIO** tab, choose an appropriate Driver Type to allow Live to communicate with your available audio hardware.

3. Choose your Audio Device.

    If you do not have a dedicated Audio Device, you can choose your computer's built-in Audio Device.

4. Select **44100** for your Sample Rate.

Configure Live's File Type and Bit Depth settings:

1. Navigate to the **RECORD / WARP / LAUNCH** tab of Live's Preferences window.

2. Set the audio File Type to **AIFF** (Mac) or **WAV** (Windows).

3. Choose **24** for the Bit Depth.

4. When finished, close the Preferences window.

Creating and Naming Tracks

For this part of the exercise, you can work in either the Session View or the Arrangement View. You can switch between views by pressing the **TAB** key. Here, you will add and remove tracks as needed and give your tracks meaningful names.

Adding Tracks

By default, a new Live Sets contain two empty audio tracks and two empty MIDI tracks. In the next series of steps, you will add some new tracks, delete unneeded tracks, rename the tracks you will use in the Set, and reorder the tracks.

Create additional tracks for the Live Set:

1. Choose **CREATE > INSERT AUDIO TRACK** to insert a new audio track.

 Try using the keyboard shortcut for creating an audio track: **COMMAND+T** (Mac) or **CTRL+T** (Windows).

2. Choose **CREATE > INSERT MIDI TRACK** to insert a new MIDI track.

 Try using the keyboard shortcut for creating a MIDI track: **COMMAND+SHIFT+T** (Mac) or **CTRL+SHIFT+T** (Windows).

This should give you a total of three audio tracks and three MIDI tracks, along with the default Reverb and Delay return tracks and the Master track.

 The number of tracks included in a new Live Set can vary, depending on the Default Template being used by Ableton Live. If the Default Template has not been changed, your Set will include two audio tracks, two MIDI tracks, and two return tracks.

Deleting Tracks

For this project, we only need two audio tracks and two MIDI tracks, so let's go ahead and remove any extra audio and MIDI tracks we have. To simplify the Set, we'll also remove the return tracks for now.

The following four tracks should be deleted from the Set:

- The third audio track
- The third MIDI track

- The Reverb return track

- The Delay return track

Delete each of the above tracks using one of the following techniques:

- Right-click on the track name and choose **DELETE** from the pop-up menu.

- Select the track, then press the **DELETE** key on the computer keyboard.

Now you'll want to rename the remaining tracks so that you'll be ready to starting producing music.

Name the four remaining tracks:

1. Right-click on the track name of the first track and select **RENAME** from the pop-up menu.

2. Change the names for the audio tracks as follows:

   - Name the first audio track Chords.

   - Name the second audio track Bass.

 Try using the Tab key to automatically move the Rename cursor to the next track.

3. Rename the MIDI tracks as follows:

   - Name the first MIDI track Drums.

   - Name the second MIDI track Melody.

4. Press **RETURN** or **ENTER** on the last track to finish renaming.

The last step is to make sure the tracks are in the correct order for the next exercise.

Move the Drums track:

- Click the on track name for the Drums track and drag it to top position in the Arrangement View or the left-most position in the Session View.

   The final track order should be:

   - Drums

   - Chords

   - Bass

   - Melody

Finishing Up

To complete this exercise, you will need to save your work under a new name and close the Live Set. Note that you will be reusing this project in Exercise 5, so it is important to save the work you've done.

Finish your work:

1.   Choose FILE > SAVE LIVE SET AS to save the Live Set and create a Live Project folder structure containing the associated Live project files.

2.   In the Save Live Set As dialog box, rename the Set as *Exercise04-XXX* (where *XXX* is your initials), and click SAVE.

3.   Press COMMAND+Q (Mac) or CTRL+Q (Windows) to quit Live and close the project.

Chapter 5

Importing and Working with Media

This chapter introduces various processes for importing audio and video files into a Live Set. We describe file formats and types that can be imported and cover how to use Ableton Live's Browser to locate and preview audio files. We go on to discuss methods for importing audio and video files in both the Arrangement View and Session View.

 Learning Targets for This Chapter

- Understand the file resolutions and formats that can be imported into Live

- Locate supported audio and video files using Live's Browser

- Use both the Arrangement View and Session View to import audio files as clips on tracks

- Import video files and perform basic video editing tasks

 Key topics from this chapter are illustrated in the Ableton Live 101 Study Guide module available through the Elements|ED online learning platform. Sign up for free at ElementsED.com.

As a music producer, composer, sound designer, or engineer, you'll encounter many situations in which a project will start with some kind of existing media. You might find inspiration in a pre-created musical loop, such as a drum loop or a chord progression, and want to use that as a starting point for a new song. A collaborator might send you tracks they created so you can continue to develop or mix the idea in your own studio. You might receive video from a director whose film needs a score. Perhaps you just want to browse and use your own samples and sound effects.

In these situations and many others, you will be working with existing media files—and you will need a way to get them into Live. In this chapter, you will learn the types of files you can import into a Live Set, as well as how to import them.

Considerations Prior to Import

Ableton Live allows you to add audio, MIDI, and video files from any available storage location to your Live Set. There are multiple ways to get media files onto tracks in your Live Set, including dragging and dropping files from a file browser and locating files through Live's built-in Browser.

Prior to attempting to add a file to your Live Set, you should understand whether it is compatible with Live.

File Characteristics

Live supports audio, MIDI, and video files of various resolutions, types, and formats. In order for a media file to be recognized in a Live Set, it must meet certain criteria.

Supported Audio Bit Depth and Sample Rate

Live supports mono and stereo audio files with bit depths of 8-bit, 16-bit, 24-bit, or 32-bit, and sample rates ranging from 44.1 kHz to 192 kHz. You can mix and match audio files of different bit depths and sample rates in a single Live Set without needing to convert them to match the Set's resolution.

Supported Audio File Formats

Ableton Live features native support for two audio file formats: Audio Interchange File Format (AIFF) and Waveform Audio File Format (WAV). WAV and AIFF are the only audio file formats that Live can load without conversion.

Live can also play Sound Designer II files, as well as compressed formats such as MP3, AAC, Ogg Vorbis, and FLAC files. These formats are converted into WAV when imported. The converted file is stored in Live's Decoding Cache:

- Windows: System Drive (C:) > Users > [username] > AppData > Roaming > Ableton > Cache > Cache > Decoding

- Mac: Macintosh HD > Users > [username] > Library > Caches > Ableton > Cache > Decoding

When compressed or encoded audio files such as MP3s are added to a Live Set, Ableton Live automatically decodes them for use and stores the decoded audio files in the Decoding Cache. You can set the maximum size and location of the Decoding Cache in Live's Preferences window, under the FILE/FOLDER section.

Here is an overview of the types of audio files that can be imported in Ableton Live:

- **Audio Interchange File Format (AIFF).** This file format is used primarily on Macintosh systems, although Live supports it natively on both Mac and Windows. AIFF files can be recorded directly or imported into a Live Set.

- **Audio Interchange File Compressed (AIFC).** A variant of the AIFF audio file standard, AIFC provides audio compression for AIFF files.

- **Waveform Audio File Format (WAV).** Live supports any standard WAV (WAVE) files. WAV files can be recorded directly and imported on either Mac or Windows systems.

- **Sound Designer II (SD II).** SD II is a mono or stereo file format supported on Macintosh systems only. This format supports sample rates up to 48 kHz.

- **MP3 (MPEG-1 Layer-3).** MP3 files are supported on all common computer platforms and employ file compression of up to 10:1, while still maintaining reasonable audio quality. Because of their small size and cross-platform support, they have traditionally been popular for streaming, social media, and file exchanges.

- **Advanced Audio Coding (AAC).** AAC files were created as a successor to MP3. This format generally achieves better sound quality than an MP3 at the same bit rate. AAC is the standard audio format for platforms such as YouTube and iOS devices.

- **OGG Vorbis (OGG).** Vorbis is an open-source compressed audio format, which is often used in conjunction with the OGG container format.

- **Free Lossless Audio Codec (FLAC).** FLAC is an audio format for lossless audio compression. FLAC compression typically reduces audio files to between 50 and 70 percent of their original size.

Supported MIDI Files

Live can import Standard MIDI Files (SMFs) in both common formats—type 0 and type 1—as well as the much less common type 2 format. Supported MIDI files are recognizable by their *.mid* or *.smf* file extensions.

Type 0 Standard MIDI Files (SMF0)

In type 0 SMFs, all MIDI data is stored in a single track, separated by the MIDI channel. When imported into Live, all MIDI data will appear in one track.

Type 1 Standard MIDI Files (SMF1)

In type 1 SMFs, individual parts are saved on different tracks within the MIDI sequence. When imported into Live, each part will appear on its own track.

 Up until Live 9, SMF1 formatted files appeared as a folder in the Browser. From there, the folder could be opened to import selected tracks, if necessary.

Type 2 Standard MIDI Files (SMF2) (Rare)

In type 2 SMFs, the MIDI file can contain multiple tracks, and each track can contain a different and complete sequence (essentially a collection of type 0 sequences in a single MIDI file). When imported into Live, each sequence will appear on its own track.

Supported Video Files

Live supports video files in Apple QuickTime format (MOV), allowing you to perform sound design and scoring to video within a Live Set. Supported video files appear in Live's built-in Browser and can be imported by dragging them into a Live Set when working in the Arrangement View.

Import Methods

Ableton Live provides several methods for bringing audio and MIDI files into your Live Set: you can import from Live's built-in Browser, use the **CREATE > IMPORT AUDIO/MIDI FILE** command, or drag and drop files from an external file browser.

 In Live 10.1 and later, you can also import MIDI to your Set by choosing **CREATE > IMPORT MIDI FILE**.

The following sections provide details for importing audio, starting with a focus on the built-in Browser, as it offers useful search and organizational features.

Live's Built-in Browser

Live's Browser makes it easy to find and audition supported media files, and ultimately to insert them as clips on tracks. While the Browser provides access to much more than just audio files, by default it displays the core media included with Live and allows you to add additional folders of media from any available storage location on your system.

Showing the Browser

The Browser is located on the left-hand side of Live's interface. The Browser display is divided vertically, with the left-hand column displaying categories of tools, sounds, and media files, and the right-hand column listing the contents of each category.

To show and hide the Browser, select **VIEW > SHOW BROWSER** or press **OPTION+COMMAND+B** (Mac) or **CTRL+ALT+B** (Windows). Alternatively, you can toggle the browser using the Show/Hide triangle in the upper left-hand corner of the Ableton Live interface.

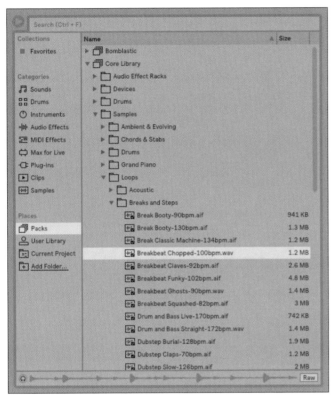

Figure 5.1 The Browser showing audio files included in Live's Core Library Pack.

When it comes to importing audio files, the Browser provides a few useful starting points:

- *Samples*: This Browser category lists all of the audio samples available to Ableton Live. If you've accumulated a large volume of samples, this list can become very long, making the search function at the top of the browser very important.

- *Packs*: This category displays any official Ableton Packs you have installed and any Packs that you have available to install (Live 10 and later). Some Packs contain a large volume of individual audio files.

- *User Library*: This is the default storage location for the various components of a Live Set, including your own samples and other audio files. When you add folders and audio files to the User Library, Ableton Live will automatically display them in this section of the Browser.

Notably, you can choose the **ADD FOLDER** option under Places in the Browser to select additional storage locations and make them available for browsing.

Navigating the Browser

Once you have selected a category, you will be able to navigate that section in the right-hand column. If the category has additional folders, you can expand and collapse them using the disclosure triangles next to each folder name. Alternatively, you can use the right and left arrows on your keyboard to expand and collapse folders, and the up and down arrows to move your selection through the list of folders and files.

Searching the Browser

It doesn't take long to accumulate a large volume of audio files in your library. The larger your audio library becomes, the more important Live's search and collections features become.

To search the browser and filter the files it displays:

1. Do one of the following:

    *   Click in the Search field at the top of the browser.

    *   Press **COMMAND+F** (Mac) or **CTRL+F** (Windows) to place your cursor in the Search field.

2. Enter a search term to browse for matching files.

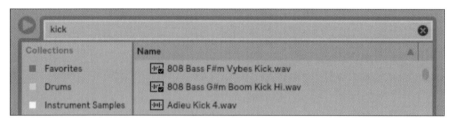

Figure 5.2 Searching the Browser for audio files with "kick" in the name

As you enter a search term, Ableton Live will automatically begin filtering the files it displays. For instance, searching for kick will cause Ableton Live to only show files with the text "kick" in their file names.

Using Collections

Collections offer an additional opportunity to organize your browser contents and ultimately find what you're seeking faster.

Ableton provides seven Collection labels that you can use to tag items in the Browser. Each label has its own unique color and name, which you can customize as desired. You might use one Collection label to mark your favorite drum samples, and another to delineate your favorite instrument samples. You can use the Collection labels to tag anything you want, including audio effects, instruments, plug-ins, and clips.

To add or remove a Collection label tag for an audio file:

1. Locate the target audio file in the Browser.

2. Do one of the following:

    *   Right-click the audio file and select the Collection label you'd like to assign or unassign.

    *   Press keys **1-7** to assign or unassign the associated Collection label.

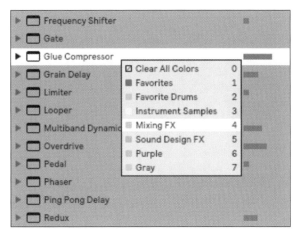

Figure 5.3 Right-click any item in the browser to assign or unassign a Collection label.

To view the contents of a Collection:

1. Click the name of the Collection in the upper, left-hand corner of the browser. The browser will display a combined list of everything contained in the Collection.

2. Use the search feature in conjunction with viewing a Collection to narrow your results even further.

3. De-select the Collection to return to normal browsing.

Previewing Audio Files in the Browser

By default, when you click on or select an audio file name, Live automatically previews the audio. You can turn off the automatic preview by clicking the **PREVIEW** button in the lower left-hand corner of the browser. (See Figure 5.4.)

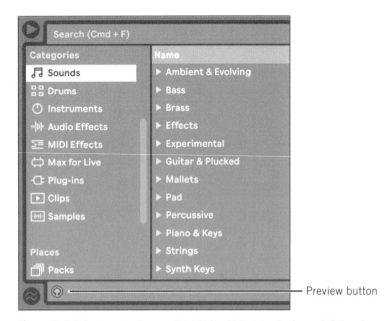

Figure 5.4 The Preview button (highlighted blue) in the lower left-hand corner of the browser.

After selecting an audio file, you will also see its waveform display at the bottom of the browser window, next to the Preview button. If the Preview button is enabled (highlighted in blue), a playhead will move across the waveform to indicate the current playback position of the sample. You can also click anywhere in a sample waveform to start playback from that specific location.

To stop the preview, you can follow any of these options:

- Press the **SPACEBAR**.

- Select another audio file or folder in the browser.

- Press the **PREVIEW** button to turn off audio previews altogether.

(i) You can trigger Preview for a selected audio file at any time by pressing the right arrow key or Shift+Return / Shift+Enter with an audio file selected in the browser. This works even with the Preview button turned off.

When applicable, Live attempts to preview any type of file in the browser in sync with the current Live Set's tempo, so you can preview it in context. To prevent this behavior, click the **RAW** button to enable it.

(i) Previews play at the current tempo only while the Set is in playback and the Raw button is not engaged.

With the Raw button engaged (highlighted in blue), files will preview at their original tempo and will not loop during previews.

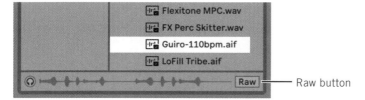

Figure 5.5 The Raw button engaged (highlighted) in the Preview display

You can adjust the volume of audio previews using the **PREVIEW/CUE VOLUME** knob on the Master track in the Session View.

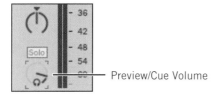

Figure 5.6 Use the Preview/Cue Volume knob on the Master track to adjust Live's preview volume.

Importing Audio from the Browser

After you have located an audio file (or files) in the Browser that you would like to use in your Live Set, your next step is to get the audio to an audio track. You can import files to existing tracks or create new tracks for the audio as you import files.

Importing Audio to Existing Tracks

You can import to existing tracks in either the Arrangement View or Session View; either way, Ableton Live will create an audio clip that you can edit however you see fit.

Import to Tracks in Arrangement View

When you're working in the Arrangement View, you'll see a linear, timeline-based view of your production.

To place audio from the browser on an audio track in the Arrangement View:

1. Select the audio file in the browser.

2. Drag the audio file onto an existing audio track. You can drag the clip anywhere in the arrangement.

> (i) Use the time rulers along the top and bottom of the Track Display window to locate the desired insert position, such as Bar 9 or the 0:30 second mark.

Import to Tracks in Session View

When you're working in the Session View, you will have access to a series of scenes and clips. You can launch clips and scenes in any order to generate performances without being tied to a linear timeline.

While the Session View environment is very different from that of the Arrangement View, the process of placing audio files as clips on tracks is very similar.

To place audio from the browser on an audio track in the Session View:

1.   Select the audio file in the browser.

2.   Click and drag the audio file to a clip slot on an audio track. The slot will update to display a play button and the associated clip name.

With the clip added to a clip slot, you can launch the audio file using either the clip launch button or the associated scene launch button.

Import Directly to a New Audio Track

You can skip the step of manually creating a destination track for an audio file, if desired.

To automatically place an audio file on a *new* audio track, drag the file from the browser to any position *below* the last track (Arrangement View) or *to the right of* the last track (Session View) in your Live Set. Live will create a new audio track at that position containing the clip.

Batch Importing Audio to Tracks

At times you might find yourself in a situation where you'd like to import multiple audio files simultaneously. In these cases, you can quickly send a set of selected files to one or more tracks.

Batch Import in Arrangement View

The Arrangement View offers two methods for importing multiple audio files to tracks. You can import the audio as a contiguous string of clips on a single track, or you can place each audio file on its own track at the same start position.

To place the audio files as contiguous clips on a single audio track:

1.   Select the audio files in the browser:

   • Hold **SHIFT** to select a contiguous range of files, or

   • Hold **COMMAND** (Mac) or **CTRL** (Windows) to select non-contiguous files

2.   Click and drag the audio files, placing them on the target audio track.

To place each audio file on its own audio track:

1. Select the audio files in the browser using the methods described above.

2. While holding **COMMAND** (Mac) or **CTRL** (Windows), drag the audio files to the audio track where you would like the first file to be placed. Subsequent files will automatically be placed on tracks below.

Figure 5.7 Simultaneously dragging multiple audio files to different tracks in the Arrangement View with the Command/Ctrl modifier

Batch Import in Session View

The Session View also offers two methods for importing multiple audio files to tracks. You can import the audio into subsequent clip slots on a single track, or you can place each audio file on a separate track in the same clip slot position.

To place the audio files into subsequent clip slots on the same audio track:

1. Select the audio files in the browser using the methods described above.

2. Click and drag the audio files to a clip slot on an audio track. The clips will be added to successive slots on the track. (See Figure 5.8.)

Figure 5.8 Simultaneously dragging multiple audio files to the same track in the Session View

To place the audio files into clip slots on separate tracks:

1.   Select the audio files in the browser using the methods described above.

2.   While holding **COMMAND** (Mac) or **CTRL** (Windows), drag the audio files onto the desired clip slot position on an audio track. The clips will be added to successive audio tracks at the same slot position.

Batch Import Directly to New Audio Tracks

You can skip the step of manually creating destination tracks for the audio files you plan to import, if desired, and instead create the tracks automatically upon import.

To place audio files on one new audio track:

■   Drag one or more files from the browser to any position below the last track (Arrangement View) or to the right of the last track (Session View) in your Live Set.

A new track will be added at that position, and the audio file(s) will be added to the track.

To place each selected file on its own new audio track:

■   Hold **COMMAND** (Mac) or **CTRL** (Windows) while dragging multiple files from the browser to any position below the last track (Arrangement View) or to the right of the last track (Session View) in your Live Set. New tracks will be added at that position as needed.

ⓘ   You can easily to recognize the new track drop area by the displayed text label, "Drop Files and Devices Here."

Audio, MIDI, and Tempo Changes

Although audio and MIDI tracks can coexist in Live Sets, they can respond differently to changes in tempo because their source material is different – audio tracks contain *samples*, while MIDI tracks contain *data*. MIDI clips easily conform to changes in your Live Set tempo, as the MIDI data is flexible. Audio clips, on the other hand, can be absolute, meaning Ableton Live will continue to play them back at their original speed regardless of the project tempo. This can be desirable for non-rhythmic audio, such as spoken words or ambient textures, but it can cause rhythmic audio to fall out of sync in the context of a song.

With Warp algorithms, Ableton Live is capable of time-warping audio clips while streaming them from disk so as to synchronize them with the Live Set's tempo. Tempo matching is done without affecting the pitch, which can be changed independently. As such, even if you mix and match audio files from various sources with MIDI data, your Live Set remains flexible to tempo changes.

To enable time-warping on audio tracks, do the following:

1. Select one or more audio clips.

2. If Clip View is not already enabled, show the Detail View as needed (**VIEW > SHOW/HIDE DETAIL VIEW**) and then switch to Clip View as needed (**VIEW > TOGGLE CLIP/DEVICE VIEW**).

3. Click the **WARP** button from the **Sample** box in the Clip View. (See Figure 5.9.)

   The selected Audio clip(s) will now automatically follow tempo changes in your Set and conform to the project tempo map.

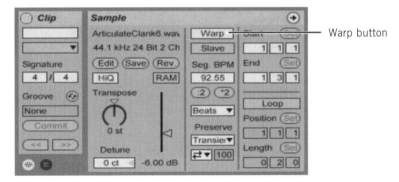

Figure 5.9 The Warp button when activate (highlighted yellow) in the Sample box within the Clip View area

 Warping audio, especially when done to extremes, can create undesired audio artifacts. Always check the results and use the Edit > Undo command if you are not happy with the outcome.

Other Methods of Importing Audio Files

Audio files can be imported using menu commands or using a file browser from your computer's operating system, rather than using the built-in Browser in Ableton Live.

Importing with a Menu Command

Ableton Live gives you the option of locating and importing audio from the **CREATE** menu. This option can be useful if you know the disk location of the audio files you want to import, such as when you've downloaded files from an online resource or when you are importing shared files from a USB drive.

To import audio using the Create menu:

1. Select the audio track on which you'd like to insert the audio file.

    - In Arrangement View, position the Insert Arrangement Marker where you want to insert the audio clip.

    - In Session View, select the clip slot in which you would like to place the audio clip.

2. Select **CREATE > IMPORT AUDIO FILE**.

3. Navigate the file browser to the location of the audio file.

4. Double-click on the file to import it.

Importing from an External File Browser

You can also import audio files by drag-and-drop from an external file browser, such as a Finder window on Mac or a File Explorer window on Windows.

To import files to a single track:

1. Locate and select the files using a file browser on your operating system.

2. Drag the files from the file browser into the Ableton Live window. The files will be added to a single track at the location where they are dropped (on an audio track, on a new track, or in a clip slot).

> (i) Hold COMMAND (Mac) or CTRL (Windows) when importing multiple files to place them on separate tracks.

Importing Video

When you are scoring and/or performing sound design for any sort of visual media, it is often best to bring the video directly into your Live Set. This way, you can not only perform basic editing—such as trimming the start and end of the clip and breaking the clip into smaller segments—but also configure your Live Set so your composition aligns with edits and key "hit points" in the video.

 Video will display in in the Arrangement View only. If you import a QuickTime file into a clip slot in the Session View, only the audio will import for playback.

To import a video into your Live Set:

1. Select the video file (MOV) from the Live browser or an external file browser.

2. Drag the file into the Track Display window in the Arrangement View. A video track will be created in the Set and will display the audio waveform from the QuickTime movie.

 Unlike some other DAWs, Ableton Live displays an audio waveform on its video tracks instead of thumbnail images of frames from the video file.

Live supports video files in Apple QuickTime (MOV) format only. You will need to have QuickTime installed on your computer in order for Live to be able to decode video files for playback in a Live Set.

Video Track Display

Regardless of whether you drop the video file on a MIDI track, an audio track, or an empty space in the Arrangement View, the track will become a video track with the video clip (waveform display) inserted in the timeline.

Ableton Live will also display a floating Video Window, reflecting the current position of the Insert Arrangement Marker (i.e., the playback position).

Figure 5.10 An imported video clip and associated video window in the Arrangement View

Ableton Live Intro and Lite editions do not support video import and playback.

The Video Window can be hidden at any time to reduce on-screen clutter and shown again later as needed.

To show or hide the Video Window, do one of the following:

■ Choose VIEW > VIDEO WINDOW.

■ Press COMMAND+OPTION+V (Mac) or CTRL+ALT+V (Windows).

The Video Window can also be resized as needed to fit comfortably within the available display space on your screen.

To resize the Video Window, do one of the following:

■ Click and drag the lower right-hand corner of the Video Window to resize it.

■ Double-click the Video Window to display it in full-screen mode.

■ OPTION-CLICK (Mac) or ALT-CLICK (Windows) anywhere on the Video Window to restore it to its original size.

Working with Video Tracks

Aside from only functioning in the Arrangement View, video clips look and function similarly to audio clips. You can move a video clip around the timeline, make separations in the clip by using the EDIT > SPLIT command (or by pressing COMMAND+E [Mac] or CTRL+E [Windows]) with the Arrangement Insert Marker positioned within the clip, and trim the start and end points of the clip.

If you attempt to perform more complex editing functions on the video clip, however, it will be converted to audio only. The Consolidate, Reverse, and Crop functions will all cause this conversion to occur.

Configuring the Start of a Video Clip

If you're scoring a piece of video, it can be helpful to reposition the start marker of your video clip so that it's right in line with the first frame of action.

To reposition the start marker within a video clip:

1. Double-click the video clip in the Arrangement View to display the Clip View for the video.

2. Click and drag the Start Marker (lower arrow in the upper left-hand corner) to the right.

3. Position the Start Marker where the first frame of the video appears in the Video Window.

(i) The Start Marker in the Clip View determines where the clip will start playing when it is launched or encountered on a track.

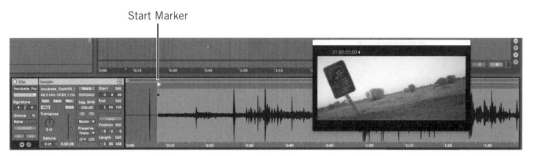

Figure 5.11 Adjusting the video Start Marker location

You can now align the start of the video with the start of your composition.

Review/Discussion Questions

1. What two audio file formats are natively supported by Live? (See "Supported Audio File Formats" beginning on page 112.)

2. Name some of the other common audio file formats that Ableton Live supports. (See "Supported Audio File Formats" beginning on page 112.)

3. What automatically happens when you import an encoded or compressed audio file into a Live Set? (See "Supported Audio File Formats" beginning on page 112.)

4. What video file format does Ableton Live support? (See "Supported Video Files" beginning on page 114.)

5. What are the three methods you can use to import an audio or video file into a Live Set? (See "Import Methods" beginning on page 114.)

6. How can you show and hide the Ableton Live browser? (See "Showing the Browser" beginning on page 114.)

7. Once you've located an audio file in the browser, how can you import it into your Live Set? (See "Importing Audio to Existing Tracks" beginning on page 119.)

8. How can you simultaneously import multiple audio files with each file being placed on its own new audio track? (See "Batch Import Directly to New Audio Tracks" beginning on page 122.)

9. How do you insert a video file that you've located in the browser as a clip on a Video track? (See "Importing Video" beginning on page 125.)

10. How can you show and hide the floating video window once you have inserted a video file on a track? How can you re-size it? (See "Video Track Display" beginning on page 125.)

11. What kinds of editing functions are available on video clips? What editing functions are *not* applicable? (See "Working with Video Tracks" beginning on page 126.)

 To review additional material from this chapter and prepare for certification, see the Ableton Live 101 Study Guide module available through the Elements|ED online learning platform at ElementsED.com.

Importing Audio

🎧 Activity

In this exercise, you will use the Browser to import audio files into the Live Set you created in the previous exercise. You will import two fragments of a musical idea: a chord progression and a bass line, both created with synths. You can choose to place these audio files on tracks using either the Arrangement View or Session View, depending on how you prefer to work.

🕑 Duration

This exercise should take approximately 10 to 15 minutes to complete.

◈ Goals/Targets

- Add a File Folder to the Browser
- Import Audio to Tracks in Arrangement or Session View

Media Files

To complete this exercise, you will need to use various audio files included in the **Media Files 2019-Live101** folder. You should have downloaded the media files in Exercise 4.

If needed, you can re-download the media files by going to www.halleonard.com/mylibrary and entering your access code (printed on the opening page of this book). From there, click the **Download** link for the **Media Files 2019-Live101** listing in your **My Library** page. The Media Files folder will begin transferring to your Downloads folder.

Getting Started

You will start by opening the Live Set you saved at the end of Exercise 4. If that file is not available, you can use the Ex04 Sample file in the 01. Completed Exercises folder within the Media Files 2019-Live101 folder.

Open the Set and save it as Exercise 5:

1. Open the Set file that you created in Exercise 4 (Storage Drive/Folder > Live101-XXX > Exercise04-XXX.als).

> **(i)** If your Exercise 4 Set is not available, you can use the Exercise 4 Sample file instead (Media Files 2019-Live 101 > 01. Completed Projects > Ex04 Sample.als).

2. Choose FILE > SAVE LIVE SET AS and name the Set *Exercise05-XXX*, keeping the Live Set inside the original Project folder. (Move the Set into your Live101-XXX folder if working from the sample file.)

The Live Set will open with the four tracks—two Audio and two MIDI—that you created in Exercise 4.

Add the Audio File Folder to the Browser

As discussed in Chapter 5, there are multiple ways of importing audio files into a Live Set. For this exercise, you will use Live's built-in Browser, as its functionality makes it well worth learning. To get started, you will add the Exercise Media folder to the Browser.

Add the sample media folder to the browser:

1. Show the Live browser by clicking VIEW > SHOW BROWSER or pressing OPTION+COMMAND+B (Mac) or CTRL+ALT+B (Windows).

2. Click the ADD FOLDER button at the bottom of the browser's left-hand column.

3. Navigate to the Media Files 2019-Live101 > 02. Exercise Media location.

4. Click SELECT FOLDER. The 02. Exercise Media folder will display in the Live Browser.

5. Click on the 02. Exercise Media folder in the Browser to display the audio files it contains.

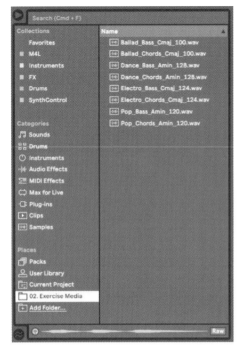

Figure 5.12   The Exercise Media folder after being added to the Live browser.

The audio files in this folder are all in WAV format. Notice that the file names include a loose genre identifier, a descriptor (**Bass** or **Chords**), a key (**C major** or **A minor**), and a tempo. In the next section, you will select a chord progression and the matching bass part to use for this exercise. For example, if you select the pop chord progression in C major at 120 BPM, you should also use the pop bass in C major at 120 BPM. This way, you will combine two distinct instruments that work together.

Preview the chord progression and bass audio files:

1.   Click through the various audio files to listen to the different options for the Live Set. As discussed in Chapter 5, you can click an audio file to preview it (assuming the Preview button is enabled).

2.   Make note of the chord progression and corresponding bass part that you like the most. In the next section, you will place the files on audio tracks and start assembling a simple musical pattern in your Live Set.

Importing Audio to Tracks

With the audio files for this exercise available through the Browser, importing them into audio tracks will be quick and easy. This is a good time to decide whether you want to work in the Arrangement View or Session View. If you prefer working in a traditional, timeline-based fashion, use the Arrangement View. If you'd like to use Live's unique features for auditioning different combinations of sounds and creating flexible arrangements, you can try the Session View instead.

Arrangement View (Option 1)

Complete this section if you'd like to work in the Arrangement View. Otherwise, skip forward to Option 2 below.

Import the audio files to tracks in the Arrangement View:

1. Set the Live Set's tempo so that it matches the tempo of the audio files you will be using.

2. Drag and drop the chord progression file you would like to use to Bar 5 of the audio track labeled **Chords**.

3. Rename the audio clip to something simpler, such as **Chords**.

4. Select the **Chords** clip and choose **EDIT > DUPLICATE** to create a second copy of the clip on the track, immediately after the original.

5. Repeat the command two more times, for a total of four identical clips, to create a longer, 16-bar song segment.

6. Drag and drop the corresponding bass part to the **Bass** track, this time starting at Bar 13.

7. Right-click on the top of the clip with the hand icon and choose **RENAME** from the pop-up menu.

8. Rename the clip to something simpler, such as **Bass**.

9. Duplicate the **Bass** clip once, so it plays from the middle to the end of the 16-bar segment.

You've now created a 16-bar segment, with a chord progression spanning the whole time and the bass part starting after 8 bars.

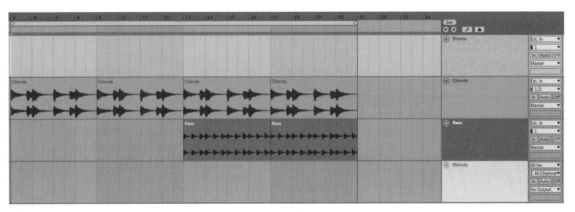

Figure 5.13 A Set with chord and bass parts completed in the Arrangement View

Review your work:

1. Position the Arrangement Insert Marker at the start of the clips.

2. Press the **SPACEBAR** to play back the Live Set and confirm your results.

3. Press the **SPACEBAR** a second time when finished.

Session View (Option 2)

Complete this section if you'd like to work in the Session View. (If you completed Option 1 above, skip forward to the next section.)

To import the audio files to tracks in the Session View:

1. Set the Live Set's tempo so that it matches the tempo of the audio files you will be using.

2. Drag and drop the chord progression file you would like to use onto the first and second clip slots of the audio track labeled Chords. This will place the clip on both Scene 1 and Scene 2.

 Instead of dragging the audio file from the Browser twice, you can press and hold OPTION (Mac) or CTRL (Windows) while a dragging the clip from clip slot 1 to duplicate it on clip slot 2.

3. Right-click on the clip on each clip slot and choose **RENAME** from the pop-up menu.

4. Rename the clip to something simpler, such as Chords.

5. Drag and drop the bass file onto the second clip slot of the Bass audio track, so the clip is only on Scene 2.

6. Right-click the clip and rename it to something simpler, such as Bass.

At this point, you will have a basic, two-scene Live Set. You can alternate playback between the chord progression in isolation (Scene 1) and the combination of the chord progression and the corresponding bass part (Scene 2).

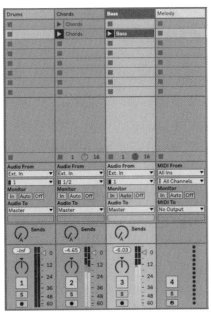

Figure 5.14 A Set with chord and bass parts added in the Session View

Review and your work:

1. Click the **SCENE LAUNCH** button on Scene 1 of the Master track. The chord clip will launch and begin playing. Left unchanged, the clip will repeat when it reaches the end.

2. When the clip is just a couple beats away from repeating, press the **SCENE LAUNCH** button on Scene 2 to queue up the next scene. When the first Scene ends, the second Scene will launch, containing both the chord progression and the corresponding bass part.

3. When finished, press the **SPACEBAR** or the **STOP ALL CLIPS** button on the Master track to stop playback.

Finishing Up

To complete this exercise, you will save your work and close the Live Set. You will be re-using this set in the next exercise, so it is important to save the work you've done.

Save your work and close the Live Set:

1. Choose **FILE > SAVE LIVE SET**.

2. Press **COMMAND+Q** (Mac) or **CTRL+Q** (Windows) to quit Live and close the project.

Chapter 6

Working with MIDI

This lesson covers the basics of recording, programming, and editing MIDI data in Ableton Live. It describes what MIDI is, how to record or manually create a MIDI performance, how to send MIDI data to a virtual instrument, and how to use many of the editing features available in Live's MIDI Note Editor.

⊕ Learning Targets for This Chapter

- Understand the basics of MIDI

- Recognize the different behaviors of MIDI clips and audio clips

- Set up a virtual instrument to generate sound using MIDI data

- Record a performance to a MIDI track using a MIDI controller

- Manually program a MIDI performance using a mouse and keyboard

- Edit and fine-tune MIDI data using the MIDI Note Editor

Key topics from this chapter are illustrated in the Ableton Live 101 Study Guide module available through the Elements|ED online learning platform. Sign up for free at ElementsED.com.

MIDI data offers music producers, sound designers, and audio engineers a tremendous amount of flexibility when carrying out their work. MIDI provides a simple and efficient way to program or record musical performances, which can then be sent to various software– or hardware–based instruments—such as synthesizers, samplers, and drum machines—to produce almost any type of sound. This chapter introduces Live's MIDI recording, programming, and editing features, as well as other general considerations to keep in mind whenever you are working with MIDI data.

MIDI Basics

MIDI, or *Musical Instrument Digital Interface*, is a protocol for connecting electronic instruments, performance controllers, and computers so they can communicate with one another. MIDI data is fundamentally different from data stored in an audio file in that MIDI data does not represent sound waves or produce any sound on its own; instead, it represents information about a performance, such as the pitch, duration, and intensity of the notes.

A *MIDI sequencer* allows you to create, edit, and play back MIDI information that can be used to control MIDI-compatible devices, such as synthesizers, samplers, drum machines, and sound modules. In modern-day music production, these devices are often virtual instrument plug-ins (i.e., software-based instruments). Virtual instruments can be added directly to MIDI tracks within Live.

MIDI data is transmitted via MIDI messages. These messages are composed of 8-bit numbers (or *bytes*) and include information such as the *note* or *pitch number* (indicating an individual note in a scale) and the *velocity* value (typically affecting an individual note's volume or intensity).

MIDI data can be transmitted in multiple ways, such as by routing to virtual instrument plug-ins within Live or by connecting to hardware MIDI devices via MIDI cable. Up to 16 separate channels of MIDI information can be sent over a single MIDI cable, allowing a single cable path to control multiple MIDI devices or to control multiple sound sources within a single device that is capable of multi-channel (or *multi-timbral*) operation.

Many other kinds of information can be conveyed via MIDI messages, such as pan and general MIDI volume information for instruments that support these, as well as program change events, or commands that tell MIDI instruments which of their available sounds, or *patches*, to use.

The Format of a MIDI Message

The most significant bit (first digit) in a MIDI message byte is reserved to distinguish between status bytes and data bytes. The remaining seven bits represent the unique data of the message byte, encompassing a range of values from 0 to 127.

The maximum length for a standard MIDI message is three bytes, consisting of one status byte and one or more data bytes. The format of each byte is as follows:

Status Byte	Data Byte 1	Data Byte 2
1tttnnnn	0xxxxxxx	0xxxxxxx

Where:

The leading 0 signifies a data byte
The leading 1 signifies a status byte
t is used to specify the type of status message being sent
n is used to specify the associated MIDI Channel Number
x is used to specify the associated data value, such as a note number (pitch) or velocity value

MIDI in Ableton Live

Ableton Live includes an integrated MIDI sequencer (or editor) that lets you program, record, import, and edit MIDI in much the same way that you work with imported audio (see Chapter 5) or recorded audio (see Chapter 7). MIDI data is stored in MIDI clips and can be edited in the Clip View regardless of whether you're working in the Session View or Arrangement View.

Press Shift+Tab to toggle between the Clip View and Device View.

The Clip View is where you will find Live's visual MIDI Note Editor, which you can use to view, write, and edit MIDI data.

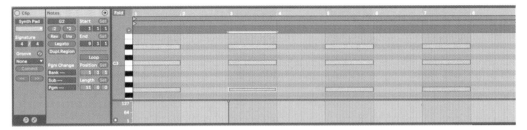

Figure 6.1 Live's MIDI Note Editor with a MIDI clip selected

As you may recall from Chapter 4, MIDI tracks can co-exist with audio tracks in a Live Set; clips on both track types reference the same timeline. Similarly, both track types feature similar mixer controls, such as volume, pan, input and output routing options, and more.

Creating MIDI Tracks

Before you can start working with MIDI, you'll need at least one MIDI track in your Live Set. To add a MIDI track, select **CREATE > INSERT MIDI TRACK** or press **COMMAND+SHIFT+T** (Mac) or **CTRL+SHIFT+T** (Windows).

You can create MIDI clips by recording a performance to a MIDI track or manually programming in the MIDI notes. Both methods are covered later in this chapter.

 For a detailed breakdown of track types and associated keyboard shortcuts, see Chapter 4 of this book.

MIDI Versus Audio Clip Operation

Audio and MIDI clips can and often do co-exist in a Live Set. However, they're very different, and it is worth understanding the differences in how audio and MIDI clips behave. We've already established one key difference in that MIDI clips don't inherently produce sound; the other key difference is how MIDI clips behave when you make changes to the tempo of your Live Set. Audio and MIDI clips respond differently to changes in tempo because their source material is different: audio clips contain *samples* whereas MIDI clips contain *performance data*.

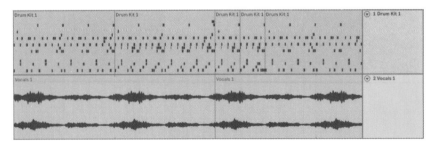

Figure 6.2 A blend of audio and MIDI clips in the Arrangement View Track Display

MIDI Clip Operation

MIDI clips easily conform to changes in your Live Set tempo, as the MIDI data is flexible. MIDI events are recorded relative to particular bar and beat locations (such as Bar 16, Beat 1), and their locations in time adjust based on the project tempo: if the tempo increases, the MIDI data will play back faster, and individual events will occur earlier in time; if the tempo decreases, the MIDI data will play back more slowly, and the same events will occur later in time.

Figure 6.3 A MIDI clip in the Arrangement View Track Display

Audio Clip Operation

Audio clips, on the other hand, are generally absolute, meaning they will continue to play back at their original speed and location after changing the project tempo—though the audio clips' positions relative to the Set's bars and beats will change. This behavior can be desirable for non-rhythmic audio, such as spoken words or ambient textures, but it can cause rhythmic audio like drum loops to fall out of sync in the context of a song.

Figure 6.4 An audio clip in the Arrangement View Track Display

 Live's Warping feature allows audio clips to automatically speed up or slow down to conform to the Live Set's tempo.

Audio Warping

With Warp algorithms, Live is capable of time-warping audio clips while streaming them from disk so as to synchronize them with the Live Set's tempo. This happens without affecting the pitch, which can be changed independently. As such, even if you mix and match audio files from various sources with MIDI data, your Live Set can remain flexible with respect to tempo changes.

To enable time-warping for audio, select an audio clip (or clips) and click the **WARP** button in the Sample box within the Clip View (see Figure 6.5). The selected audio clips will stretch or compress as needed to automatically follow tempo changes and conform to the Set's tempo.

Live provides a variety of Warp modes, as illustrated in Figure 6.5. The different modes change the way warping is applied, allowing you to select the best option for different program material.

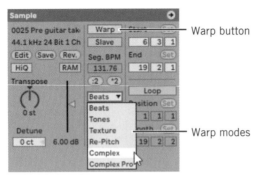

Figure 6.5 The Warp button and available Warp modes for a selected audio clip

 Warping audio, especially when done to extremes, can create undesired audio artifacts. Always check the results and use the Edit > Undo command if you are not happy with the outcome.

Setting the Tempo and Time Signature

Before you begin recording MIDI data, you should determine the required tempo and time signature for the performance. The following sections describe how to configure these options for your composition.

Setting the Base Tempo

When you create a new Live Set, the tempo defaults to 120 beats per minute (BPM). If you need to work at a different tempo—and especially if you are planning to record a performance with the metronome—make sure to set the tempo in Live accordingly.

Entering a Tempo Value

If you know the tempo that you wish to use, you can enter it directly into the Control Bar.

To configure the Live Set's tempo directly, do the following:

1. Click the **TEMPO** field in the Control Bar.

2. Drag up and down to adjust the value, or type a value in BPM. This will change the tempo for the entire Live Set in real time.

Figure 6.6 The Tempo field in the Control Bar (highlighted in yellow)

Tap Tempo

If you have a tempo in mind but you're not sure of the exact value, click the **TAP** button in the Control Bar once per beat; the Live Set's tempo will follow your tapping. For example, to set the tempo based on a performance you will be recording, have the musician(s) begin playing through the piece while you tap along using a mouse or trackpad with the cursor on the Tap button.

Figure 6.7 The Tap button in the Control Bar (highlighted in yellow)

 You can use something other than a mouse or trackpad to tap a tempo. To do so, click on the KEY switch in the Control Bar to enable the Key Map mode. Click the TAP button and then press the target key to use for tapping. Press the KEY switch again to exit the Key Map mode and use the newly assigned key.

Automating Tempo Changes with Breakpoints

Your Live Set does not have to stick to one static tempo throughout its duration. You can use an automation envelope to change the tempo at any time in your Live Set.

 Adding tempo changes with automation requires that you work in the Arrangement View.

To add tempo change breakpoints to your arrangement, do the following:

1. If necessary, switch to the Arrangement View.

2. Right-click the **TEMPO** field in the Control Bar and select **SHOW AUTOMATION**. This will show the Song Tempo automation envelope on the Master track.

   The automation envelope will display as a dotted orange line on the Master track in Arrangement View.

 The automation envelop in Ableton Live is also sometimes referred to as the automation graph.

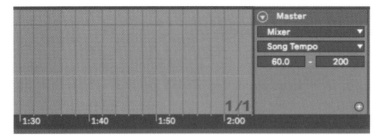

Figure 6.8 The automation envelope on the Master track before adding breakpoints

3. Disable the **DRAW MODE** switch in the Control Bar, if necessary.

4. Click anywhere on the dotted line to add a breakpoint at the existing tempo. A small circular node will display on the automation envelope, and the envelope graph will change to a solid orange line.

5. Click again on the line to add a second breakpoint.

6. Drag breakpoints up or down to set the desired tempo; drag breakpoints forward or backward to set the position for the tempo change and adjust the tempo ramp.

   Tempo changes can either take effect instantly or ramp smoothly over time (see Figure 6.9).

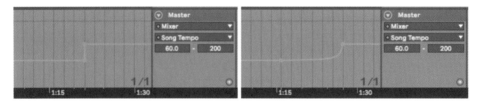

Figure 6.9 An instant tempo change (left) and a gradual tempo change (right)

 Automation is covered in more detail in Chapter 10 of this book.

Setting the Base Time Signature

When you create a new Live Set, the time signature defaults to 4/4. If you intend to record and work in another time signature, you'll need to set it accordingly. You can either alter the time signature for the entire Live Set or have the time signature change within an arrangement.

To set the time signature for the entire Live Set, do the following:

1. Click the **TIME SIGNATURE NUMERATOR** in the Control Bar.

2. Drag up or down, or type a numeric value.

3. If necessary, click the TIME SIGNATURE DENOMINATOR in the Control Bar.

4. Drag up or down, or type a numeric value.

Figure 6.10 The Time Signature field in the Control Bar

Adding Time Signature Changes

Your Live Set does not have to stick to one time signature for the entire piece. You can change the meter at any point in your Live Set using time signature markers.

 Adding time signature changes requires that you work in the Arrangement View.

To add time signature markers to your arrangement, do the following:

1. If necessary, switch to the Arrangement View.

2. Place the Arrangement Insert Marker where you want a time signature change to occur.

3. Do one of the following:

    • Select CREATE > INSERT TIME SIGNATURE CHANGE.

    • Right-click at the desired location in the scrub area of the beat-time ruler and select INSERT TIME SIGNATURE CHANGE from the pop-up menu.

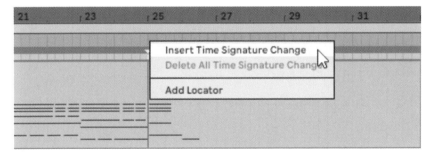

Figure 6.11 Right-click in the scrub area below the beat-time ruler to insert a time signature change.

4. Enter the desired time signature. For instance, you can type 4/4, 3/4, or some other valid time signature.

5. Press RETURN or ENTER.

This will create a marker beneath the beat-time ruler where all time signature changes appear, as shown in Figure 6.12. A red dot will also appear on the TIME SIGNATURE field in the Control Bar, indicating that it has been automated (see Figure 6.13).

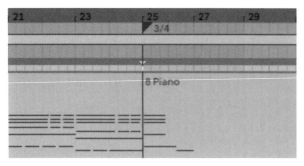

Figure 6.12 A time signature change marker in the Arrangement View

Figure 6.13 The Time Signature field with the automation indicator displayed (red dot)

You can click and drag time signature markers to move them along the timeline. Right-click a time signature marker and select EDIT TIME SIGNATURE to make changes to it or select DELETE to remove it.

Preparing to Record MIDI

With at least one MIDI track added to your Set and the tempo and time signature configured as desired, you will next need to prepare your Live Set for recording.

The general processes you will use to prepare for recording MIDI are as follows:

1. Configure the metronome to aid in making a well-timed recording, if desired.

2. Configure your Record Quantization settings to automatically correct timing errors during the performance, if desired.

3. Connect a MIDI device, if available.

> (i)   In the absence of a dedicated MIDI device, you can record MIDI using your computer keyboard or manually program MIDI using your mouse and keyboard.

4. Check the track inputs/outputs.

5. Record-enable the track(s).

Enabling the Metronome

When you're recording parts for a song or other composition that is based on a specific tempo (or tempos) with established bar and beat divisions, you might want to perform along with a metronome-based tick. The metronome may help you synchronize your performance to the composition when you're recording – whether it's MIDI data or audio – and ultimately align the recorded parts to musical divisions. Having your recorded parts in alignment with the Live Set's tempo makes it easy for you to make selections according to the musical grid, and perform such tasks as copying and pasting entire song sections as you work on your arrangements.

To enable or disable the metronome, click the **METRONOME** switch in the Control Bar along the top of the Ableton Live interface. When you press the **PLAY** button in the Control Bar, launch a clip from the Session View, or begin recording, the metronome will play a tick at each beat.

Customizing the Metronome

Ableton Live provides several metronome options, which you can access by clicking the menu triangle on the **METRONOME** switch.

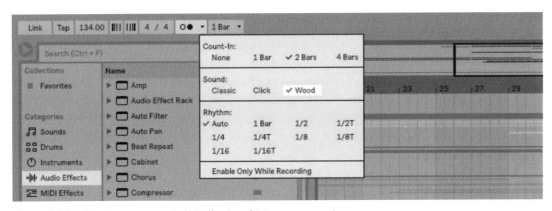

Figure 6.14 The Metronome switch (yellow) and Metronome settings menu

Options available in the Metronome settings menu include the following:

- **Count-In**: determines the number of bars the metronome will tick before recording commences.

- **Sound**: allows you to choose between three styles of metronome ticks (Classic, Click, and Wood).

- **Rhythm**: determines the musical divisions that will be represented by the metronome.

- **Enable Only While Recording**: causes the metronome to sound during recording only – not during playback.

You can control the volume level of the metronome by adjusting the Preview/Cue Volume on the Master track (see Figure 6.15).

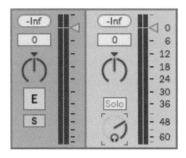

Figure 6.15 Use the Preview/Cue Volume knob (blue) on the Master track to adjust the metronome volume relative to the level of the Live Set

Configuring Record Quantization

You can set up Live so that it automatically aligns, or quantizes, MIDI notes during a recording.

To set up Record Quantization, do the following:

1. Select EDIT > RECORD QUANTIZATION.

2. From the list of options, choose the musical divisions to which you would like to align your notes. Larger divisions will result in a more noticeable quantization.

If you want to retain the original feel of the performance, do not use quantization during the recording. You can always quantize your performance after the recording. Quantization is covered in the last section of this chapter, "Creating and Editing MIDI Performances."

Connecting a MIDI Device

Recording MIDI data often involves connecting a keyboard, a drum machine, or another MIDI device as an input to your system. Before starting to record, you should verify that the MIDI device you will use for input (also called a *MIDI controller*) is connected to your system through an input on your MIDI interface or a USB port on your computer.

You can view connected MIDI devices in the PREFERENCES window (choose LIVE > PREFERENCES on Mac or OPTIONS > PREFERENCES on Windows) by selecting the LINK / MIDI tab (see Figure 6.16).

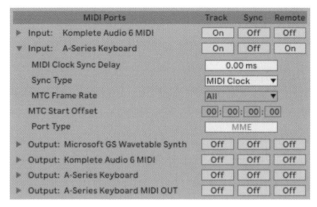

Figure 6.16 MIDI devices, as listed in the Live Preferences menu

Using the Computer Keyboard for MIDI

To use your computer keyboard as a MIDI device, press the **M** key or click the **COMPUTER MIDI KEYBOARD** switch in the Control Bar. This will make the computer keyboard available to function as a MIDI device, as described below.

Figure 6.17 The Computer MIDI Keyboard switch (yellow) in the Control Bar

When active, the Computer MIDI Keyboard uses the top and middle rows of alphabetic keys on the QWERTY keypad to play the black and white notes on a piano, as indicated in Figure 6.18. The octave targeted by the computer keys can be adjusted up or down using the **Z** and **X** keys.

You can adjust the velocity that will be used for the played notes using the **C** and **V** keys. Each key press will shift the velocity value up or down in 20 unit intervals.

Figure 6.18 MIDI mapping for the Computer MIDI Keyboard

Selecting MIDI Inputs

Once your MIDI device is connected, you will need to route its signal into the input of your MIDI track.

Before moving forward, make sure that the In/Out controls are visible by clicking **VIEW > IN/OUT** or **COMMAND+OPTION+I** (Mac) or **CTRL+ALT+I** (Windows). This will reveal input and output options for all the tracks in your Live Set in both the Session View and Arrangement View.

Input Type and Input Channel

Each MIDI track has an *Input Type chooser* and an *Input Channel chooser* at the top of the track's I/O section. These input options allow you to choose the MIDI device you would like to use with the track.

To select your MIDI device, do the following:

1. Locate the In/Out section of the track on which you will record.

2. Use the **INPUT TYPE** dropdown menu to select the MIDI controller you will use to record a MIDI performance.

3. Select an **INPUT CHANNEL**. For now, **All Channels** will suffice.

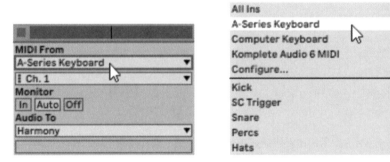

Figure 6.19 The MIDI In/Out options (left) and Input Type chooser menu (right)

Record-Arming MIDI Tracks

To enable recording on a MIDI track, click the track's **ARM** button in either the Session View or Arrangement View. The **ARM** button turns red when the track is record-ready.

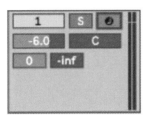

Figure 6.20 The track Arm button in the Session View (left) and Arrangement View (right)

Using MIDI Arrangement Overdub Mode

In certain MIDI recording workflows, you may wish to enable MIDI Arrangement Overdub mode. This feature allows you to record additional MIDI notes into a clip without overwriting existing notes. This recording method can be useful for many purposes, such as adding layers to an instrumental performance or recording layers of a drum kit in separate passes.

When the **MIDI ARRANGEMENT OVERDUB** button is active, you can record a MIDI performance while merging it in with existing MIDI data on the track, overdubbing the track. When this button is not active, recorded MIDI data will replace existing track material.

To enable MIDI Arrangement Overdub do one of the following:

- Select **OPTIONS > MIDI ARRANGEMENT OVERDUB.**

- Click the **MIDI ARRANGEMENT OVERDUB** button (plus sign) in the Control Bar.

Figure 6.21 The MIDI Arrangement Overdub button (yellow) in the Control Bar

 Before starting a MIDI recording on a track that already contains MIDI data, be sure to verify the status of the MIDI Arrangement Overdub mode to ensure you get the intended results.

Using Virtual Instruments

While the MIDI track is now ready to record, at this stage it will not produce any sound. In order for the MIDI signal to generate sound, it needs to be sent to a *virtual instrument*. Virtual instruments are the software equivalents of outboard synthesizers, samplers, or sound modules. Ableton Live Suite includes a selection of native virtual instruments and also supports third-party virtual instruments as plug-ins.

Ableton Live Suite ships with an assortment of popular software-based virtual instruments, including Wavetable, Operator, and Sampler. Ableton Live Standard includes a smaller number of sample-based instruments. In order to experience MIDI recording and editing, you will need at least one software-based instrument.

Inserting a Virtual Instrument on a MIDI Track

You can add a native or third-party virtual instrument to a MIDI track at any time.

To add a virtual instrument to a MIDI track, do the following:

1. Show the Browser by choosing **VIEW > SHOW BROWSER** or by pressing **COMMAND+OPTION+B** (Mac) or **CTRL+ALT+B** (Windows).

2. Do one of the following:

    *   Select the **INSTRUMENTS** category to view the available Ableton Live virtual instruments.

    *   Select the **PLUG-INS** category to view any third-party plug-ins you've installed (including virtual instruments).

3. Expand the instrument as needed to navigate the available contents, using the disclosure triangles in the Browser content pane.

4. With the destination MIDI track selected, double-click the virtual instrument device you want to insert. Your MIDI signal will now be routed to the virtual instrument.

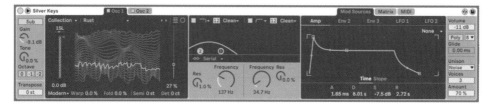

Figure 6.22 The Wavetable virtual instrument device on a MIDI track

5. Set the track's **VOLUME** slider to the desired output level.

6. Record-enable the track and play some notes on your MIDI controller. The meters on the MIDI track will register the instrument's audio output.

Deactivating Virtual Instruments

You can deactivate a virtual instrument without removing it from a track. Deactivating the instrument will free up the CPU resources that the instrument was using, while retaining the instrument settings.

To deactivate a virtual instrument:

■ Click the round Device Activator in the upper left-hand corner of the device.

Figure 6.23 The Device Activator (yellow) on a virtual instrument

Using Drum Rack

The Drum Rack is a simple but powerful drum sampler that is bundled with Ableton Live Standard and Suite editions. It has a grid-based layout that is reminiscent of many drum machines, allowing you to create your own drum kits and trigger the drum sounds with MIDI signals. Each cell in the Drum Rack corresponds to a single a MIDI note, such as C1, C#1, D1, and so on. When you drag and drop an audio file to a cell, the MIDI note assigned to it will trigger playback of the sound, making the drum kit playable by using a MIDI device or by manually programming MIDI notes.

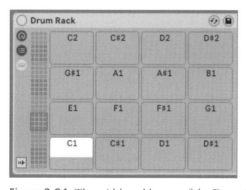

Figure 6.24 The grid-based layout of the Drum Rack instrument

The flexibility of this instrument comes from the amount of control you have over each sample you load into the Drum Rack. For instance, you can configure basic mix controls, such as volume and pan, as well as filter, LFO (or low-frequency oscillator), and sample length parameters for each individual sample.

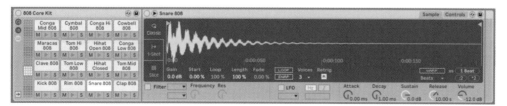

Figure 6.25 A Drum Rack preset with drum samples that can be triggered with MIDI data

If you are not feeling ready to construct your own kit using the Drum Rack, you can browse pre-created kits in the Browser. Click the Drums category in the browser to audition available drum kits. Double-click a drum kit that you'd like to add to a MIDI track.

Using Simpler

Simpler is an instrument that allows you to trigger any piece of recorded audio—instrument sounds, vocal recordings, drum and synth one-shots, and more—using MIDI data. In order to use this sample-based instrument, you must have an audio file to load into the Simpler.

Simpler is a useful tool for making playable instruments out of any source material, as well as performing realistic recreations of acoustic instruments through MIDI. Sampling is a deep and complex art, so to start to understand how it works, you might want to explore some of Ableton's Simpler presets.

Figure 6.26 A Simpler-based preset called "BBass" loaded on a MIDI track

To browse Simpler presets, click the disclosure triangle next to Simpler in the Browser. You can explore different categories of sounds and audition them by clicking their name. Once you have found one you like, double-click it to insert it on the currently selected MIDI track. Be aware that this will overwrite any existing instrument device for the track.

Using Wavetable (Ableton Live 10 Suite only)

Wavetable is a wavetable synthesizer that was introduced with Ableton Live 10 Suite. It is particularly useful for creating dynamic, morphing sounds through wavetable modulation. However, synthesis is also a complex topic, so at this time you might consider browsing for a preset, or a pre-created sound, rather than creating your own from scratch in Wavetable.

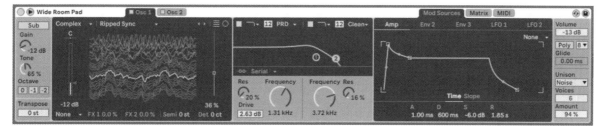

Figure 6.27 A Wavetable preset called "Wide Room Pad" loaded on a MIDI track

To browse Wavetable presets, click the disclosure triangle next to Wavetable in the Browser. You can explore different categories of sounds and audition them by clicking their names. Once you have found one you like, double-click it to insert it on the currently selected MIDI track. Be aware that this will overwrite any existing instrument device on the track.

 For more information on navigating the Browser and using its controls, see Chapter 5 in this book.

Recording a MIDI Performance

With a MIDI controller selected, a MIDI signal feeding a virtual instrument device, and the track armed for recording, you are ready to begin recording.

Session View

Recording in Session View allows you to create individual clips and launch other clips while recording.

To begin recording MIDI in Session View, do the following:

1. Record-arm at least one MIDI track as described earlier in this chapter. Once the track is armed, each clip slot in the track will display a round Record button in place of its square Clip Stop button.

2. Click the **RECORD** button on one of the clip slots to record a new clip to that slot.

3. The record button will flash red and the metronome count-in will begin, if enabled.

4. Once recording has commenced, the record button will turn into a red Clip Launch button.

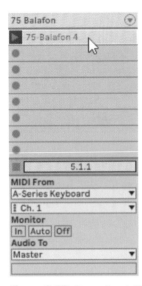

Figure 6.28 Recording MIDI to a clip slot in the Session View

5. When you have finished your record take, click the **STOP** button in the Control Bar (or press the **SPACEBAR**).

> (i) Alternatively, you can press the red Clip Launch button at the end of a record pass to continue playback of the current scene, including the new MIDI recording.

Recording to Multiple Tracks

If you have multiple tracks armed for recording, you can click the **SESSION RECORD** button (hollow circle) in the Control Bar to record onto all armed tracks on a selected scene.

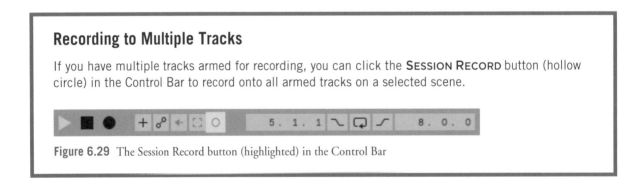

Figure 6.29 The Session Record button (highlighted) in the Control Bar

---

Customizing Session View Recording

When recording in the Session View, you can optionally select a value from the Quantization Menu. When the value is set to anything other than **None**, Live will automatically cut the boundaries of your recorded clip so it aligns with your Live Set. This will aid in keeping clips in rhythmic alignment.

Figure 6.30 The Quantization Menu with a value of 2 Bars selected

The Session View can also be configured so that recording begins on all armed tracks upon launching a given scene. To do this, you need to enable the Start Recording on Scene Launch option in the Preferences window. This option is located under the RECORD / WARP / LAUNCH tab.

Arrangement View

The Arrangement View gives you a linear, timeline-based view of your recording progress. It is best suited for recording to multiple tracks simultaneously.

To begin recording MIDI in Arrangement View, do the following:

1. Arm at least one MIDI track for recording.

2. Position the Arrangement Insert Marker where you want the recording to begin.

3. Click the **ARRANGEMENT RECORD** button (solid circle) in the Control Bar.

Figure 6.31 The Arrangement Record button (red) in the Control Bar

4. The Arrangement Record button will turn red and recording will begin immediately, starting with the metronome count-in (if enabled). The track(s) to which you are recording will be highlighted red during the recording.

5. When you have finished your record take, click the **STOP** button in the Control Bar (or press the SPACEBAR).

Customizing the Arrangement Record Button

You can change the behavior of the Arrangement Record button by toggling the **START PLAYBACK WITH RECORD** option in the Ableton Live Preferences window. This option is located under the RECORD/WARP/LAUNCH tab. When disabled, recording does not start until the Arrangement Record button is triggered **and** the **PLAY** button (or the SPACEBAR) is pressed.

 You can use function key F9 as a shortcut to activate the Arrangement Record button.

You can also hold Shift while activating the Arrangement Record button to override the current Start Playback with Record setting, saving you from having to open the Preferences window and manually switch modes.

Creating a MIDI Performance Manually

Sometimes, you might want or need to create a MIDI performance manually (by programming notes using the mouse and keyboard). This requires that you create a MIDI clip and draw notes in the MIDI Note Editor.

First, you'll need to create an empty MIDI clip; there are multiple ways of doing this in both Session View and Arrangement View.

To create a MIDI clip in Session View:

- Double-click an empty clip slot on a MIDI track.

- Select an empty clip slot on a MIDI track and choose CREATE > INSERT MIDI CLIP(S).

To create a MIDI clip in Arrangement View:

- Double-click on a MIDI track in the Track Display window.

- Select an empty range of time on a MIDI track in the Track Display window and choose CREATE > INSERT MIDI CLIP(S), or press COMMAND+SHIFT+M (Mac) or CTRL+SHIFT+M (Windows).

The next section covers the MIDI Note Editor in detail, including its features for creating and editing notes.

Creating and Editing MIDI Performances

Live's MIDI Note Editor allows you to both create new MIDI performances and edit existing ones. To access Live's MIDI Note Editor, select a MIDI clip (if Clip View is active) or double-click a MIDI clip (if Clip View is not active). This will display the clip contents in Clip View, within the MIDI Note Editor.

 Click and drag the divider between the Clip View and Track Display to expand the MIDI Note Editor, if necessary.

The MIDI Note Editor

The MIDI Note Editor shows individual MIDI notes in a piano-roll format, with note pitch shown on the vertical axis, and note position and duration in time shown on the horizontal axis. MIDI notes are represented as colored bars of different brightness, depending on their respective velocities.

A dedicated velocity editor is located along the bottom of the MIDI Note Editor, with the current grid spacing value indicated in the lower right-hand corner (see Figure 6.32).

 If the velocity editor is not visible, click the triangle icon at the bottom of the note ruler area in the MIDI Note Editor (bottom left corner).

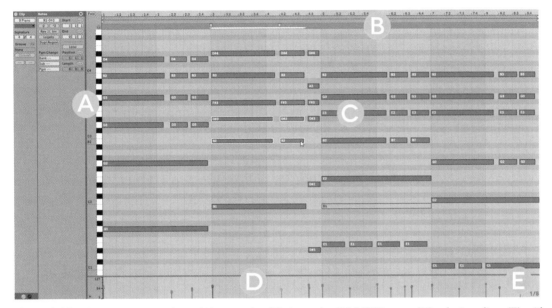

Figure 6.32 The MIDI Note Editor: (A) note ruler (B) time ruler (C) MIDI notes (D) velocity editor (E) grid spacing

The visual nature of the MIDI Note Editor makes it easy to see musical performances as well as create, select, and edit notes. This section covers editing functions that will allow you to create the exact performance you desire.

Creating MIDI Notes

During the production process, you may want to enter MIDI notes by hand. For many producers, this is a faster way of entering MIDI data than playing a keyboard or other controller.

There are two methods of creating MIDI notes by hand:

■ Double-click in the MIDI Note Editor at the desired note and position in time. Before releasing the mouse, drag to the right to extend the duration of the note. (You can also trim note durations after adding them by dragging on a note edge with the trim icon.)

- Press the **B** key or the **DRAW MODE** button in the Control Bar to enable Draw Mode. This enables the pencil tool, allowing you to "draw" MIDI notes in the editor. Note lengths will match the current grid size of the MIDI Note Editor.

Figure 6.33 The Draw Mode button (yellow) in the Control Bar

When adding notes using the above methods, note start and end points will snap to the current grid lines. To change the grid size, right-click in the MIDI Note Editor and choose a different Fixed Grid setting. You can also press and hold **COMMAND** (Mac) or **ALT** (Windows) to remove grid constraints when adding new notes.

 With the cursor in the MIDI Note Editor, press COMMAND+1 and COMMAND+2 (Mac) or CTRL+1 and CTRL+2 (Windows) to narrow or widen the grid, respectively.

 Clicking on an existing note in Draw Mode (or double-clicking in Edit Mode) will delete the note.

Selecting MIDI Notes

Whether you have recorded or manually created MIDI notes, you can make selections for editing in multiple ways.

To make a selection of MIDI notes, do one of the following:

- Click an individual note in Edit Mode.

- Starting from an empty space, click and drag within the MIDI Note Editor in Edit Mode to draw a marquee around multiple notes.

- **SHIFT+CLICK** a note in Edit Mode to add a note to a selection or remove a note from a selection.

- Click and drag within the MIDI Note Editor in Edit Mode *without* selecting any notes to select a timespan, or click and drag within the MIDI Note Editor Scratch Area in either mode to create a timespan. Then press **RETURN** or **ENTER** to select all notes that start within the timespan.

- With the cursor located in the MIDI Note Editor or any note selected, press **COMMAND+A** (Mac) or **CTRL+A** (Windows) to select all notes in the clip.

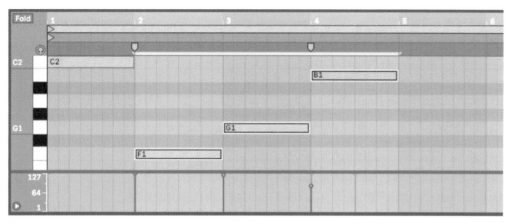

Figure 6.34 A multi-note selection in the MIDI Note Editor

Moving a Selection to a Different Note

Once you've made a selection of one or more MIDI notes, you can easily move the selection to a different note.

To move a selection from note to note using the keyboard, do one of the following:

- With at least one note selected, you can cycle between the previous and next note by pressing **OPTION+UP/DOWN ARROW** (Mac) or **CTRL+UP/DOWN ARROW** (Windows).

- With at least one note selected, you can cycle between the previous and next note *of the same pitch* by pressing **OPTION+LEFT/RIGHT ARROW** (Mac) or **CTRL+LEFT/RIGHT ARROW** (Windows).

Editing MIDI Notes

The MIDI Note Editor provides many ways to edit notes, allowing you to develop your own workflows. It is possible to edit MIDI notes using a mouse or trackpad, and also directly from the computer keyboard.

Editing MIDI Notes Using a Mouse or Trackpad

You can quickly change the pitch, position, and length of MIDI notes using the mouse.

To edit MIDI notes using a mouse or trackpad:

- Click and drag a note in Edit Mode to move it to another pitch and position in time.

- Click and drag the edges at the start or end of a note to trim its duration in either direction.

- Right-click and select **DEACTIVATE NOTE(S)** to prevent a note from playing without deleting it.

- Right-click and select **DUPLICATE** to duplicate a note or a selection of notes.

■ While holding **OPTION** (Mac) or **CTRL** (Windows), click and drag a note or selection of notes to duplicate it.

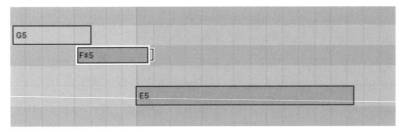

Figure 6.35 A deactivated MIDI note (G5) and a note being trimmed with the mouse (F#5)

Editing MIDI Notes with the Computer Keyboard

You can also perform some of the same editing tasks described above using the computer keyboard.

To edit MIDI notes using the computer keyboard:

■ With a note selected, press any directional arrow to move it to adjacent pitches and positions in time.

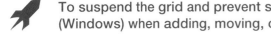 Hold **SHIFT** while pressing the **UP** or **DOWN ARROW** to move a note or notes by an entire octave.

■ To change the duration of a selected note (or notes), press **SHIFT+LEFT/RIGHT ARROW**.

■ Press the **O** key to activate or deactivate a note; deactivating a note will prevent it from playing without deleting it.

■ Press **COMMAND+D** (Mac) or **CTRL+D** (Windows) to duplicate a selected note or notes.

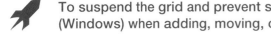 To toggle notes snapping to the grid, select **OPTIONS > SNAP TO GRID** or press **COMMAND+4** (Mac) or **CTRL+4** (Windows).

To suspend the grid and prevent snapping, hold **COMMAND** (Mac) or **ALT** (Windows) when adding, moving, or trimming a note.

Editing Velocity

Velocity is MIDI data that indicates how hard a key or pad was pressed when recording from a MIDI controller. This data is stored within the MIDI performance. Velocity information can help you create more lifelike MIDI performances, as different velocity values can trigger different audio samples and different volume levels from virtual instruments. Even if you don't perform MIDI using a velocity-sensitive MIDI controller, you can manually edit velocity data for each note in a clip.

Velocity is represented both by the brightness of a note and by the velocity stalk at the bottom of the MIDI Note Editor. Higher velocity notes are brighter and more vibrant in color. Their velocity stalk in the velocity editor is also taller than lower-velocity notes.

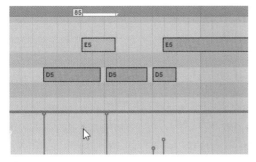

Figure 6.36 Editing velocity by clicking and dragging a velocity stalk

To quickly adjust the velocity for one or more notes:

1. Select one or more MIDI notes.

2. Do one of the following:

   - Click and drag a velocity stalk up and down in the velocity editor.

   - While holding **COMMAND** (Mac) or **ALT** (Windows), click and drag up and down on a MIDI note.

The velocity value will display at the top of the MIDI Note Editor window, using a range spanning from 1 to 127. When multiple notes are selected, the velocity of all notes will change relative to one another.

Additional Editing Features

Just to the left of the MIDI Note Editor display is the Notes section of the Clip View. Several handy MIDI editing features are located here:

- *Transpose*: Allows you to move all selected notes up and down by semitones by typing in a positive or negative value.

- *Play at half or double tempo*: Halves or doubles the duration of all selected notes and the spacing between notes.

- *Reverse Notes*: Reverses the order of a selection of notes.

- *Invert Notes*: Inverts the pitch of a selection of notes, while retaining the intervals between notes.

■ *Legato*: Shortens or lengthens selected notes so that the end of each note reaches the start of the next note without overlapping.

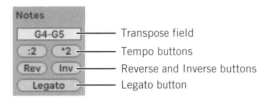

Figure 6.37 Additional MIDI editing features in the Notes section

MIDI Quantization

Quantization allows you to align, or quantize, MIDI notes to a specified timing grid. This creates a style of recording similar to working with a hardware sequencer or drum machine. While you might want that sort of strict timing for your performance in some cases, Live's quantization feature also allows you to improve the accuracy of your MIDI performance without sacrificing its natural human quality.

To quantize a MIDI note or multiple notes:

1. Select one or more notes using any of the methods described earlier in this chapter.

2. Select **EDIT > QUANTIZE SETTINGS**, or Right-click a selected note in the MIDI Note Editor and select **QUANTIZE SETTINGS**. The Quantize Settings dialog box will display.

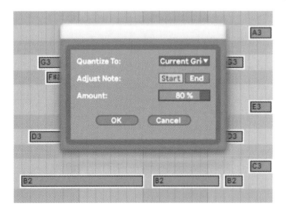

Figure 6.38 The Quantize Settings dialog box

3. In the dialog box, select the desired quantization grid, whether you want to quantize the start or end of the notes (or both), and the intensity of the quantization.

4. Click **OK** to apply the change.

By using a quantization value of less than 100%, you can improve the timing of the performance without losing its human touch.

 To skip the Quantization Settings dialog box and apply the previous quantization settings, select EDIT > QUANTIZE or press COMMAND+U (Mac) or CTRL+U (Windows).

Navigating the MIDI Note Editor

Depending on the complexity of your MIDI performance, it may be very useful to zoom the MIDI Note Editor to increase the visual resolution of the recorded notes. You can navigate and zoom the vertical and horizontal axes independently, allowing you to isolate specific notes and make fine-tuning adjustments, or show all of the MIDI data in a clip for broad edits.

Scrolling and Zooming with Time Ruler (Horizontal Axis)

The horizontal axis, or time ruler, represents the position and duration of MIDI notes. There are multiple ways to zoom the time ruler for specific editing tasks.

Figure 6.39 The cursor will display a magnifying glass when positioned over the time ruler

To zoom horizontally using the timer ruler:

- Click and drag up and down on the time ruler to zoom the MIDI Note Editor horizontally.

- Double-click the time ruler to show the contents of the entire selected MIDI clip.

- With one or more notes selected, double-click the time ruler to fit the selection horizontally to the MIDI Note Editor window.

 With the cursor placed in the MIDI Note Editor (or with a note selected), you can also press the PLUS (+) and MINUS (–) keys on the keyboard to zoom horizontally.

Once you have zoomed in, you can click and drag left and right on the time ruler to scroll the MIDI Note Editor horizontally. You can also scroll left and right with the keyboard by pressing COMMAND+PAGE UP/PAGE DOWN (Mac) or CTRL+PAGE UP/PAGE DOWN (Windows).

Scrolling and Zooming with the Note Ruler (Vertical Axis)

The vertical axis, or note ruler, represents all the notes or pitches that you can send to a MIDI instrument. This display format is known as a piano roll. Ableton Live provides multiple ways to zoom using the note ruler for specific editing tasks.

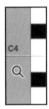

Figure 6.40 The cursor will display a magnifying glass when positioned over the note ruler

To zoom vertically using the note ruler:

■ Click and drag left and right on the note ruler to zoom the MIDI Note Editor vertically.

■ Double-click the note ruler to show the entire range of notes used in the selected clip.

■ With multiple notes selected, double click the note ruler to fit the selection vertically to the MIDI Note Editor window.

 When zooming in vertically on selected notes, the range will scroll to begin at the top of the MIDI Note Editor. If the range of notes does not fill at maximum vertical zoom, additional pitches will be displayed below the selected range.

Once you have zoomed in, you can click and drag up and down on the note ruler to scroll vertically through the octaves of available notes. You can also scroll up and down from the keyboard using the **PAGE UP** and **PAGE DOWN** keys.

 Click the FOLD button in the upper left-hand corner of the MIDI Note Editor to hide any MIDI pitches that are unused in the selected clip.

Review/Discussion Questions

1. What does the term MIDI stand for? How is MIDI data different from the data stored in an audio file? (See "MIDI Basics" beginning on page 138.)

2. What are two key differences between the behavior of MIDI clips and audio clips? (See "MIDI Versus Audio Clip Operation" beginning on page 140.)

3. What is the default tempo in a Live Set? How would you go about changing the tempo? (See "Setting the Base Tempo" beginning on page 142.)

4. What is the default time signature in a Live Set? How would you go about changing the time signature in the middle of an arrangement? (See "Setting the Base Time Signature" beginning on page 144.)

5. How would you go about locating and placing a virtual instrument device on a MIDI track? (See "Using Virtual Instruments" beginning on page 151.)

6. What steps would you take to record a MIDI performance to a new clip in the Session View? (See "Recording a MIDI Performance" beginning on page 155.)

7. What steps would you take to record a MIDI performance to a new clip in the Arrangement View? (See "Recording a MIDI Performance" beginning on page 155.)

8. What are two ways you can manually create MIDI notes using a mouse and keyboard in the MIDI Note Editor? (See "Creating a MIDI Performance Manually" beginning on page 158.)

9. How do you display Live's MIDI Note Editor? What are the main components of the MIDI Note Editor? (See "The MIDI Note Editor" beginning on page 158.)

10. What is velocity in the context of MIDI data? What are two ways you can go about editing the velocity values of MIDI notes? (See "Editing Velocity" beginning on page 162.)

11. What is MIDI quantization? How would you go about using quantization to improve the timing of a MIDI performance without sacrificing its "performed" feeling? (See "MIDI Quantization" beginning on page 164.)

To review additional material from this chapter and prepare for certification, see the Ableton Live 101 Study Guide module available through the Elements|ED online learning platform at ElementsED.com.

Working with MIDI

🎧 Activity

In this exercise, you will continue work on the Set that you started in Exercises 4 and 5. You will add character to the project by creating both a drum part and a melody part to accompany the chord progression and bass part.

This exercise provides three approaches: Option 1 lets you record MIDI performances from a MIDI controller; Option 2 lets you manually create MIDI performances using the MIDI Note Editor; and Option 3 lets you import existing MIDI clips to use for the new parts. Each of the three options is covered separately.

🕐 Duration

This exercise should take approximately 10 to 15 minutes to complete.

◈ Goals/Targets

- Configure the Set
- Assign Instruments to MIDI tracks
- Prepare the Set for recording
- Record or manually create a MIDI performance

Media Files

To complete this exercise, you may need to use various media files included in the **Media Files 2019-Live101** folder. You should have downloaded the media files in Exercise 4.

If needed, you can re-download the media files by going to www.halleonard.com/mylibrary and entering your access code (printed on the opening page of this book). From there, click the **Download** link for the **Media Files 2019-Live101** listing in your **My Library** page. The Media Files folder will begin transferring to your Downloads folder.

Getting Started

You will start by opening the Live Set you saved at the end of Exercise 5. If that file is not available, you can use the Ex05 Sample file in the 01. Completed Exercises folder within the Media Files 2019-Live101 folder.

Open the Set and save it as Exercise 6:

1. Do one of the following:

    • Open the Set file that you created in Exercise 5 (Storage Drive/Folder > Live101-XXX > Exercise05-XXX.als).

    • Alternatively, you can use the Ex05 Sample file (Media Files 2019-Live101 > 01. Completed Projects > Ex05 Sample.als).

2. Choose FILE > SAVE LIVE SET AS and name the Set *Exercise06-XXX*, keeping the Live Set inside the original Project folder. (Move the Set into your Live101-XXX folder if working from the sample file.)

In Exercise 5, you created the foundation of a song segment using imported audio files. You had the choice of four bass and chord progression options, spanning several styles of music and several tempos. To review the genre and BPM you chose, click any of the audio clips. Then press SHIFT+TAB, as needed, to display the Clip View, where you can see the file name of the referenced audio. This will include the genre, key, and tempo of the file.

Figure 6.41 Audio file information in the Clip View

 For the full name and location of an audio file referenced in a clip, hover over the clip on a track or clip slot and see the Status Bar at the bottom of the Live window.

From here, you will augment this song segment using the two MIDI tracks: Drums and Melody.

Configuring the Set

Before continuing, you will configure the Live Set to ensure that the tempo is correct and that Record Quantization is enabled.

Configure the Set:

1. Make sure the tempo of your Live Set matches the tempo of your audio clips.

(i) **As noted above, the tempo is listed on the file names of the audio files you selected in Exercise 5.**

2. Select EDIT > RECORD QUANTIZATION and choose a value. Higher quantization values, such as Quarter-Note Quantization, will have a more dramatic effect on your MIDI performance when you record from a MIDI controller.

(i) **Alternatively, you can leave Record Quantization disabled and quantize your MIDI performance after recording using the MIDI Note Editor.**

Assigning Instruments to MIDI Tracks

You will now assign instrument devices to both of the MIDI tracks in your project so that they can produce sound. The Drums track will use the Drum Rack instrument, and the Melody track will use the Simpler instrument.

Assign a virtual instrument to each MIDI track:

1. Show the Browser by selecting VIEW > SHOW BROWSER or by pressing OPTION+COMMAND+B (Mac) or CTRL+ALT+B (Windows).

2. Select the Drums MIDI track.

3. In the browser, choose the DRUMS category.

4. Audition the pre-created drum kits by clicking on each one to select one for use in your Live Set.

5. With the Drums track still selected, double-click the name of the your selected drum kit to insert a Drum Rack device.

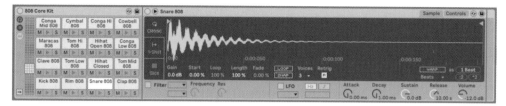

Figure 6.42 A Drum Rack preset on the Drums MIDI track

6.   Select the **Melody** MIDI track.

7.   In the browser, select **INSTRUMENTS**.

8.   Click the disclosure triangle next to Simpler to browse the different synth options, then expand the categories and click on the sounds to audition them. Some good places to look for the purposes of this exercise are **Pianos & Keys** and **Synth Lead**.

9.   Once you've found a sound you like that fits with your existing audio clips, double-click its name to add the Simpler instrument to the **Melody** track.

Getting Ready to Record

This section will help you prepare to record a MIDI performance using a MIDI controller device or the computer keyboard. If you are not using a MIDI controller, you can skip this section.

Select a MIDI controller to use on each MIDI track:

1.   Make sure that the In/Out controls are visible by selecting **VIEW > IN/OUT** or pressing **OPTION+COMMAND+I** (Mac) or **CTRL+ALT+I** (Windows).

2.   Locate the In/Out section of the **Drums** MIDI track.

3.   Use the **INPUT TYPE** dropdown menu to select the MIDI controller you will use to record your performance.

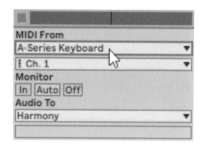

Figure 6.43 In this example, an A-Series Keyboard is selected as the MIDI input device

4.   Repeat this process for the **Melody** MIDI track.

If you are not using a MIDI controller to record a performance, you can either import MIDI data from the Exercise Media folder or manually create a MIDI performance. Both options are described later in this exercise.

Enable the metronome and count-in to aid in recording:

1. Click the **METRONOME** switch in the Control Bar to enable the metronome.

2. Click the down arrow on the **METRONOME** switch to enable the count-in from the pop-up menu.

3. Select a count-in value of 1 or 2 Bars.

 You can also customize the sound of the metronome tick, if desired, as described in Chapter 6.

Recording a MIDI Performance (Option 1)

In this section, you will record a MIDI performance for both the Drums track and the Melody track. If you prefer not to perform live recording passes, skip this section and continue with Option 2 or Option 3 later in this exercise.

Recording in Session View

To get started, you will record MIDI clips into Clip Slots in the Session View.

Record the MIDI drum and melody performance:

1. Press **TAB** as needed to display the Session View.

2. **ARM** the Drums MIDI track for recording.

3. Click the **RECORD** button in the second clip slot of the Drums track. This will initiate the count-in.

4. After the count-in, begin recording your drum pattern.

   A good length is 4 bars, matching the audio clip length in the Live Set. However, you can record a clip of any length, and Live will continue to loop the clip as you play Scene 2 in Session View.

5. Once you have recorded your drum pattern, press **SPACEBAR** to stop the recording.

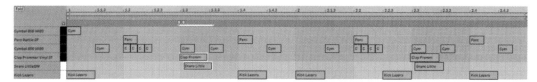

Figure 6.44 A 2-bar MIDI drum performance with Fold mode enabled

6. Launch Scene 2 by clicking the Scene Launch button on the Master track to listen to your MIDI performance along with the existing clips.

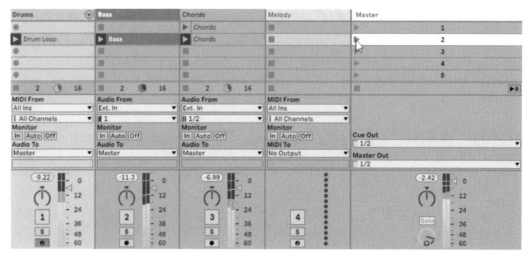

Figure 6.45 Listening to Scene 2 to audition the drum recording along with the bass and chord clips

7. If you're not satisfied with the results, you can either delete the clip and try again, or edit and quantize the performance to improve the timing. You will have an opportunity to edit the MIDI performance later in this exercise.

You can also use the MIDI Arrangement Overdub feature at this point, if desired, to layer additional MIDI notes over your initial performance.

> (i) **To add notes without overwriting your performance, click the MIDI ARRANGEMENT OVERDUB button, then begin recording by pressing the SESSION RECORD button (hollow circle) in the Control Bar.**

8. Once you are satisfied with your recording, copy the clip to the first clip slot of the **Drums** track by holding **OPTION** (Mac) or **ALT** (Windows) while dragging the clip to the top slot position.

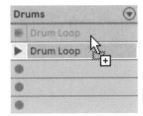

Figure 6.46 Duplicating a clip to another slot on the Drums track by Option-/Alt-dragging (Mac/Windows)

(i) Alternatively, you could choose to leave the drums only on Scene 2, allowing you to introduce the drums along with the bass.

9. Repeat the above process on the **Melody** MIDI track. This time, you will record a simple melody to accompany the drums, bass, and chords.

(i) All of the provided audio clips for this exercise are in the key of either C major or A minor. Try using the notes C, D, E, F, G, and A to construct your melody.

Recording in Arrangement View

In this section, you will record MIDI onto tracks using Arrangement View.

Record the MIDI drum and melody performance:

1. Press **TAB** to toggle the display to the Arrangement View.

2. Click the red **BACK TO ARRANGEMENT** button in the Arrangement View to reactivate playback for the Arrangement View, as needed.

Figure 6.47 Clicking the Back to Arrangement button

 For details on the Back to Arrangement button, see Chapter 3 in this book.

3. **ARM** the Drums MIDI track for recording.

4. Place the Arrangement Insert Marker at the start of the arrangement.

(i) Clicking the STOP button in the Control Bar at anytime while playback is stopped will return your Arrangement Insert Marker to the start of the Live Set.

5. Click the **ARRANGEMENT RECORD** button (solid circle) in the Control Bar. This will initiate the count-in.

6. After the count-in completes, begin recording for a 16-bar drum pattern.

    You can record an entire 16-bar clip, or record a shorter clip—such as 4 or 8 bars—and duplicate it to fill the required length.

7. Once you have completed the recording, press **SPACEBAR** to stop the recording.

8. Duplicate the clip as needed to span 16 bars. (Select the clip and choose **EDIT > DUPLICATE**.)

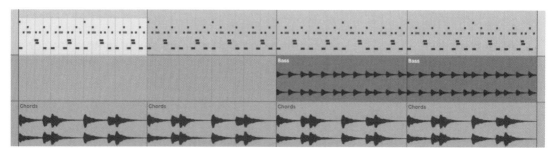

Figure 6.48 A 4-bar MIDI drum performance (light blue), duplicated to span the entire arrangement

9. Place the Arrangement Insert Marker at the start of the arrangement again and press **SPACEBAR** to listen to your work.

    • If you're not satisfied with the results, you can either delete the performance and try again, or edit and quantize the performance to improve the timing.

    • You can also use the MIDI Arrangement Overdub feature to layer additional MIDI notes over your base performance. Click the **MIDI ARRANGEMENT OVERDUB** button; then repeat the recording process above to add additional notes without overwriting your original performance.

10. Repeat the above process to record a part on the Melody MIDI track. On this track, compose a simple melody to accompany the drums, bass, and chords.

(i) All of the provided audio clips for this exercise are in the key of either C major or A minor. Try using the notes C, D, E, F, G, and A to construct your melody.

Edit Your MIDI Performances

In this section, you will have the opportunity to fine-tune your MIDI performances as needed.

Tweak your MIDI performances using the MIDI Note Editor:

1. Double-click a MIDI clip you that would like to edit in the MIDI Note Editor.

2. Using editing features such as moving, trimming, and quantizing, tweak the MIDI performance to your liking.

 To quantize your performance, select all of the notes in the MIDI Note Editor by pressing COMMAND+A (Mac) or CTRL+A (Windows), and then select EDIT > QUANTIZE SETTINGS to configure the quantize behavior.

Manually Creating a MIDI Performance (Option 2)

If you are unable to record a MIDI performance using a MIDI controller or your computer keyboard, you can instead create a MIDI performance manually using the MIDI Note Editor. (If you have completed the recording process in Option 1, you can skip this section.)

Creating a Performance in Session View

In this section, you will create MIDI clips for Clip Slots in the Session View.

Manually create a MIDI drum and melody performance in the Session View:

1. Double-click the second clip slot on the **Drums** track to create an empty clip.

2. Under the **NOTES** section in the Clip View, set the clip Length to 4 bars (4 . 0 . 0)

Figure 6.49 Clip length set to 4 bars

3. Create notes for different drum sounds at different points in time. For instance, you might start by inserting a kick drum note on beats 1 and 3 of each measure and then add snare hits on beats 2 and 4. Then you can add hi-hats and other drums and experiment with timing patterns from there.

 Double-click at the desired location in the MIDI Note Editor to add a new note in Edit Mode (or single-click with the Pencil tool in Draw Mode).

 Press the B key at any time to toggle between Edit Mode and Draw Mode in the MIDI Note Editor.

4.   Once you are satisfied with your performance, copy the clip to the first clip slot of the **Drums** track by holding **OPTION** (Mac) or **ALT** (Windows) while dragging the clip to the top slot position.

Figure 6.50 Duplicating a clip to another slot on the Drums track by holding Option (Mac) or Alt (Windows) while dragging

(i)   Alternatively, you could choose to leave the drums only on Scene 2, allowing you to introduce the drums along with the bass.

5.   Repeat the above process to create a part for the **Melody** MIDI track. On this track, compose a simple melody to accompany the drums, bass, and chords.

(i)   All of the provided audio clips for this exercise are in the key of either C major or A minor. Try using the notes C, D, E, F, G, and A to construct your melody.

Creating a Performance in Arrangement View

In this section, you will create a MIDI performance for each track using the Arrangement View.

Manually create a MIDI drum and melody performance in the Arrangement View:

1.   Press **TAB** to toggle the display to the Arrangement View.

2.   Click the red **BACK TO ARRANGEMENT** button in the Arrangement View to reactivate playback for the Arrangement View, as needed.

Figure 6.51 Clicking the Back to Arrangement button

 For details on the Back to Arrangement button, see Chapter 3 in this book.

3. Click and drag on the Drums MIDI track in the Track Display window, selecting from the start of the Arrangement (at Bar 1) up to the start of Bar 5 (a 4-bar timespan).

4. Select **CREATE > INSERT MIDI CLIP(S)**, or press **COMMAND+SHIFT+M** (Mac) or **CTRL+SHIFT+M** (Windows), to create an empty 4-bar clip.

Figure 6.52 An empty MIDI clip

5. Double-click the empty MIDI clip to open it in the MIDI Note Editor.

6. As you did when creating the drum clip in Session View, create notes for different drum sounds at different points in time. Again, you could start by inserting kick drum notes on beats 1 and 3 of each measure, then add snare hits on beats 2 and 4, and then add hi-hats, other drums, and pattern variations from there.

 Double-click at the desired location in the MIDI Note Editor to add a new note in Edit Mode (or single-click with the Pencil tool in Draw Mode).

Press the B key at any time to toggle between Edit Mode and Draw Mode in the MIDI Note Editor.

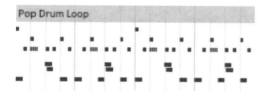

Figure 6.53 A clip including MIDI note data

7. Once you have created a drum pattern you like, you can move and duplicate the clip in the Track Display window so that it plays at the times you desire.

   To duplicate the clip, select it and choose **EDIT > DUPLICATE**.

8. Repeat the above process on the Melody MIDI track. On this track, compose a simple melody to accompany the drums, bass, and chords.

All of the provided audio clips for this exercise are in the key of either C major or A minor. Try using the notes C, D, E, F, G, and A to construct your melody.

Importing MIDI Clips (Option 3)

Finally, if you would prefer to use pre-created MIDI clips, you can simply import MIDI data into your Live Set. If you are satisfied with the MIDI performances you recorded or created in Option 1 or Option 2, you can skip this section; otherwise you can follow the steps below to import MIDI in lieu of completing Option 1 or 2 or as a replacement for the MIDI performances you created under Option 1 or 2.

Importing MIDI in Session View

In this section, you will import MIDI clips into the Session View.

Import pre-created MIDI files in the Session View:

1.   Press **TAB** as needed to toggle to the Session View.

2.   Select the second clip slot of the Drums MIDI track.

3.   Select **CREATE > IMPORT MIDI FILE**.

4.   In the Import dialog box, navigate to the Media Files 2019-Live101 folder; then select an appropriate MIDI drum pattern to match your audio from the 02 Exercise Media > [MIDI] folder.

5.   Click **OPEN**. The selected clip will be added to the clip slot in the Session View.

6.   Right-click the clip and select **DUPLICATE** to copy it to the second clip slot on the Drums track.

7.   Edit the MIDI performance as desired by double-clicking the clips and using the MIDI Note Editor.

8.   Repeat this process for the Melody MIDI track, selecting an appropriate melody clip for your Set.

Importing MIDI in Arrangement View

In this section, you will import MIDI clips into the Arrangement View.

Import pre-created MIDI files in the Arrangement View:

1.   Press **TAB** to toggle to the Arrangement View.

2.   Click the red **BACK TO ARRANGEMENT** button in the Arrangement View to reactivate playback for the Arrangement View, as needed.

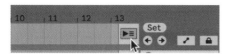

Figure 6.54 Clicking the Back to Arrangement button

 For details on the Back to Arrangement button, see Chapter 3 in this book.

3. Place the Arrangement Insert Marker at the start of the arrangement.

(i) **Clicking the STOP button in the Control Bar at anytime while playback is stopped will return your Arrangement Insert Marker to the start of the Live Set.**

4. Select **CREATE > IMPORT MIDI FILE**.

5. In the Import dialog box, navigate to the **Media Files 2019-Live101** folder; then select an appropriate MIDI drum pattern to match your audio from the **02 Exercise Media > [MIDI]** folder.

6. Click **OPEN**. The selected clip will be added to the track in Arrangement View, and a dialog box will appear prompting you to select an option for importing tempo and time signature information.

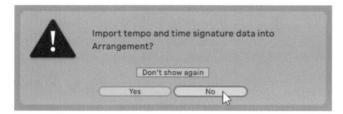

Figure 6.55 MIDI import options in the Arrangement View

7. Select **No** in the dialog box, as you have already set the tempo of the Live Set.

8. Duplicate the drum clip across the arrangement by selecting it and pressing **COMMAND+D** (Mac) or **CTRL+D** (Windows).

9. Edit the MIDI performance as desired by double-clicking the clips and using the MIDI Note Editor.

10. Repeat this process for the **Melody** MIDI track, selecting an appropriate melody clip for your Set.

Finishing Up

To complete this exercise, you will need to save your work and close the Live Set. You will be reusing this project in Exercise 7, so it is important to save the work you've done.

Review and your work in the Session View:

1.   Press **TAB** to toggle the display to the Session View.

2.   Click the **PLAY** button on Scene 1 of the Master track to play back the clips in Scene 1.

3.   Click the **PLAY** button on Scene 2 of the Master track to play back the clips in Scene 2.

4.   Repeat for any other Scenes that include clips.

5.   Press the **SPACEBAR** or the **STOP ALL CLIPS** button on the Master track to stop playback.

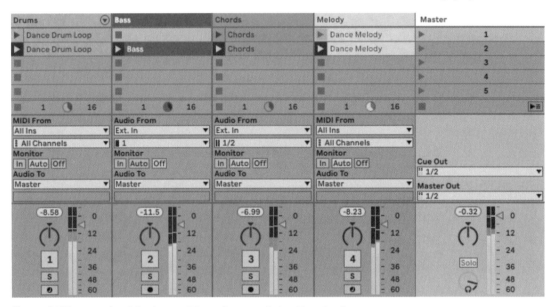

Figure 6.56 Example of the Session View after completing Exercise 6

Review your work in the Arrangement View:

1.   Press Tab to toggle the display to Arrangement View.

2.   Click the red **BACK TO ARRANGEMENT** button to reactivate playback for the Arrangement View.

3.   Click the Stop button in the Control Bar to position the Arrangement Insert Marker at the start of the clips.

4.   Press the **SPACEBAR** to play back the Live Set and confirm your results.

5.   Press the **SPACEBAR** a second time when finished.

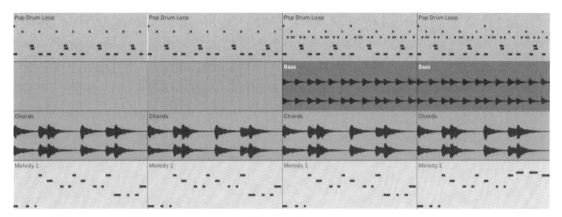

Figure 6.57 Example of the Arrangement View after completing Exercise 6

Save your work and close the Live Set:

1. Choose FILE > SAVE LIVE SET.

2. Press COMMAND+Q (Mac) or CTRL+Q (Windows) to quit Live and close the project.

Chapter 7

Making Your First Audio Recording

This chapter covers the steps required to begin recording audio into a Live Set. It also describes the types of audio files your project will include and covers processes for keeping your audio files organized.

 ## Learning Targets for This Chapter

- Configure the metronome to aid in recording audio

- Record audio onto tracks in your Live Set from external and internal sources

- Record in both the Arrangement View and Session View

- Recognize the difference between audio clips and audio files

- Manage audio files after recording to minimize clutter and optimize your Live Set

 Key topics from this chapter are illustrated in the Ableton Live 101 Study Guide module available through the Elements|ED online learning platform. Sign up for free at ElementsED.com.

Many Ableton Live productions require some amount of audio recording, whether the source is live instruments and voices or other tracks within the Live Set. While the recording controls and processes in Ableton Live are intuitive in many respects, getting optimal results can be challenging if you are new to recording audio.

This lesson provides the background information on recording that you'll need to get started on the right foot. Whether your audio endeavors involve a simple setup in a home studio or an elaborate system in a professional environment, this information will help you take the first steps toward capturing quality audio recordings in Ableton Live.

Before Recording

Before you begin recording in a Live Set, you should ensure that your system has enough storage space for the parts you plan to record. The amount of storage space consumed by audio files will vary, depending on the bit depth and sample rate of the project. (See the "Converting Audio to Digital Format" section in Chapter 1 for a detailed discussion of bit depth and sample rate.)

Audio Storage Requirements

Ableton Live records all audio at sample rates ranging from 44.1 kHz to 192 kHz – the upper limit depends on the capabilities of your audio hardware, as discussed in Chapter 4 – and with bit depths between 16-bit and 32-bit floating point. At a sample rate of 44.1 kHz, each track consumes approximately 5 megabytes (MB) of disk space per minute for 16-bit audio (mono), 7.5 MB per minute for 24-bit audio (mono), and 10 MB per minute for 32-bit floating-point audio. With increasing bit depth and sample rates, hard disk space consumption increases correspondingly; recording at a sample rate of 88.2 kHz, therefore, consumes twice as much space as recording at 44.1 kHz. Similarly, recording in stereo consumes twice the space of recording in mono.

Table 4.1 in Lesson 4 shows approximate storage consumption at the different data rates supported by Ableton Live.

 Ableton Live creates a separate analysis file (.asd) for each audio file loaded into a Live Set or previewed in the Browser. These files reference their respective audio files, and contain data that helps Live optimize stretching quality, speed up the waveform display, and automatically detect the tempo of long samples.

 Clip settings files consume a small but variable amount of additional disk space, depending on the size of the audio file they each reference.

Calculating File Sizes

The sample rate and bit depth of a recorded audio file are directly related to the resulting file size. In fact, you can calculate file sizes using these two parameters with the following equations:

Sample Rate x Bit Depth = Bits per Second

Sample Rate x Bit Depth x 60 = Bits per Minute

In the binary world of computers, 8 bits make a byte, 1,024 bytes make a kilobyte (KB), and 1,024 KB make a megabyte (MB). Therefore, the file size equation can be restated as follows:

(Sample Rate x Bit Depth x 60) / (8 bits per byte x 1,024 bytes per kilobyte x 1,024 kilobytes per megabyte) = Megabytes (MB) per Minute

Reducing terms gives us the following:

Sample Rate x Bit Depth / 139,810 = MB per Minute

For example, recording audio at a sample rate of 44,100 samples per second with a bit depth of 24 bits per sample would generate files that consume space at the following rate:

44,100 x 24 / 139,810 = 7.57 MB per Minute

Determining Available Disk Space

Now that you have an understanding of how much disk space is required to store recorded audio files at different sample rates and bit depths, you can estimate whether your system or storage drive has enough space available to allow you to complete your project. There are many ways to check the amount of available space on the hard drive where Ableton Live saves your audio files, but Ableton Live does not directly provide such information. Consult your operating system manual for more information.

Preparing to Record

Once you have created a Live Set, added an audio track (or tracks) on which to record, and verified that you have adequate disk space available, you will need to prepare your hardware and Live Set for recording. You might also want to enable and configure the metronome (sometimes called the *click* or *tick*) to use as a tempo reference while recording. Whether or not you use the metronome, the general processes you will use to prepare for recording audio are as follows.

To prepare to record audio:

1. Check the hardware connections, if you're using external instruments.

2. Route the signal to be recorded to an audio track.

3. Record-arm the audio track on which you'd like to record.

4. Set the input level of the signal to be recorded.

Enabling the Metronome

As discussed in Chapter 6, when you're recording for a song that is based on a specific tempo (or tempos) with established bar and beat divisions, it can help to perform along with a metronome. The metronome will help performers synchronize to the composition while tracking and will ultimately help align the recorded parts to the bars and beats in the Set. Having your recorded parts in alignment with the tempo will help you to make selections according to the musical grid, and can simplify tasks such as copying and pasting an entire song section as you work on your arrangements.

To enable or disable the metronome, click the **METRONOME** switch in the Control Bar. When enabled, the metronome will begin ticking to the beat whenever you press the **PLAY** button in the Control Bar, launch a clip from the Session View, or start a record pass.

Customizing the Metronome

As described previously in Chapter 6, Ableton Live includes several metronome options, which are available by clicking the down arrow icon on the Metronome switch.

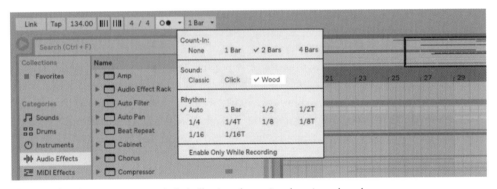

Figure 7.1 The Metronome switch (yellow) and associated settings dropdown menu

By way of recap, the available options for the Metronome include:

- **Count-In:** determines the number of bars the metronome will tick before recording commences

- **Sound:** allows you to choose between three styles of metronome ticks: Classic, Click, and Wood

- **Rhythm:** determines the musical divisions that will be represented by the metronome

- **Enable Only While Recording:** causes the Metronome to sound during recording only, and not during playback

You can control the volume level of the metronome by adjusting the Preview/Cue Volume on the Master track.

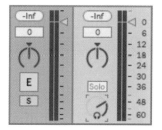

Figure 7.2 Use the Preview/Cue Volume knob (blue) on the Master track to adjust the metronome volume relative to the level of the Live Set

Checking Hardware Connections

When recording audio from an external source, such as an instrument, microphone, or other sound source, you first need to connect the source to the system that is running Ableton Live. This is generally done through an audio interface, which is capable of converting incoming signals to digital audio and typically also lets you amplify the incoming signal using a preamp or gain control.

Most audio interfaces have inputs designated for different sound sources and input types. Before starting to record, you should verify that your sound source is connected to an appropriate input on the audio interface, and that the signal is being passed through the interface correctly. For basic recording, it is simplest to use the lowest available inputs on your audio interface (for example, Input 1 for a mono source or Inputs 1 and 2 for a stereo pair).

If necessary, check the configuration of your audio interface and/or the **AUDIO** tab of Ableton Live's Preferences window to ensure that your audio device's hardware inputs will be available on audio tracks.

  For details on configuring Preferences in Ableton Live, see Chapter 4.

Selecting and Routing the Sound Source

With your sound source connected to the inputs of your audio interface, you are now ready to configure an audio track to receive a signal from your source and to pass the signal through the system for recording and monitoring purposes.

Displaying In/Out Controls

Before moving forward, make sure that the In/Out controls are visible by selecting **VIEW > IN/OUT** or pressing **OPTION+COMMAND+I** (Mac) or **CTRL+ALT+I** (Windows). This will reveal input and output choosers for all the tracks in your Live Set in both the Arrangement View and Session View.

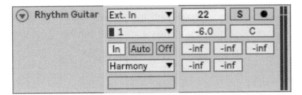

Figure 7.3 In/Out controls in the Arrangement View

Selecting Input Type and Input Channel

Each audio track has an *Input Type* chooser and an *Input Channel* chooser at the top of the track's In/Out section. This selector allows you to route a signal from an input on your interface to the track for recording.

To set the incoming signal in both the Arrangement View and Session View, do the following:

1. Locate the In/Out section of the track on which you will record.

2. Using the top chooser, select the **INPUT TYPE** (if using an external audio interface or the computer's built-in audio inputs, select **Ext. In**).

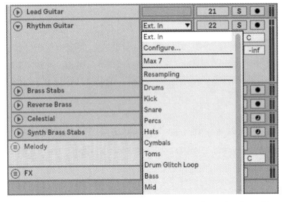

Figure 7.4 The Input Type chooser on the Rhythm Guitar audio track in Arrangement View

3. Using the second chooser (underneath the Input Type), select the appropriate **INPUT CHANNEL**. Select a single channel (such as 1 or 2) to record a mono sound source or a channel pair (such as 1/2 or 3/4) to record a stereo sound source. (See Figure 7.5.)

 Make sure that the selection displayed on the Input Channel chooser matches the input number(s) that your sound source is plugged into on your audio interface. Otherwise you may record the wrong signal (or no signal) to the track.

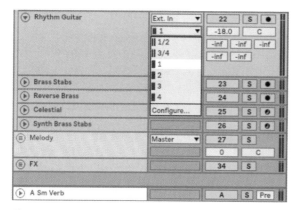

Figure 7.5 Selecting a mono source from the Input Channel chooser on an audio track in Arrangement View

Setting Input Channels for Recording on Multiple Tracks

When recording to multiple tracks simultaneously, each track will need to have a unique input channel. For example, suppose you are recording a vocalist on Track 1 and an acoustic guitar accompaniment on Track 2 of your Live Set. You might have the vocal microphone connected into Input 1 of your audio interface, and the guitar microphone connected into Input 2.

In the Live Set window, you would set the Input Channel for your first track to 1 (or the corresponding input channel name, such as Analog 1). Similarly, you would set the Input Channel for your second track to 2 (or its corresponding input channel name).

This setup will allow you to record and process the vocal signal on the first track separate from the guitar signal on the second track.

Recording an Existing Track to a New Audio Track

Many composers who work in Ableton Live commonly record the output of a track already existing within their Live Set to a new audio track. This workflow offers many creative editing possibilities, such as Warping, stretching, re-pitching, and reversing the resulting audio, while preserving the original source material. Additionally, repeating this process offers an opportunity to process sounds in subsequent layers, which can result in full sound transformations. For example, you could print an existing track to a new audio file, process it with creative effects, record it again to a new audio track, and process it again with additional effects. You can repeat this process again and again to create interesting sounds.

> To record an existing track to a new audio track, simply change the Input Type of the new audio track from an external input (Ext. In) to the name of the existing track you would like to record. When you initiate recording on the new audio track, the output of the existing track will be captured in a new audio file.

Arming (Record-Enabling) Tracks

To set up an audio track for recording, click the track's **ARM** button (the button with a solid circle icon) in either the Arrangement View or Session View. The button will turn red when the track is armed and ready to record.

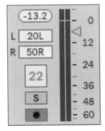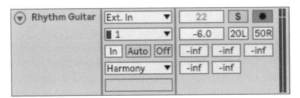

Figure 7.6 The track Arm button in the Session View (left) and in the Arrangement View (right)

 To arm multiple tracks for recording, COMMAND-CLICK (Mac) or CTRL-CLICK (Windows) on the ARM buttons on additional tracks.

Monitoring Modes

In order to hear your sound source through Ableton Live, you need to choose a Monitoring mode. The three modes are listed in the In/Out section below the Input Type and Input Channel choosers.

- **Off:** In this mode, monitoring is turned off, meaning you will not hear the sound source through Ableton Live. This might be useful if you are recording an acoustic instrument and want to exclusively hear the sound of the instrument, rather than the recorded sound.

- **Auto:** In general, this Monitoring mode will be best for most recording applications. As long as the track is armed for recording, your input signal will be passed through any processing to the output so you can hear what is being recorded onto the track. The only time you *won't* hear your sound source is during normal playback, making it easy to listen to what you've recorded.

- **In:** With this Monitoring mode, you will always be monitoring your input signal – regardless of whether the track is armed for recording or the Live Set is playing. This mode can be useful to allow the talent to rehearse a part while listening to playback from other tracks in the set.

Controlling Input Level and Pan

Adjusting input levels and panning is essential to a smooth recording process.

Input Level

As a general rule, input levels should be adjusted to obtain a strong, clean signal while avoiding clipping. You do not, however, need to record at the highest possible level. Recording too hot can leave little room for subsequent gain-based processing (such as EQ) and can lead to digital clipping, which is detrimental to audio quality.

For best results, aim for an average peak input level around –6 dBFS or lower, and ensure that the track meter never turns red. To do this, adjust the level of your analog source while monitoring the volume meter of your track within the Live Set.

 The amplitude of digital audio is represented in decibels relative to full-scale audio (dBFS), with full scale indicating the loudest signal that can be recorded at a given bit depth. Digital clipping occurs whenever a signal exceeds 0 dBFS at an input or output.

 The Ableton Live mixer includes a Peak Level indicator button to the left of the track meter. Use this indicator to help set record levels. When the Peak Level meter exceeds 0.00, the button will highlight in orange.

Adjusting the input level will typically require you to change the source volume, adjust the microphone placement, or modify the incoming signal strength using a mixer or preamplifier. Note that although a track's Track Volume slider can be used to increase or decrease playback levels, the Track Volume slider *does not* affect record levels.

Many audio interfaces provide preamplifier gain controls for their inputs. For all other I/O devices, record levels are set entirely from the source or pre-I/O signal processing.

Pan Position

Setting the pan affects the stereo placement of a signal for monitoring and playback purposes only; it has no effect on how the audio files are recorded.

Ableton Live provides a graphical Track Pan control (pan knob) for audio tracks in the Session View by default and a Track Pan value display for audio tracks in the Arrangement View.

Track Pan in Session View

To set the pan position of the signal in the Session View, change the position of the STEREO PAN knob for the track in the track mixer section.

To control panning independently for the left and right channels of a stereo source, right-click the Stereo Pan knob and click SELECT SPLIT STEREO PAN MODE. The pan knob will be replaced by Left and Right pan value displays.

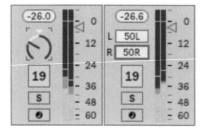

Figure 7.7 Stereo Pan knob display (left) and Split Stereo Pan display (right) in Session View

Arrangement View

To set the pan position of the signal in the Arrangement View, click and drag in the **TRACK PAN** value display in the track mixer section. The pan value is initially set to C, signifying the center of the stereo field. Pan settings range from 50L (hard left) to 50R (hard right).

 To control panning independently for the left and right channels in Arrangement View, right-click on the Track Pan value display and choose SELECT SPLIT STEREO PAN MODE.

Figure 7.8 Stereo Pan display (left) and Split Stereo Pan display (right) in Arrangement View

Recording and Managing Audio

With your sound source routed to one or more tracks and the desired tracks armed for recording, you are ready to begin recording audio.

Depending on whether you are working in the Arrangement View or Session View, the recording process will vary.

Recording in Arrangement View

Arrangement View gives you a linear, timeline-based view of your recording progress. It is best suited for recording to multiple tracks simultaneously.

To begin recording audio in Arrangement View, do the following:

1. Arm at least one audio track for recording.

2. Position the Arrangement Insert Marker where you want the recording to begin.

3. Click the **ARRANGEMENT RECORD** button (solid circle) in the Control Bar. The Arrangement Record button will turn red when enabled.

Figure 7.9 The Arrangement Record button armed (red) in the Control Bar

  Press function key F9 as a shortcut to activate the Arrangement Record button.

4. Depending on your Preferences settings, recording may begin immediately when you enable the Arrangement Record button. If not, click the **PLAY** button (triangle) or press the **SPACEBAR** to begin the record pass, starting with the metronome count-off (if enabled).

  The Preferences setting under the RECORD/WARP/LAUNCH tab called START PLAYBACK WITH RECORD can be enabled to automatically start a record pass whenever the Arrangement Record button is clicked.

  To override the current Preferences setting for START PLAYBACK WITH RECORD, using the opposite behavior, SHIFT-CLICK the Arrangement Record button when starting a record pass.

5. When you have finished your record take, click the **STOP** button (solid square) in the Control Bar, or press the **SPACEBAR**.

Recording in Session View

Recording in Session View allows you to create individual clips and launch other clips while recording.

To begin recording audio in Session View, do the following:

1. Arm at least one audio track for recording. Once armed, each clip slot in the track will have its own record button.

2. Click the **RECORD** button on one of the clip slots to record a new clip to that slot.

If you have multiple tracks armed for recording, you can click the Session Record button (hollow circle) in the Control Bar to record onto all armed tracks on a selected scene. (See Figure 7.10 below.)

Figure 7.10 The Session Record Button (highlighted) in the Control Bar

3. The clip slot record button will flash red, and the metronome count-off will begin (if enabled).

4. Once recording has commenced, the record button will turn into a red Clip Launch button.

Figure 7.11 Recording audio to a clip slot in the Session View

5. When you have finished your record take, click the **STOP** button in the Control Bar (or press the **SPACEBAR**).

    Alternatively, you can press the red Clip Launch button to continue the playback of the current scene, including the new audio recording.

Session View Recording Quantization

When recording in the Session View, you might want to select a value from the Quantization Menu. When the value is set to anything other than **None**, Ableton Live will automatically cut the clip boundaries of your recorded audio so they align with your Live Set. This will aid in keeping clips in rhythmic alignment.

Figure 7.12 The Quantization Menu (right) with a value of 2 Bars selected

Recording on Scene Launch

The Session View can also be configured so that recording begins on all armed tracks upon launching a given scene. To do this, you need to enable the **START RECORDING ON SCENE LAUNCH** option in the Ableton Live Preferences window. This option is located under the **RECORD/WARP/LAUNCH** tab.

Organizing after Recording

Once you've completed a record pass, it is recommended that you complete a few steps to preserve and organize the audio file(s) that were created in the process.

Disarm the Record Tracks and Adjust Playback Settings

First, disarm the track(s) to which you recorded to prevent inadvertently recording further audio and overwriting clips. Once you've done that, you can also dial in basic mixing controls, such as the track volume and panning.

To return a track to playback mode and adjust the playback settings, do the following:

1. Click the **ARM** button on the audio track to take it out of record-enable mode.

2. Click **PLAY** in the Control Bar (Arrangement View) or on the recorded clip slot (Session View) to hear your performance.

3. Adjust the playback level and panning as necessary.

Organize Audio Files and Clips

Each time you record audio into Ableton Live, you create a single audio file. This single audio file is the original, unedited, continuous audio recording. It is referenced by a clip (or clips) within the Live Set, but is stored externally. Organizing audio files involves maintaining information both within the Live Set and in the Live Project folder.

 When you record audio into a Live Set, the audio files are stored in the project's **SAMPLES** > **RECORDED** folder by default.

As you begin to edit your recording within the Live Set, you will likely end up creating multiple clips that reference the original audio file. These clips are simply electronic pointers within the Live Set to the audio file—they do not store audio information directly, but instead are used to display, edit, and play back audio information contained within the referenced file. Clips can range in duration from a single sample to many minutes.

Working with Clips

Audio clips represent pieces of audio data that can be moved or edited within the Live Set. They are block-like containers that can be positioned along the horizontal timeline in the Arrangement View and in dedicated slots in the Session View. Clips are created during normal editing and can refer to any type of supported audio file.

For instance, after a file has been recorded to disk, a corresponding clip will display in the Arrangement that points to the recorded audio file. You can copy, paste, split, trim, duplicate, fade, and perform other editing functions on the clip within the Live Set without affecting the original audio file.

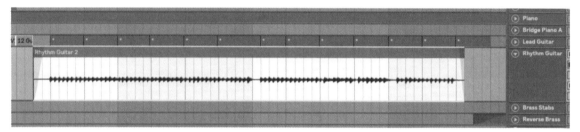

Figure 7.13 A clip referencing recorded audio, selected in Arrangement View

Naming Audio Files and Clips

During recording, Ableton Live automatically assigns names to audio files and clips. You can change these names from within the Live Set, if needed, to make them more meaningful or to help with organization.

Default Naming Conventions

When you record audio on a track, Ableton Live names the resulting file according to the track name. It also appends a take ID—a sequential number based on the number of times you've recorded on that track—followed by the exact date and time of recording in brackets.

Here is an example of the file name generated after recording on a new audio track for the first time:

> **1-Audio 0001 [2018-01-01 120000]**   Where 1-Audio is the track name, 0001 is the take number, and 2018-01-01 120000 is the date and time of recording

Similarly, Ableton Live automatically assigns names to clips that have been created within a Live Set after recording. Clips are named by default according to the track name, with a sequential number appended for each *new clip* that is created. When copying or duplicating existing clips, they retain their original name, meaning there can be many clips with the same name.

Here is an example of the type of name Ableton Live will automatically generate for a clip:

1-Audio 3   Where 1-Audio is the name of the audio track on which the clip was created, and 3 is the clip number

Changing Clip Names

You can change the default names that Ableton Live has applied to clips at any time.

To rename a clip, select a clip in the Arrangement View or Session View and do one of the following:

■ Right-click on the clip and select **RENAME** from the pop-up menu; then type the new name for the clip and press **ENTER**.

■ Press **COMMAND+R** (Mac) or **CTRL+R** (Windows), enter a new name, and press **ENTER**.

■ In the Clip View, click in the **CLIP NAME** field and enter a new name.

You can apply the same name to multiple clips by first selecting all the clips you'd like to rename simultaneously.

Changing File Names

You can change the default names that Ableton Live has applied to audio files at any time, assuming the files aren't in use by another process.

To rename an audio file, use one of the following processes:

■ Process 1:

  • Select a clip that references the audio file you'd like to rename.

  • In the Clip View, under the Sample section, click the file name referenced by the clip to select the audio file in the Browser on the left-hand side. (See Figure 7.14.)

  • Right-click the file name in the Browser and select **RENAME** from the pop-up menu.

    After renaming, all clips pointing to the audio file within the Live Set will now point to the newly renamed version.

■ Process 2:

  • In the Ableton Live Browser, click **CURRENT PROJECT** to list all of the audio files that belong to the current Live Set.

  • Right-click the file name you wish to change and select **RENAME** from the pop-up menu.

    After renaming, all clips pointing to the audio file within the Live Set will now point to the newly renamed version.

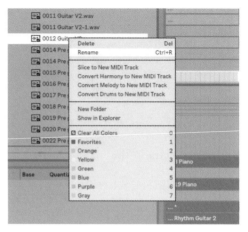

Figure 7.14 Clicking an audio file name in the Clip View (left) selects it in the Browser (right), where it can quickly be renamed

   Renaming an audio file may prevent other projects or programs that reference the file from being able to locate it. Use this feature with caution for files in loop libraries and sample collections.

Removing Audio Clips and Deleting Audio Files

Ableton Live makes an important distinction between removing clips from a Set and deleting files from disk:

■   When you remove a clip from a Live Set, the parent audio file remains on the storage drive and can be used in other clips elsewhere in the Live Set or in other Live projects.

■   When you delete an audio file from disk, clips referring to that file will no longer be able to locate it and will not produce any sound.

Removing Audio Clips

To remove audio clips from your Live Set:

1.   Select one or more clips on tracks in Arrangement View or in Clip Slots in Session View.

2.   Press the **DELETE** key, or right-click the selection and choose **DELETE** from the pop-up menu.

Removing audio clips from a set does not delete the audio files, so this action will have essentially no effect on the drive space used for the project.

Deleting Audio Files

As you work on your Live Set, you may accumulate unwanted audio files from test recordings or unusable takes. You might want to delete these unneeded audio files to clean up your Live project and free up drive space.

Deleting files from disk will permanently remove them from your system. This can affect other Live Sets that reference the same audio files.

To remove or delete audio files associated with the current Live Set from your drive, do the following:

1. In the Ableton Live Browser, click **CURRENT PROJECT**.

2. Select the audio file(s) you wish to remove from the Live Set and your storage drive.

3. Right-click the selection and choose **DELETE**. A confirmation dialog box will appear.

4. Select **YES** in the dialog box to send the selected audio file(s) to the trash.

Finding Unused Audio Files

Another option is to use Ableton Live's File Manager to isolate the audio files that are contained within the current Live project but not used by the current Live Set.

 Using this process doesn't guarantee that the identified files are not used by a *different* Live Set. Use caution when deleting files with this method.

To search for unused audio files, do the following:

1. Select **FILE > MANAGE FILES** to display Live's File Manager on the right side of both the Session View and Arrangement View.

(i) You can also display the File Manager by choosing **VIEW > FILE MANAGER**.

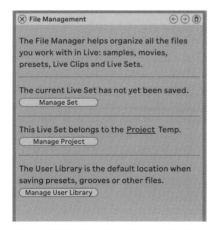

Figure 7.15 The File Manager display in Ableton Live

2. Click the **MANAGE PROJECT** button in the File Manager. The display will change to show information and tools for managing the current project.

3. In the Unused Files section, you'll see a report of the number of audio files that are not currently in use in the current Live Set, as well as the amount of disk space they consume.

(i) If needed, click the disclosure triangle next to Unused Files to expand the list.

4. Click the **SHOW** button for the relevant type of audio file—in this case, recordings. The unused files will display in the Browser on the left-hand side of the screen.

5. Select the audio file(s) you wish to remove from the Live Set and your storage drive.

6. Right-click the selection and choose **DELETE**. A confirmation dialog box will appear.

7. Select **YES** in the dialog box to send the selected audio file(s) to the trash.

Review/Discussion Questions

1. Aside from the length of the recording and the number of channels (mono or stereo) being recorded, what two factors ultimately determine the amount of disk space consumed by an audio recording? (See "Audio Storage Requirements" beginning on page 186.)

2. How can you enable the metronome in a Live Set? What are some of the metronome settings you can customize? (See "Enabling the Metronome" beginning on page 188.)

3. How do you route an external sound source into the input of an audio track in a Live Set? (See "Selecting Input Type and Input Channel" beginning on page 190.)

4. How can you adjust the input level of a sound source on an armed track? Can you use the Track Volume slider to affect the strength of the incoming signal? (See "Input Level" beginning on page 193.)

5. How do you arm an audio track for recording in the Session View and Arrangement View? (See "Arming (Record-Enabling) Tracks" beginning on page 192.)

6. What function key can be used as a shortcut for triggering the Arrangement Record button? (See "Recording and Managing Audio" beginning on page 194.)

7. Where are recorded audio files stored within the Live project? (See "Organize Audio Files and Clips" beginning on page 197.)

8. How do audio clips differ from audio files? (See "Working with Clips" beginning on page 198.)

9. How can you rename a recorded audio file from within Ableton Live? (See "Changing File Names" beginning on page 199.)

10. How would you go about removing audio files that are associated with your project but unused in the current Live Set? (See "Deleting Audio Files" beginning on page 200.)

11. Which Ableton Live view can be used to locate unused audio files? (See "Finding Unused Audio Files" beginning on page 201.)

12. Why should you use caution when deleting unused audio files from a project? (See "Finding Unused Audio Files" beginning on page 201.)

To review additional material from this chapter and prepare for certification, see the Ableton Live 101 Study Guide module available through the Elements|ED online learning platform at ElementsED.com.

Recording Audio

 Activity

In this exercise, you will be recording a new part to accompany the tracks you have set up in previous exercises. You have two options available to complete this exercise.

Option 1: Live Recording. For this option, you will first need to connect an external sound source, such as a microphone, guitar, or other instrument, to your audio interface. If you do not have an audio interface, you may be able to connect a microphone directly to a computer input or USB port, or use the computer's built-in microphone, if available. Don't worry too much about the quality of the recording—at this time, the goal is to understand how to route a signal into an audio track and capture a recording.

 This exercise does not include instructions for routing audio from a USB microphone into Ableton Live.

 Refer to the section in Chapter 2 called "Accessing Connected Audio Devices" for basic setup information for audio interfaces and USB microphones. Consult the documentation that came with your device for additional details.

Option 2: Internal Recording. If the above live recording options are not available or are impractical, you can instead record from an existing track in your Live Set to a new audio track.

◷ Duration

This exercise should take approximately 10 to 15 minutes to complete.

✦ Goals/Targets

- Configure a Set for audio recording
- Record an external audio source or record internally

Getting Started

You will start by opening the Live Set you completed in Exercise 6. If that file is not available, you can use the Ex06 Sample file in the 01. Completed Exercises folder within the Media Files 2019-Live101 folder.

 To re-download the media files, go to **www.halleonard.com/mylibrary** and enter the access code printed on the opening page of this book. Then click the DOWNLOAD link for Media Files 2019-Live101 listing in your **My Library** page.

Open the set and save it as Exercise 7:

1. Do one of the following:

   • Open the set file that you created in Exercise 6 (Storage Drive/Folder > Live101-XXX > Exercise06-XXX.als).

   • Alternatively, you can use the Ex06 Sample file (Media Files 2019-Live101 > 01. Completed Projects > Ex06 Sample.als).

2. Choose **FILE > SAVE LIVE SET AS** and name the Set *Exercise07-XXX*, keeping the Live Set inside the original Project folder. (Move the Set into your Live101-XXX folder if working from the sample file.)

3. Create a new audio track to use as a record track. Choose **CREATE > INSERT AUDIO TRACK**, or use the keyboard shortcut **COMMAND+T** (Mac) or **CTRL+T** (Windows).

Live Recording (Option 1)

Before getting too much further, think about what you plan to record. Since we have already created the foundation of a song segment, you can either record another layer to accompany the four existing tracks, or record a new part to replace one of the existing tracks. Remember that this musical idea is rooted in the key of C Major, so the notes C, D, E, F, G, A, and B will sound most natural.

Configure the Set

If you plan to capture a live recording from an external sound source, you will need to route its signal to the input of your new audio track.

Route the external signal to the input of the new audio track:

1. Locate the **IN/OUT** section of the new track you created.

2. Select the **INPUT TYPE** (in the case of an external audio interface, select Ext. In).

3. Select the appropriate **INPUT CHANNEL**.

4. Select the **AUTO** Monitoring mode for the audio track. (See Figure 7.16.)

In Auto mode, the incoming signal will pass through to the output while tracking so you can hear what is being recorded onto the track in your headphones or monitor speakers. During playback, monitoring will switch to play the track content, making it easy to listen to what you've recorded.

Figure 7.16 The In/Out settings for recording an external sound source

 If you are using your computer's built-in audio for recording and playback, enabling the Auto Monitoring mode may lead to feedback. In this case, use Off mode instead.

5.   Verify that the input displayed on the **INPUT CHANNEL** chooser matches the input that your sound source is plugged into on your audio interface.

6.   If necessary, click the **INPUT CHANNEL** chooser to make changes, selecting the correct input channel from the drop-down menu. (Note: Stereo sources will have a pair of inputs routed to the track.)

Check Levels

Once you have your sound source routed to an audio track, it's time to check the level of the signal to ensure you're receiving a strong signal, but not exceeding 0 dBFS and introducing digital clipping.

Monitor the incoming signal and check the level:

1.   Arm the audio track for recording.

2.   Test the input level from your external sound source by playing the connected instrument, speaking or singing into a connected microphone, or otherwise activating the incoming signal.

3.   Adjust the strength of the incoming signal, as needed.

 Remember, the Track Volume slider does not affect the strength of the input signal. If your input signal is too strong or too soft, you need to adjust the instrument volume, microphone position, or audio interface gain.

Be careful not to push the meter past 0 dBFS and into the red zone, as this could lead to irreversible clipping in the recorded audio file.

Record Your Performance

Once you've tweaked your sound source and arrived at a good input level, it's time to try recording the part to your audio track. If you plan to replace one of the existing tracks with your recording, you might want to disable/mute the track before recording.

 To mute a track, click the Track Activator button below the pan control in the Session View or left of the Solo button in the Arrangement View.

Record in Arrangement View

Record the performance to an audio track in Arrangement View:

1.   First, name the record track appropriately; for example, Guitar or Vocal.

2.   Click the **METRONOME** switch to enable the metronome.

3.   Click the down arrow next to the Metronome switch and select a 2-bar count-in (or more, if needed).

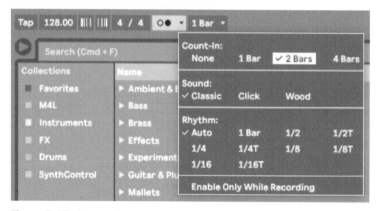

Figure 7.17 Setting the Metronome Count-In to 2 Bars

4.   Position your Arrangement Insert Marker where you would like the recording to begin.

5.   Click the **ARRANGEMENT RECORD** button or press function key **F9** to initiate recording.

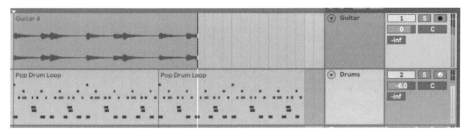

Figure 7.18 Recording audio in the Arrangement View

6. After completing the record pass, press **SPACEBAR** to stop the recording.

Repeat this process, if necessary, until you are satisfied with your results. If you don't want to delete or overwrite a recorded take but want to perform the part again, simply move the clip to a later point in the arrangement.

Record in Session View

Record the performance to an audio track in Session View:

1. First, verify that the record track has been named appropriately; for example, Guitar or Vocal.

2. Click the **METRONOME** switch to enable the metronome.

3. Click the down arrow next to the Metronome switch and select a 2-bar count-in (or more, if needed).

4. From the Quantization Menu, select a value of 1 Bar.

Figure 7.19 Setting the Quantization value to 1 Bar

5. Click the record button on an empty clip slot. If you want to play along with other clips in the Live Set, you can manually launch them by pressing their Clip Launch buttons before performing the recorded part.

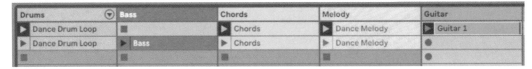

Figure 7.20 A red Clip Launch Button indicates that a track is currently recording

6. As the recording begins the fourth bar, click the **PLAY** button on Scene 1. This will launch the scene, and conclude the record pass. The quantization setting of 1 bar will guarantee that the length of the recording is an exact amount in full bars (such as 4 bars).

Repeat this process, if necessary, until you are satisfied with your results. You can either delete a record take from the selected clip slot, or move on to another slot for subsequent recordings. When you settle on a take, move that clip to the scene containing the other elements of the song.

Internal Recording (Option 2)

If you plan to record internally, you will need to route the output of an existing track to the input of your new audio track. To complete this part of the exercise, you will use the Melody track that you created Exercise 6 as the source of the recording.

Configure the Set

Route the existing track to the input of the new audio track:

1. Name the audio track Melody Recording.

2. Locate the **IN/OUT** section of the Melody Recording audio track.

3. From the **INPUT TYPE** chooser, select the Melody MIDI track. This routes the output of the existing Melody track to the new audio track.

4. Set the Monitor Mode of the Melody Recording track to **AUTO**.

Figure 7.21 The In/Out settings and Monitor Mode for internal recording

5. Arm the Melody Recording audio track for recording.

Record the Audio to the New Track

Now that you've routed the existing track to your new audio track, you're ready to record.

Record in Arrangement View

Record the existing track to your new audio track in Arrangement View:

1. In Arrangement View, position the Arrangement Insert Marker at the location where you want to begin recording from the **Melody** track.

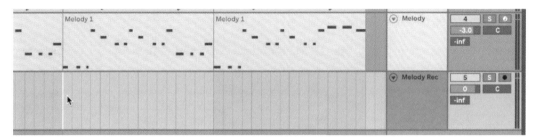

Figure 7.22 Placing the Arrangement Insert Marker

2. Click the **ARRANGEMENT RECORD** button or press function key **F9**.

3. After completing the record pass, press **SPACEBAR** to stop the recording.

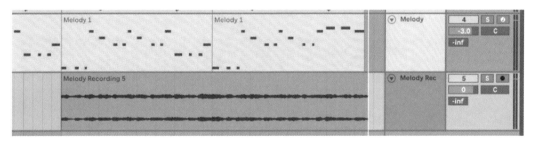

Figure 7.23 The completed record pass in Arrangement View

Record in Session View

Record the existing track to your new audio track in Session View:

1. From the Quantization Menu, select a value of **1 BAR**.

2. Open the Ableton Live Preferences window by selecting **LIVE > PREFERENCES** (Mac) or **OPTIONS > PREFERENCES** (Windows).

3. Under the **RECORD/WARP/LAUNCH** tab, enable the **START RECORDING ON SCENE LAUNCH** option.

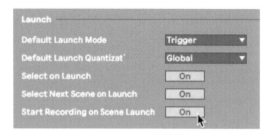

Figure 7.24 Enabling the Start Recording on Scene Launch preference

4.   Close the Preferences window when finished.

5.   Click the **PLAY** button on Scene 1 of the Master track. This will simultaneously launch the clips on the scene and initiate recording on the Melody Recording track.

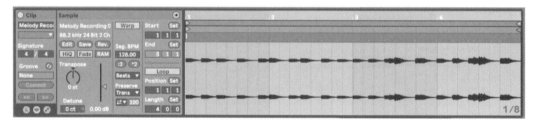

Figure 7.25 A red Clip Launch Button indicates that a track is currently recording.

6.   As the recording begins the fourth bar, click the **PLAY** button on Scene 1 again. This will re-launch the scene, and conclude the record pass. The quantization setting of 1 bar will ensure that the length of the recording is an exact multiple of full bars.

Figure 7.26 The recorded clip is exactly four bars long.

After completing the internal recording, you can deactivate/mute the Melody MIDI track, as it is essentially a duplicate of the audio recording you just created.

 To mute a track, click the Track Activator button below the pan control in the Session View or left of the Solo button in the Arrangement View.

Finishing Up

To complete this exercise, disarm your record track(s) so that you don't overwrite any of your takes. After that, you can review your work and save the Live Set.

Review your work in the Arrangement View:

1. Position the Arrangement Insert Marker at the start of the clips.

2. Press the SPACEBAR to play back the Live Set and confirm your results.

3. Press the SPACEBAR a second time when finished.

Review your work in the Session View:

1. Click the PLAY button on Scene 1 of the Master track to play back the Live Set and confirm your results.

2. Press the SPACEBAR or the STOP ALL CLIPS button on the Master track to stop playback when finished.

Save your work and close the Live Set when finshed:

1. Choose FILE > SAVE LIVE SET.

2. Press COMMAND+Q (Mac) or CTRL+Q (Windows) to quit Live and close the project.

Chapter 8

Selection, Navigation, and Configuration

This chapter covers various selection and navigation techniques that can add efficiency to your workflow in Ableton Live. It includes descriptions of how to quickly navigate even complex Live Sets, make different types of selections on tracks in the Arrangement View, customize the order and size of tracks, and work with locators to organize and add notes to an arrangement.

 ## Learning Targets for This Chapter

- Navigate an arrangement with the Overview

- Make selections in tracks based on clips and time

- Quickly zoom and scroll through an arrangement

- Customize the order and size of tracks

- Add, delete, and work with locators

 Key topics from this chapter are illustrated in the Ableton Live 101 Study Guide module available through the Elements|ED online learning platform. Sign up for free at ElementsED.com.

Understanding how to navigate, select content in, and customize the display of a Live Set can dramatically speed up your production workflow. Whether you need to make broad edits or zoom in and isolate a specific moment, being able to quickly locate and select material is the key. In this lesson, you will learn to streamline your creative process with methods for quickly navigating, selecting content, and customizing the layout of your Live Set.

How you navigate a Live Set will vary, depending on whether you are working in the Session View or Arrangement View. Whereas the Session View displays tracks and clips on a non-linear grid, the Arrangement View displays tracks and clips along a linear timeline.

Using the Arrangement Overview

The Arrangement View is meant to display an entire—and perhaps finished—piece of music, and thus offers a series of unique navigation features and techniques. One of those features is the Overview, which is essentially a bird's-eye view of an arrangement.

The Overview is located at the top of the Arrangement View or Session View and shows all MIDI, audio, and video material on tracks in the Arrangement. Clips are represented by narrow, horizontal lines, in the same color as the clips on the tracks in Arrangement View.

To toggle the display of the Overview, do one of the following:

■   Choose **VIEW > OVERVIEW**.

■   Press **OPTION+COMMAND+O** (Mac) or **CTRL+ALT+O** (Windows).

Figure 8.1 The Overview situated at the top of the Arrangement View

  Ableton Live 10.1 introduced the ability to change the height of the Overview by clicking and dragging at the bottom of the Overview area.

The Overview Outline (Arrangement View only)

When working in the Arrangement View, you can use the Overview as one method to navigate and zoom an arrangement. This can be very useful when you are working with complex or lengthy pieces of music. The Overview displays a black outline (rectangle) surrounding the entire Overview area (when zoomed out completely) or framing a portion of the Overview (when zoomed in). This outline represents the part of the arrangement that is currently displayed in the Arrangement View.

If you change the display of the Arrangement View by zooming or scrolling, the framed outline area in the Overview will relocate and resize accordingly. During playback, if the Follow behavior is set to scroll, the outline area in the Overview will also scroll.

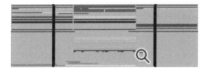

Figure 8.2 The Overview outline with the Arrangement View zoomed in on a specific song segment

Zooming and Scrolling with the Overview (Arrangement View Only)

The Overview offers a simple way to zoom and scroll a Live Set.

To zoom and scroll using the Overview, do the following:

1. Click anywhere in the Overview area to move the framed outline to the selected location, scrolling the Arrangement View to that location.

2. Do one of the following:

    •   To zoom in or out on an arrangement, click within the black Outline area in the Overview and drag up or down (or click and drag either edge to resize the rectangle).

    •   To scroll left or right in an arrangement, click within the black Outline area and drag left or right.

    •   To zoom out completely, double-click anywhere within the Overview Outline.

 You can also zoom by holding COMMAND (Mac) or CTRL (Windows) and scrolling with the mouse wheel or trackpad while hovering over the Overview.

Making Selections in the Arrangement View

Making selections allows you to quickly edit material on audio, MIDI, and video tracks, as well as the contents of Group Tracks. Being able to quickly make selections will allow you to perform editing tasks with ease and efficiency. Most of the track-based selections techniques take place within the Arrangement View.

 This chapter covers selections of clips and time on any kind of track. Selections within clips and automation selections are covered in greater detail in later chapters.

Selecting Clips and Time

There are two distinct methods of making selections when you are working in the Arrangement View. You can select *clips* or you can select spans of *time*. Once you have made a selection of either type, you can perform any action available under the **EDIT** menu.

Selecting Clips

Making selections often starts with selecting audio, MIDI, or video clips. To select a clip, click within the top half of the clip, where the hand icon appears (see Figure 8.3).

 When a track display is folded (collapsed), you can click anywhere on a clip to select it.

 Information on folding and unfolding tracks is provided in the section on "Adjusting Your Live Set" later in this Chapter.

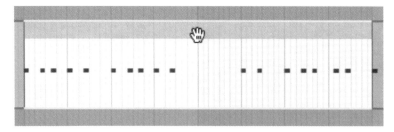

Figure 8.3 Selecting a single clip on an unfolded track using the solid colored bar at the top of the clip

To add clips to an existing selection, hold **SHIFT** and click on another clip with the hand icon. This will select everything between the existing and new selections, even across multiple tracks.

Selecting Time

Selecting time allows you to perform broad editing tasks, such as duplicating a song segment, as well as making selections *within* a clip's boundaries. This can be accomplished by clicking and dragging within the bottom half of a clip with the arrow pointer icon or clicking and dragging from anywhere on a track outside of a clip.

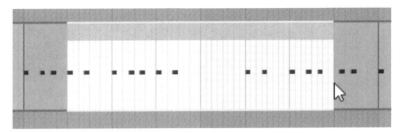

Figure 8.4 Selecting time within clip boundaries

To add time to an existing selection, hold **SHIFT** and click at another point in time with the arrow pointer icon. This will extend the selection to include everything between the existing and new selections, even across multiple tracks.

 When you hover your mouse cursor over a selection, Live will display the start and end locations, as well as the selection length, in the Status Bar at the bottom of the Live interface.

Selections On and Off the Grid

By default, when you click and drag within the Track Display, your selection start and end will snap to the current grid. This is often desired behavior, but at times you may want to make a more precise selection. To prevent a selection from snapping to the grid, hold **COMMAND** (Mac) or **ALT** (Windows) while clicking and dragging a selection.

Multi-Track Selections

You can make selections across any number of available tracks in your Live Set. Ableton Live provides several methods of doing this.

To make a selection across adjacent tracks, do one of the following:

- Click and drag horizontally and vertically across multiple tracks. (Do not click and drag a clip, as that will move the clip to another location and track.)

- Make a selection on one track, hold **SHIFT**, and press the **UP** or **DOWN ARROW** keys to extend the selection across additional tracks.

- Make a selection on one track, hold **SHIFT**, and click at the end location on another track to make a contiguous selection across all tracks in between.

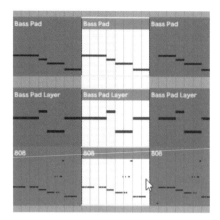

Figure 8.5 A selection across adjacent tracks

To make a selection across non-adjacent tracks, do the following:

1. Make a selection on one track.

2. While holding **COMMAND** (Mac) or **CTRL** (Windows), click on another non-adjacent track with the arrow pointer icon. The selection will be added to the second track non-contiguously.

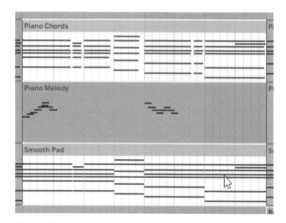

Figure 8.6 A selection across non-adjacent tracks

 For details on making selections within an Automation envelope, see the "Automation" section in Chapter 10 of this book.

Zooming and Scrolling the Arrangement View

The Arrangement Overview, discussed at the start of this chapter, is a useful tool for quickly determining your position within a more complex arrangement, as well as locating and zooming into other areas.

However, there are many other methods of navigating and zooming in the Arrangement View, and they may provide additional efficiency for your production process.

Zooming In and Out

One of the quickest methods of zooming into a specific location is done using the beat-time ruler.

To zoom using the beat-time ruler, do the following:

1. Hover your pointer over the beat-time ruler. The cursor will change into a magnifying glass.

2. Click the location you would like to zoom into and drag up or down to zoom out or in, respectively.

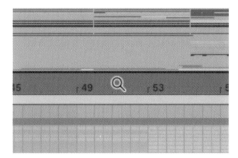

Figure 8.7 Zooming using the beat-time ruler at the top of the Arrangement View

 You can also zoom on your current mouse cursor location by scrolling the mousewheel or trackpad up and down while holding COMMAND (Mac) or CTRL (Windows).

Zooming In and Out on Selections

Whether you have a clip selected or simply have the Insert Marker positioned in a specific location, you can zoom in on the location using the keyboard.

To zoom using the keyboard, do the following:

1. Place the insert marker on a track or make a selection.

2. Press the **PLUS (+)** or **MINUS (–)** keys to zoom in or out on the location or selection.

 You can zoom to fit the current selection to the Arrangement View by double-clicking the beat-time ruler. If nothing is selected, this action will zoom out to show the entire length of the arrangement.

Zooming to Fit the Screen

At times, you may need to zoom a selection such that it fills the screen horizontally. One way to do this is to select VIEW > ZOOM TO ARRANGEMENT TIME SELECTION, or press the Z key.

To zoom back out from this view, press X or select VIEW > ZOOM BACK FROM ARRANGEMENT TIME SELECTION. Once you are zoomed out again, you can also use the X shortcut to show the entirety of an arrangement.

 Ableton Live 10.1 introduced the ability to use the W key to zoom out to show the entirety of an arrangement, and the H key to zoom track heights to fit the screen.

 The above shortcuts will not work when the Computer MIDI Keyboard switch is active in the Arrangement View.

To toggle the Computer MIDI Keyboard on/off, press the M key.

You can also zoom a selection to fit the screen by double-clicking the beat-time ruler or by Right-clicking within a selection and choosing Zoom to Arrangement Time Selection from the pop-up context menu.

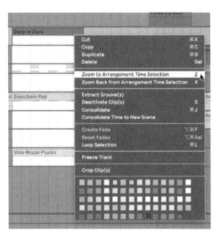

Figure 8.8 Zooming a selection to fit the screen using the right-click menu

Scrolling

Ableton Live provides multiple methods of scrolling the Arrangement View to the left and right.

To scroll the Arrangement View, do one the following:

- Click and drag the beat-time ruler (at the top of the Track Display) to the left or right.

- Click and drag the Time Ruler (at the bottom of the Track Display) to the left or right.

- Hold **OPTION+COMMAND** (Mac) or **CTRL+ALT** (Windows), click anywhere in the Track Display, and drag left or right.

Adjusting Your Live Set

Live offers several methods of organizing your project and customizing the display of individual tracks. While these are subtle optimizations to your Live Set, they have the potential to make your production and editing processes faster.

Changing the Track Order

Ableton Live allows you to change the order of tracks in your Live Set at any time. Arranging tracks in a logical order can speed up your workflow and project navigation. You might consider arranging the tracks in your Live Set such that related tracks are displayed together, instruments are displayed in a logical order, or commonly used tracks are located at the left (Session View) or the top (Arrangement View).

 Any changes you make to the track order in the Session View will also affect the display in the Arrangement View, and vice versa.

To change the track order, do the following:

- In the Session View, click the name of a track you wish to move and drag it left or right. The destination location will be represented by a vertical black line as you drag.

- In the Arrangement View, click the name of the track and drag it up or down. The destination location will be represented by a horizontal black line as you drag.

 To move multiple tracks simultaneously, select the target tracks prior to dragging.

 Hold the SHIFT key while clicking to select multiple adjacent tracks or hold COMMAND (Mac) or CTRL (Windows) while clicking to select non-adjacent tracks.

Folding and Unfolding Tracks

Each track in the Arrangement View includes a **FOLD/UNFOLD TRACK** button to the left of the track name. Clicking this button will fold the track display in and out.

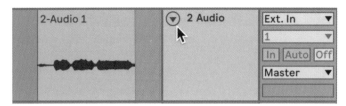

Figure 8.9 The Fold/Unfold Track button on an audio track (shown unfolded)

Folding a track collapses the track display to its minimum size, allowing you to fit more tracks in the Arrangement View simultaneously.

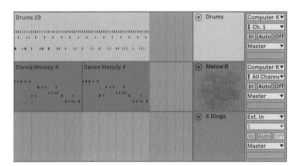

Figure 8.10 Tracks shown unfolded (left) and folded (right)

To toggle a track display between a folded and unfolded state, do one of the following:

- Click the triangular **FOLD/UNFOLD TRACK** button next to the track name.

- Select the track and press the **LEFT** and **RIGHT ARROW** keys on your computer keyboard to fold and unfold the track, respectively.

 Hold OPTION (Mac) or ALT (Windows) while clicking on the Fold/Unfold Track button for any track to fold/unfold all tracks in the Set simultaneously.

Adjusting Track Size

Live allows you to customize the size of each track in both the Session View and Arrangement View. Larger track sizes are particularly useful for precision editing because they show more detail. Smaller track sizes are useful for conserving screen space in large projects.

Adjusting Track Width in Session View

In the Session View, tracks are displayed as vertical strips. In this view, you can change the width of individual tracks as needed.

To expand a track in the Session View, do the following:

- Click and drag the track border to the right of the track name. In the Session View, making tracks wider can be useful to view long clip names on Clip Slots; making tracks narrower is useful for reducing track size and freeing up screen real estate.

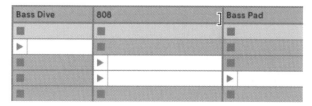

Figure 8.11 When changing the track size in the Session View, the cursor turns into a bracket icon

Adjusting Track Height in Arrangement View

In the Arrangement View, tracks are displayed as horizontal strips along the timeline.

To expand a track in the Arrangement View, do the following:

1. Position your pointer over the lower boundary of any track in the Mixer area; the cursor will change into a double-headed arrow.

2. Click on the track boundary and drag up or down. The track height will change as you drag.

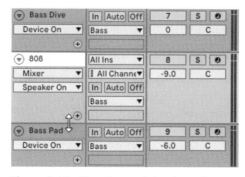

Figure 8.12 Changing track height in the Arrangement View

(i) To change the height of all tracks simultaneously, hold OPTION (Mac) or ALT (Windows) while dragging the track boundary of any track.

(i) To change track height using a mousewheel or trackpad, select the target track(s) and hold OPTION (Mac) or ALT (Windows) while scrolling up or down with the mouse cursor anywhere in the Track Display.

You can also resize all tracks in a Live Set by selecting **VIEW > SHOW ALL TRACKS** or by pressing the **H** key. This will fit as many tracks as possible into the Track Display by folding them into their most condensed form.

 The H key shortcut will not work when the Computer MIDI Keyboard switch is active in the Arrangement View.

Working with Locators (Arrangement View Only)

Locators can be used to bookmark important locations in your arrangement, making it easy to organize song sections, create notes on important hit points when scoring or sound designing with video, or simply leave reminders of ideas to keep your creative process flowing. The following sections describe how to add, edit, recall, and delete locators, and how to create selections and loops using locators.

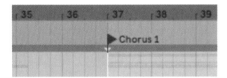

Figure 8.13 A "Chorus" locator at bar 37 of an arrangement

Adding Locators

Locators can be added at any point in an arrangement.

To add a locator, do one the following:

- Click the **SET LOCATOR** button next to the beat-time ruler. This can be done in real-time during recording or playback, or while the transport is stopped. A new locator will be added at the playhead location, Arrangement Insert Marker location, or selection start location.

Figure 8.14 Adding a locator at the currently selected location using the Set button

- Right-click in the scrub area and choose **ADD LOCATOR** to add a locator at the selected location.

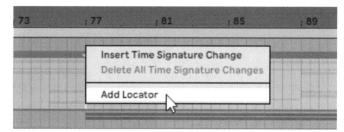

Figure 8.15 Adding a locator by right-clicking in the scrub area below the beat-time ruler

- Select **CREATE > ADD LOCATOR** to add a locator at the Insert Marker position.

 When you add a locator, it will be quantized according to the Quantization setting specified in the Control Bar. This is done to keep locators on musical divisions; however, you can freely edit the position of the locator after adding it, as described in the next section.

With a locator selected or the Insert Marker placed at the position of a locator, the Set Locator button becomes a **DELETE** button for quick removal of the locator.

Editing Locators

Once you've created a locator, you have a few options to move, rename, and add text information to it.

Moving Locators

Locators can be moved by clicking and dragging on the locator arrow in the Scrub Area, or by selecting the locator arrow and pressing the left and right arrow keys on your computer keyboard.

 As is the case with other editing operations in Live, you can hold COMMAND (Mac) or ALT (Windows) while dragging a locator to prevent it from snapping to the grid.

Renaming Locators

Ableton Live provides a few different ways that you can name or rename an exiting locator.

To rename a locator, do one of the following:

- Right-click the locator arrow and select **RENAME** from the pop-up menu.

- Click on a locator arrow to select it and then do one of the following:

  - Choose **EDIT > RENAME**.

  - Press **COMMAND+R** (Mac) or **CTRL+R** (Windows).

Adding Info Text to Locators

In addition to naming your locators, you also have the opportunity to add informational text to each locator in your Set.

To add info text to a locator:

1. Right-click on a locator arrow and select EDIT INFO TEXT or, with a locator arrow selected, choose EDIT > EDIT INFO TEXT.

   This action will place your cursor in the Info View section of the Live interface.

2. Type additional notes about the locator in the Info View section.

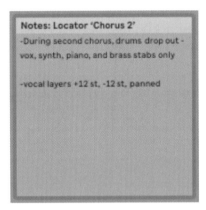

Figure 8.16 You can add notes to a locator using the Edit Info Text option

Recalling and Playing from Locators

Once you have set locators in your Live Set, you can recall the locator positions and begin playback from those locations for quick access to different song sections or components of your project.

To recall a locator position, do one of the following:

- Click on a locator to select it.

- Click the PREVIOUS LOCATOR or NEXT LOCATOR buttons below the SET LOCATOR button to cycle through locator positions sequentially.

Double-click on a locator arrow to begin playback from that position.

Using Locators for Loops and Selections

If you have at least two locators in your Live Set, you can use them to create selections and loop points based on the locator positions.

To create a selection between two locators:

1. Right-click on the first of the two locator arrows where you'd like to create a selection.

2. Choose **SELECT TO NEXT LOCATOR** from the pop-up menu.

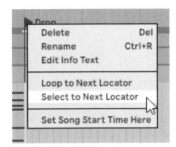

Figure 8.17 Making a selection or loop between two locators

To create loop points between two locators:

1. Right-click the first of the two locator arrows where you'd like to create a loop area.

2. Choose **LOOP TO NEXT LOCATOR**. The loop brace will be added to the Scrub Area, spanning between the two locators.

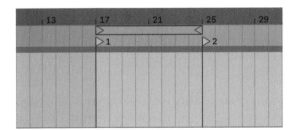

Figure 8.18 The loop brace after creating loop points based on locator positions 1 and 2

Deleting Locators

You can remove locators from an arrangement at any time using one of a variety of commands.

To delete a locator, do one of the following:

- With a locator selected or the Insert Marker at the position of a locator, press the **DELETE LOCATOR** button next to the beat-time ruler.

- Right-click a locator and select **DELETE**.

- With a locator selected, press **DELETE** or **BACKSPACE** on your computer keyboard.

- With a locator selected, choose **CREATE > DELETE LOCATOR**.

Navigating the Arrangement

Clicking in the Track Display area in the Arrangement View selects a point in time, represented by the flashing insert marker. The insert marker can be placed on any track and at any position by clicking at the desired location. The insert marker position determines where playback will begin in Arrangement View.

The insert marker can also be used to navigate within the arrangement using the arrow keys on your computer keyboard.

Navigating Time

The insert marker can be moved forward or backward in time from the keyboard, based on the current Edit Grid settings. This can be useful for repositioning the playback point or edit location without having to reach for the mouse.

To move the insert marker in time:

■ Press the **Left** and **Right Arrow** keys. Each key press will move the insert marker to the next or previous Edit Grid line.

Navigating Tracks

The insert marker can also be moved vertically between tracks from the keyboard. This can be useful for moving the edit point up or down through your track. The same technique can be used to move a selection up or down between tracks.

To move the insert marker or selection to an adjacent track:

■ Press the **Up** and **Down Arrow** keys. Each key press will move the insert marker or selection to the next or previous track in the Arrangement View.

Navigating Through Clips and Locators

At times, you may want to move the insert marker forward to the start of next clip, backward to the end of the previous clip, or to another clip boundary or marked location. Using modifiers with the arrow keys, you can easily navigate horizontally between the clips on a track and any locator positions in a Set.

To move though clip boundaries and locators:

1. Position the insert marker on the track where you wish to navigate.

2. Press **Option+Left/Right Arrow** (Mac) or **Ctrl+Left/Right Arrow** (Windows).

    Each key press will move the insert marker to the next or previous clip boundary on the track; the insert marker will also stop at each locator position in the Set.

Making Selections while Navigating

Navigating from the keyboard can also be useful for making selections on a track. You can select horizontally and vertically from the current insert marker location or existing selection by holding **SHIFT** while navigating using any of the above techniques.

To select horizontally using the keyboard:

■ Hold **SHIFT** while pressing the **LEFT** or **RIGHT ARROW** keys to select forward or backward in Edit Grid increments.

■ Hold **OPTION+SHIFT** (Mac) or **CTRL+SHIFT** (Windows) to select forward or backward to the next/previous clip boundary or locator position.

■ Hold **SHIFT** while pressing the **UP** or **DOWN ARROW** keys to extend the insert marker or existing selection to adjacent tracks.

Review/Discussion Questions

1. What is the purpose of the Overview? How can you use this feature to zoom and scroll an arrangement? (See "Using the Arrangement Overview" beginning on page 216.)

2. How can you make a selection based on a range of time (rather than a selection based on a clip's boundaries)? (See "Selecting Clips and Time" beginning on page 218.)

3. How can you prevent a selection from snapping to the grid when clicking and dragging? (See "Selections On and Off the Grid" beginning on page 219.)

4. What key modifier allows you to extend a selection to additional, *non-adjacent* tracks? (See "Multi-Track Selections" beginning on page 219.)

5. What are some of the ways you can zoom in and out in the Arrangement View? (See "Zooming In and Out" beginning on page 221.)

6. How do you change the order of tracks in the Session View and Arrangement View? What are some reasons you might want to re-order tracks? (See "Changing the Track Order" beginning on page 223.)

7. What are locators, and why might you use them in an arrangement? (See "Working with Locators" beginning on page 226.)

8. What are some ways to add locators to a Live Set? Can you add locators in real time during recording or playback? (See "Adding Locators" beginning on page 226.)

9. How can you quickly start playback from a locator position? (See "Recalling and Playing from Locators" beginning on page 228.)

10. How can you use locators to make a selection or to designate a loop area? (See "Using Locators for Loops and Selections" beginning on page 228.)

11. What keys can you use to move the insert marker forward or backward in time from the keyboard? (See "Navigating Time" beginning on page 230.)

12. What keys can you use to move the insert marker forward or backward on a track through clip boundaries? (See "Navigating Through Clips and Locators" beginning on page 230.)

To review additional material from this chapter and prepare for certification, see the Ableton Live 101 Study Guide module available through the Elements|ED online learning platform at ElementsED.com.

Recording, Configuring, and Adding Locators to an Arrangement

🎧 Activity

In this exercise, you will extend and configure an arrangement using the techniques discussed in Chapter 8. You will make basic selections, duplicate a segment of an arrangement, and add locators that indicate changes in the arrangement.

🕐 Duration

This exercise should take approximately 10 to 15 minutes to complete.

⊕ Goals/Targets

- Record from Session View into an Arrangement
- Edit an Arrangement
- Extend an Arrangement
- Configure your Live Set
- Use Locators

Media Files

To complete this exercise, you may need to use various media files included in the **Media Files 2019-Live101** folder. You should have downloaded the media files in Exercise 4.

If needed, you can re-download the media files by going to www.halleonard.com/mylibrary and entering your access code (printed on the opening page of this book). From there, click the **Download** link for the **Media Files 2019-Live101** listing in your **My Library** page. The Media Files folder will begin transferring to your Downloads folder.

Getting Started

You will start by opening the Live Set you completed in Exercise 7. If that Set is not available, you can use the **Ex07 Sample** file in the **01. Completed Exercises** folder within the **Media Files 2019-Live101** folder.

Open the Live Set and save it as Exercise 8:

1. Do one of the following:

    • Open the Set file that you created in Exercise 7 (**Storage Drive/Folder > Live101-XXX > Exercise07-XXX.als**).

    • Alternatively, you can use the Ex07 Sample file (**Media Files 2019-Live101 > 01. Completed Projects > Ex07 Sample.als**).

2. Choose **FILE > SAVE LIVE SET AS** and name the Set *Exercise08-XXX*, keeping the Live Set inside the original Project folder. (Move the Set into your **Live101-XXX** folder if working from the sample file.)

Recording from Session View into an Arrangement

Up until this point, you've had the option of completing exercises in either the Session View or the Arrangement View. For this exercise, you will need to be working in the Arrangement View. If you have been working in the Session View, you will first record your work into the Arrangement View. Live makes this process of translating your Session View scenes into an arrangement fairly simple.

If you have been working exclusively in the Arrangement View thus far, you can simply review these steps to familiarize yourself with the process, as it may be useful for you in the future.

Complete a Record Pass

Record from the Session View to the Arrangement View:

1. Click the **STOP** button in the Control Bar twice to place the Arrangement Position at 1 . 1 . 1—the very beginning of bar 1. This will ensure that your recording begins at the start of the arrangement.

2. Click the **ARRANGEMENT RECORD** button (solid circle) in the Control Bar. The button will turn red, preparing the Live Set for recording into an arrangement. However, recording will not begin until you launch a clip or scene.

Figure 8.19 The Arrangement Record button (red) in the Control Bar

3. Launch Scene 1 by clicking its **PLAY** button on the Master track.

4. Allow the scene to repeat twice.

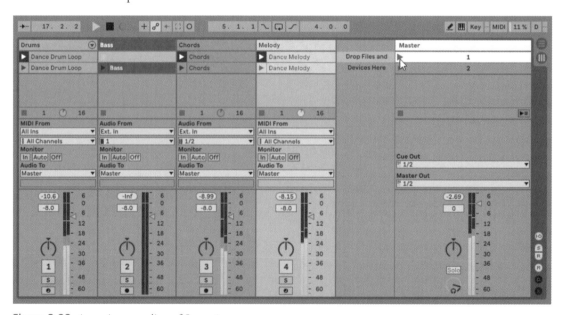

Figure 8.20 An active recording of Scene 1

5. Roughly two beats before the second repetition ends, launch Scene 2 from the Master track.

Figure 8.21 You can use the track status indicator in the Session View to see the progress of clip playback

6.   Allow the scene to repeat twice.

7.   After the second repetition of Scene 2, click the **STOP** button in the Control Bar or press the **SPACEBAR** to end the recording.

You've now recorded your scenes to an arrangement.

Clean Up the Recording

Next, you will verify your recorded results and clean up the ending of the arrangement, if necessary.

Switch to the Arrangement View and verify your results:

1.   Press **TAB** to switch to the Arrangement View and see your recorded scenes. The recorded material is displayed on tracks along a horizontal timeline.

> (i) You can also choose VIEW > TOGGLE ARRANGEMENT/SESSION VIEW to swap to the Arrangement View or click the ARRANGEMENT VIEW SELECTOR button.

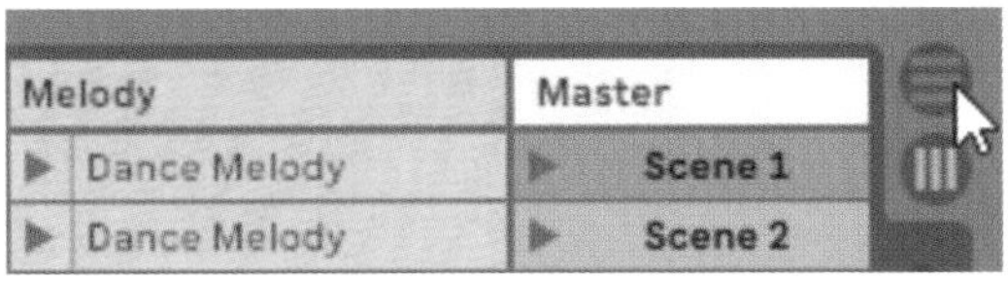

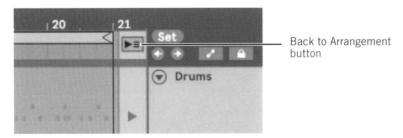

Figure 8.22 The Arrangement View Selector button

2.   Click the **BACK TO ARRANGEMENT** button in the upper right-hand corner of the Arrangement View to activate the tracks for playback in the arrangement.

Back to Arrangement
button

Figure 8.23 The Back to Arrangement button (red)

3.   Trim the ends of clips as necessary. Your recording should be 16 bars in length; you can trim any clips that extend slightly past 16 bars so you have a clean ending to the arrangement.

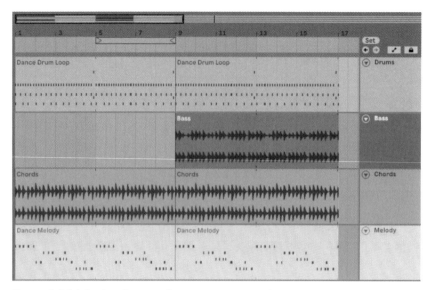

Figure 8.24 The Set after recording two scenes into the Arrangement View and cleaning up the tracks

Extending the Arrangement

In this part of the exercise, you will make a basic selection and use it to extend the duration of your existing 16-bar song segment.

Extend the arrangement by selecting and duplicating time:

1.   Make a selection across the first eight bars of the composition. (See Figure 8.25.)

   You can make your selection by selecting time, by selecting an 8-bar clip, or by using any of the other selection techniques you've learned.

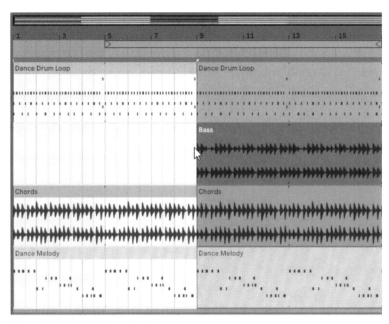

Figure 8.25 An 8-bar selection

2. From the menu bar, select **EDIT > DUPLICATE TIME**. This will duplicate all the content existing in tracks across the selected time range, extending your 16-bar arrangement to 24 bars.

3. Select the first eight bars on the **Drums** track.

4. Deactivate the selected drum clip(s) by pressing the **O (ZERO)** key or by selecting **EDIT > DEACTIVATE CLIP(S)**. This will prevent the clip(s) from playing.

Figure 8.26 Deactivating clips allows you to effectively mute clips without deleting them

You'll now have three eight-bar segments, each with different levels of activity.

Configuring the Live Set

In this part of the exercise, you will adjust the track order and height to your liking.

Change the track order according to your preferences:

■   Click the name of any track that you wish to change and drag it up or down. The destination location will be represented by a horizontal black line.

Change the track height to a size of your choosing:

1.   Position your pointer over the lower boundary of any track you wish to resize in the Mixer area; the cursor will change into a double-headed arrow.

2.   Click on the track boundary and drag up or down. The track height will change in increments.

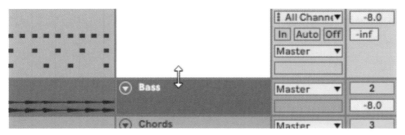

Figure 8.27 Changing track height in the Arrangement View

Adding Locators

To finish configuring the arrangement, you will add three locators to your Live Set. Here you will use locators to mark where changes occur in the arrangement.

Add locators at each change:

1.   Place the Insert Marker at the start of your arrangement.

2.   Right-click in the Scrub Area and choose **ADD LOCATOR**, or select **CREATE > ADD LOCATOR** from the menu bar.

3.   Name the locator Intro and press **RETURN** (Mac) or **ENTER** (Windows) to accept the name.

4.   Place the Insert Marker at the start of the bar 9 of your arrangement.

5.   Add a second locator and name it Drums.

6.   Place the Insert Marker at the start of the bar 17 of your arrangement.

7.   Add a third locator and name it Bass.

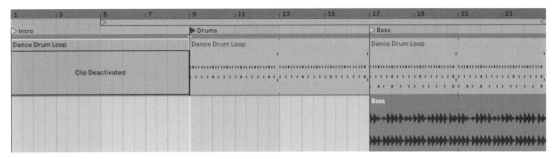

Figure 8.28 Exercise 8, after adding locators at each 8-bar increment

Finishing Up

Using the knowledge you have gained thus far, you can continue to edit and extend this basic musical idea to your liking, if desired. For now, to complete this exercise, you will need to save your work and close the Live Set.

Review your work:

1. Place the Insert Marker at the start of your arrangement.

2. Press the **SPACEBAR** to play back the Live Set and confirm your results.

3. Press the **SPACEBAR** a second time when finished.

Save your work and close the Live Set:

1. Choose **FILE > SAVE LIVE SET**.

2. Press **COMMAND+Q** (Mac) or **CTRL+Q** (Windows) to quit Live and close the project.

Chapter 9

Editing Your Media

This chapter covers the basics of editing audio and MIDI data in Ableton Live. It provides details on playback options, Edit Grid options, edit commands, and moving and resizing operations. It also introduces techniques for creating fades and for undoing edit actions.

◈ Learning Targets for This Chapter

- Set options for scrolling (follow behavior) and looping during playback

- Recognize the difference between Fixed Grid mode and Zoom-Adaptive Grid mode

- Configure Grid values

- Apply standard editing commands to clips

- Understand the effects of the Edit Grid on moving and trimming operations

- Create fade-in, fade-out, and crossfade effects on your tracks

 Key topics from this chapter are illustrated in the Ableton Live 101 Study Guide module available through the Elements|ED online learning platform. Sign up for free at ElementsED.com.

Any time you add audio or MIDI data to the tracks in your set, you are likely to need to do some editing. Whether you need to adjust timing, smooth out a transition, or improve a performance, editing techniques will play a large part in transforming a project from a basic recording to a polished final product. The processes described in the following sections will help you make that transformation, enabling your recordings and compositions to sound their best.

Selecting Playback Options

To simplify your navigation and workflow, Ableton Live provides several playback options to choose from while working on a Set. Two configurations you will likely want to explore include the *follow* behavior and the loop playback option.

Follow Behavior

Ableton Live offers three different scrolling options or "follow" behaviors. The current settings determine how the contents of the Arrangement View and Clip View are displayed during playback and recording.

Available options include no scrolling (follow behavior off), follow by page, and follow with a continuous scroll of the track display:

- **Follow: Off (No Scrolling).** This option prevents the screen from following the current play position. Use this option to keep the display located on an area that you are editing while playing back an area that starts or ends off screen.

- **Follow: Page.** This option scrolls on a page-by-page basis whenever the play position reaches right edge of the screen or jumps to a new location.

- **Follow: Scroll.** This option scrolls the timeline continuously, keeping the current play position centered on the screen. This option works best at lower zoom settings.

Toggling Follow On/Off

To toggle the follow behavior on or off, do one of the following:

- Click the **FOLLOW** switch in the toolbar.

Figure 9.1 The Follow switch enabled in the toolbar (yellow highlight)

- Choose **OPTIONS > FOLLOW**.

- Press **COMMAND+SHIFT+F** (Mac) or **CTRL+SHIFT+F** (Windows).

Setting the Follow Behavior in Preferences

To select the desired follow behavior, do the following:

1. Open the Ableton Live Preferences window by selecting **LIVE > PREFERENCES** (Mac) or **OPTIONS > PREFERENCES** (Windows).

2. Click on the **LOOK/FEEL** tab.

3. Click the indicator box to the right of the Follow Behavior label to toggle between the Page and Scroll settings.

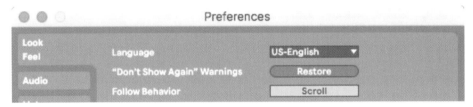

Figure 9.2 The Follow Behavior setting in the Look/Feel tab of Ableton Live's preferences

Arrangement Loop

During editing, you will often want to listen to a selection repeatedly. Enabling Ableton Live's Arrangement Loop feature allows you to repeat your selection continuously, looping from the end of the selection back to the start without interruption. This allows you to easily review the continuity of an edit or transition point.

To loop a selection in the Arrangement View, do the following:

1. Make the desired selection in the Arrangement View.

2. Choose **EDIT > LOOP SELECTION**. This will accomplish two tasks at once:

    • The Loop Brace will move to match the current selection.

    • The Loop switch in the Control Bar will become highlighted to show that Arrangement loop is enabled.

3. Click **PLAY** or press the **SPACEBAR** to start continuous looped playback.

Figure 9.3 The Control Bar with Arrangement Loop active (yellow highlight)

You can adjust the start and end points of the Arrangement loop during playback by modifying the Loop Brace. By dragging the corresponding triangle markers in the Loop Brace (start and end arrows), you can resize the loop area.

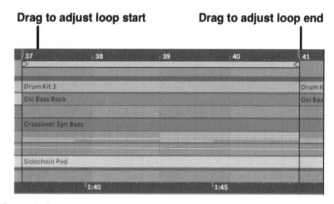

Figure 9.4 Adjusting the Loop length using the triangular start and end arrows in the Loop Brace

 The Arrangement loop requires a selection of at least one quarter-note (0. 1. 0) in duration. You will not be able to set the Loop Brace to a smaller size, regardless of the Edit Grid setting.

Using the Edit Grid

As you learned in Chapter 3, Ableton Live provides two Edit Grid modes: fixed grid and zoom-adaptive grid. The Edit Grid mode can affect the size of the grid increments at different zoom settings, which in turn affects selections and edits you make to audio and MIDI clips. Both Edit Grid modes allow you to place a clip on a track without affecting the placement of other clips, leaving space between clips or overlapping clips as desired.

- **Fixed Grid.** In fixed grid mode, selections, clip movements, and resizing operations are constrained to a specific grid value that does not change based on the zoom level.

- **Zoom-Adaptive Grid.** In zoom-adaptive grid mode, selections, clip movements, and trim operations are constrained to a grid value that changes based on the zoom level. As you zoom in, the grid increments get successively smaller, allowing you to edit with greater precision.

Configuring the Edit Grid Settings

Ableton Live allows you to set the Edit Grid value based on an interval of your choosing. This helps maintain the timing of clips, notes, events, and selections as you edit your track material. The Edit Grid value affects edit operations whenever the Snap to Grid function is enabled (see "Snap to Grid" below).

The Edit Grid can also be used for display purposes, allowing it to serve as a visual reference whether or not Snap to Grid is enabled.

In Ableton Live, the Edit Grid value is always based on bars and beats.

To set the Edit Grid value to a Fixed Grid increment, do the following:

1. Right-click in the Arrangement View or Clip View.

2. From the pop-up menu, choose a value under the Fixed Grid heading (such as 1/8). The menu will close after you make a selection.

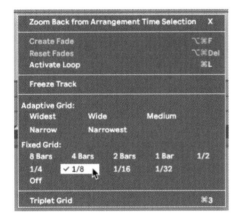

Figure 9.5 Selecting a Fixed Grid value

To set the edit grid value to a Zoom-Adaptive Grid increment, do the following:

1. Right-click in the Arrangement View or Clip View.

2. From the context menu, choose an option under the Adaptive Grid heading (such as Medium). The menu will close after you make a selection.

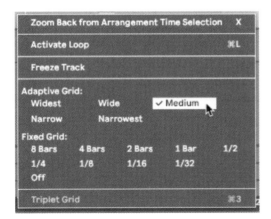

Figure 9.6 Selecting a Zoom-Adaptive Grid value

To enable a Triplet Grid, value first select a Fixed Grid value, then open the menu a second time and select Triplet Grid at the bottom.

Once you've set the Edit Grid to an appropriate value, the corresponding grid lines will appear in the Arrangement View to serve as a visual reference.

Snap to Grid

Ableton Live's Snap to Grid function is enabled by default when the Edit Grid value is set to something other than **NONE**. With Snap to Grid enabled, you can make edits based on the timing interval defined by the grid. (See "Configuring the Edit Grid Settings" above.) Selections snap to grid intervals, which in turn affects cut, copy, and paste operations. Move and resize operations either align to the grid or move in grid increments relative to their origination point.

- If a clip is already positioned on a grid line, moving the clip snaps the clip start to an exact grid line. In this scenario, resizing a clip snaps the clip edge to an exact grid line as well.

- If a clip's start point falls between grid lines, moving the clip will snap the clip start two separate incremental locations as you drag:

  - The clip start will snap to exact grid lines, aligning with absolute grid locations.

  - The clip start will also snap to a secondary interval that shares the same offset from the grid line as the original clip start point. This alternate snap position allows you to move clips in grid increments while preserving the clip's relative offset from the grid.

- Similarly, if a clip's start or end point falls between grid lines, trimming the clip will snaps the associated clip edge both to successive grid lines and to the offset grid interval, preserving the relative starting point or ending point location.

Disabling Snap to Grid

Disabling Snap to Grid allows you to move or arrange the parts of your set freely and to place material anywhere on the timeline.

 When Snap to Grid is disabled, the grid lines will retain their previous value but will appear greyed out.

To toggle Snap to Grid on/off, do one of the following:

- Choose **OPTIONS > SNAP TO GRID**.

- Press **COMMAND+4** (Mac) or **CTRL+4** (Windows).

You can temporarily suspend Snap to Grid by holding down the COMMAND key (Mac) or CTRL key (Windows). The same modifiers work to temporarily enable Snap to Grid when it has been toggled off.

 Setting the Edit Grid Value to OFF will automatically disable Snap to Grid.

Editing Clips

Ableton Live offers a variety of common editing commands—such as Copy and Paste—as well as application-specific commands—such as Split and Consolidate—that affect clips.

As we've seen previously, Ableton Live supports both audio clips and MIDI Clips. The editing techniques described in this section apply to both types of clips, unless otherwise specified.

Basic Editing Commands

Like most commercial applications, Ableton Live offers standard Cut, Copy, Paste, and Delete commands. The Ableton Live Duplicate command also offers functionality similar to that found in other media applications. Ableton Live performs each of these editing functions nondestructively, meaning that the operations do not alter the original media files on disk.

Each of these commands can be performed on a single track or on multiple tracks simultaneously, depending on the selection or the Clipboard contents. Edits can apply to the following material:

- Part of a clip or parts of multiple clips (selected by clicking in the lower half of clips)

- A whole clip or multiple whole clips (selected by clicking in the upper half of clips)

Selections can cross multiple clip boundaries, can include entire clips or partial clips, and can even include silence, if desired.

The Cut Command

Using the Cut command, you can remove selected material from its current position and place it on the Clipboard (in the computer's RAM) to be used elsewhere via the Paste command.

To cut a selection and place the material on the computer's Clipboard, do the following:

1. Make a selection of any length on a single track or multiple tracks.

2. Choose EDIT > CUT, or press COMMAND+X (Mac) or CTRL+X (Windows). The selected audio and/or MIDI data will be removed from the original location and copied to the Clipboard.

The Copy Command

The Copy command is much like the Cut command, but instead of removing the selected range, it leaves the original in place and creates a copy of it on the Clipboard so that you can paste it elsewhere.

To copy a selection, do the following:

1. Make a selection of any length on a single track or multiple tracks.

2. Choose EDIT > COPY, or press COMMAND+C (Mac) or CTRL+C (Windows). The selected audio and/or MIDI data will be copied to the Clipboard.

 When you place a selection on the computer's Clipboard using a Cut or Copy command, you replace any material previously stored on the Clipboard.

The Paste Command

Using the Paste command, you can insert the contents of the Clipboard at a location that you have selected. You can paste data only after something has been cut or copied to the Clipboard.

To use the Paste command, do the following:

1. Select the desired paste destination using one of the following methods:

    *   Place the insert marker on the desired destination track at the location where you want the start of the paste to occur.

    *   Make a selection of any length on the desired destination track, with the beginning of the selection at the location where you want the start of the paste to occur.

    (i) To paste a multi-track selection from the clipboard, place the insert marker on the topmost track where you would like to paste the clipboard contents.

2. Choose EDIT > PASTE, or press COMMAND+V (Mac) or CTRL+V (Windows). The material on the Clipboard will be pasted in, beginning at the insert marker or selection start point.

    (i) If the Clipboard contains material from multiple tracks, the data will be pasted to tracks starting where the insert marker resides, filling subsequent tracks from top to bottom, provided the destination track types match the source tracks.

    (i) To paste data immediately after a clip, move the insert marker to the ending clip boundary by pressing Option+Right Arrow (Mac) or Alt+Right Arrow (Windows) before using the Paste command.

The Delete Command

The Delete command allows you to remove any selected material without placing it on the Clipboard.

To delete a selection, do the following:

1. Make a selection of any length on a single track or multiple tracks.

2. Choose **EDIT > DELETE.** This command has the same result as pressing the **DELETE** key on the keyboard.

The Duplicate Command

The Duplicate command makes a copy of any selected material and places it immediately after the end of the selection. This command provides a quick way to repeat a selection, extend a sound, or create a simple looping effect—it is faster and more convenient than copying and pasting data to achieve the same result.

To duplicate audio or MIDI data, do the following:

1. Make a selection of any length and content on one or more tracks.

2. (Optional) Play the selection using Arrangement Loop to ensure that it plays smoothly in succession. If the selection loops smoothly, you can duplicate it without creating an audible edit point.

3. (Optional) Adjust the selection as needed to create a smooth loop transition.

4. Choose **EDIT > DUPLICATE** or press **COMMAND+D** (Mac) or **CTRL+D** (Windows). The selection will be duplicated and pasted at the end of the selected area or clip.

The Split Command

Splitting a clip is the process of breaking a clip in two or separating a selection as a new, independent clip.

You can split a clip for one of several purposes:

- To divide a source clip into two new clips on a track. (See Figure 9.7.)

- To separate a selection from a parent clip or from the material on either side. Use this process to create a clip from a selection, creating new byproduct clips on either side. (See Figure 9.8.)

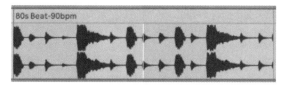 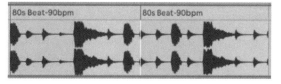

Figure 9.7 Splitting a clip at the insert marker: before (left) and after (right)

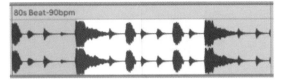 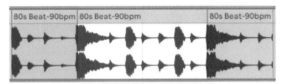

Figure 9.8 Splitting a selection as a new clip: before (left) and after (right)

When you split clips, you create byproduct clips from the material on either side of the selection.

To split a clip, do the following:

1. Place the insert marker at the location where you want a split to occur, or make a selection of any length within a clip or across multiple clips.

2. Do one of the following:

   • Choose **EDIT > SPLIT**.

   • Press **COMMAND+E** (Mac) or **CTRL+E** (Windows).

   • Right-click within the selection and choose **SPLIT** from the pop-up menu.

Ableton Live will create new clips based on the insert marker or the selection start and end points.

 Ableton Live does not automatically rename the clips that result from using the Split command, so you will have two different clips that share the same name.

Moving and Resizing Clips in the Arrangement View

The following sections describe techniques for moving and resizing clips and discuss the effects of the Edit Grid and the clip Loop option on these operations. The nudge function is also introduced.

Moving Clips

In Ableton Live, you can easily move clips within the Arrangement View. You can drag a clip to a different location within the same track or to a different track. Regardless of the Snap to Grid setting, you can always place clips so that they overlap or so that they have space between them on a track. During playback, you will hear silence in any open areas.

Moving Clips with Snap to Grid Enabled

When editing clips with Snap to Grid enabled, moving and dragging operations are constrained by the current Edit Grid value as configured in the Arrangement View.

To move a clip with Snap to Grid enabled, do the following:

1. Verify that the Edit Grid value has been set as desired. (See "Configuring the Edit Grid Setting" earlier in this chapter.)

2. Position the mouse cursor over the top half of the clip that you'd like to move. The cursor will change into a hand icon.

3. Click and drag the clip to the desired destination. A preview of the clip will appear on the track, snapping to each successive grid line as you drag.

4. Release the mouse to position the clip at the desired location.

Moving Clips with Snap to Grid Disabled

With Snap to Grid disabled, you can move clips freely.

To move a clip with Snap to Grid disabled, do the following:

1. Position the mouse cursor over the top half of the clip that you'd like to move. The cursor will change into a hand icon.

2. Click on the clip and drag it to the desired destination. A preview of the clip will appear as you drag, moving smoothly across the Track Display area.

3. Release the mouse to position the clip at the desired location.

 As you drag a clip, the Status Bar at the bottom left of the Arrangement View will dynamically update to show you the precise insert position.

Resizing Clips (Arrangement View))

The resize function in Ableton Live allows you to easily trim clips within the Arrangement View. You can shorten or lengthen clips as desired by trimming their heads or tails at any time.

Resizing a Clip

By resizing the head or tail of a clip, you can eliminate unwanted material or reveal additional material that precedes or follows the currently visible data. If the clip Loop switch is engaged, you can also loop a clip or clip segment by resizing.

To resize a clip, do the following:

1. If needed, zoom in on the clip you want to resize in the Arrangement View.

2. Position the mouse cursor at the top of the clip near the start or end. The cursor will change to a left or right bracket shape. (See Figure 9.9.)

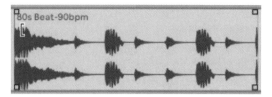 

Figure 9.9 The resize cursor, as displayed near the start (left) or end (right) of the clip

3. Click and drag to resize the clip in either direction.

4. Release the mouse button at the desired location to complete the trim.

Looping Clips

The resize behavior in Live will vary, depending on whether the target clip has its Loop switch engaged. The Loop switch can be found in the Notes box (for MIDI clips) or Sample box (for audio clips). Enabling Loop functionality for a clip will allow that clip to loop indefinitely when resized.

 Audio clips that are not Loop-enabled can only be resized to the up to the outer boundaries of the original audio sample or audio file recorded on disk.

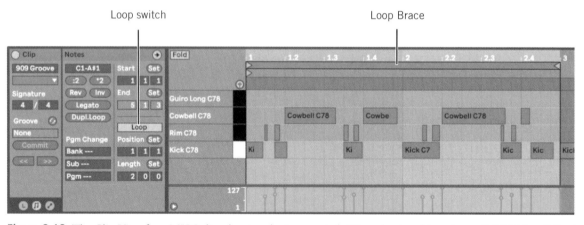

Figure 9.10 The Clip View for a MIDI clip, showing the Loop switch (Notes box) and loop brace (MIDI Note Editor)

The Warp switch must be activated prior to enabling the Loop switch for an audio clip. Unwarped audio clips cannot be looped.

To activate warping for an audio clip, do the following:

- Click the **Warp** button from the **Sample** box in the Clip View. (See Figure 9.11.) When active, the audio clip will automatically conform to tempo changes in your Set and the project tempo map.

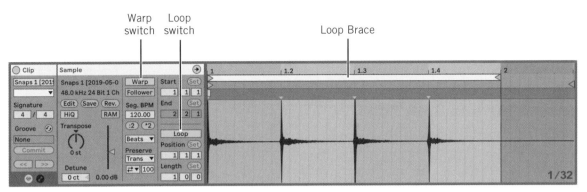

Figure 9.11 The Clip View for an audio clip showing the Warp and Loop switches in the Sample box and the loop brace in the Sample Editor

In the Arrangement View, any Loop-enabled clip can be resized beyond the length of its original media, with Ableton Live automatically adding successive iterations (repetitions) of the clip contents to achieve the desired length. The looped area of the clip will correspond to the loop position and length, as demarcated by the loop brace in the Sample Editor.

To enable clip looping:

1. Double-click on the target clip to open it in the Clip View.

2. If necessary, enable warping for the clip as described above (required for audio clips).

3. Click the **LOOP** switch in the Notes box (for MIDI clips) or in the Sample box (for audio clips).

You can drag the triangle markers (start and end arrows) in the loop brace to change length of the loop brace, or you can type exact values into the Loop Length and Position fields. You can also use various keyboard commands to adjust the loop length and position.

To modify the loop, do one of the following:

■   Click and drag a triangle marker at either end of the loop brace to change its position.

■   Type in exact position and length values in the Notes box (for MIDI clips) or the Sample box (for audio clips).

■   Click on the loop brace to select it, and do one of the following:

•   Press the **LEFT** or **RIGHT ARROW** keys to nudge the loop brace to the left/right by the Grid value.

•   Hold **COMMAND** (Mac) or **CTRL** (Windows) while pressing the **LEFT** or **RIGHT ARROW** keys to shorten or lengthen the loop brace by the Grid value.

Regardless of the position of the loop brace, clip playback will begin at the clip start marker. This means you can configure a clip to run into a loop by setting the clip start location earlier than the loop brace start location.

Nudging Clips and Selections

Ableton Live allows you to adjust the placement of clips and selections by nudging them with the keyboard. With Snap to Grid enabled, nudging moves clips and selections by the Edit Grid Value. With Snap to Grid disabled, nudging moves in very small increments and adapts to the zoom level.

Nudging Clips

To nudge a single clip or multiple clips by the Edit Grid Value, do the following:

1. Verify that that Snap to Grid is enabled.

2. Select the clip or clips you want to nudge.

3. Press the **LEFT ARROW** key to move the clip(s) earlier in the track or the **RIGHT ARROW** key to move the clip(s) later in the track. The clip(s) will move incrementally by the Edit Grid Value.

To nudge a single clip or multiple clips by a small, zoom-adaptive value, do the following:

1. Do one of the following to disable Snap to Grid:

    *   Choose **OPTIONS > SNAP TO GRID**.

    *   Press **COMMAND+4** (Mac) or **CTRL+4** (Windows)

    *   Set the Edit Grid Value to **OFF**.

2. Select the clip or clips you want to nudge.

3. Press the **LEFT ARROW** key to move the clip(s) earlier in the track or the **RIGHT ARROW** key to move the clip(s) later in the track. The clip(s) will move incrementally by a small, zoom-adaptive value.

 Hold the COMMAND key (Mac) or ALT key (Windows) while nudging to flip the nudge behavior so that clips nudge by the Edit Grid Value when the Edit Grid is disabled or by a small zoom-adaptive value when the Edit Grid is enabled.

 You can snap clips to the next or previous Locator by holding down the OPTION key (Mac) or CTRL key (Windows) while nudging.

Nudging Selections

In addition to nudging clips, you can also nudge selections using the **LEFT ARROW** and **RIGHT ARROW** keys on the computer keyboard.

To nudge a selection, do the following:

1. Make a selection on any track or tracks.

2. Press the **LEFT ARROW** key to move the selection earlier in the track or the **RIGHT ARROW** key to move the selection later in the track. The selection and its contents will move earlier or later following the nudge behavior described above relative to the Snap to Grid status.

To change the length of a selection by nudging:

- Hold the **SHIFT** key while pressing the **LEFT ARROW** key or the **RIGHT ARROW** key on the computer keyboard. The selection will lengthen or shorten incrementally following the nudge behavior relative to the Snap to Grid status.

Nudging to Clip Boundaries and Locators

You can perform macro-level nudging to move to successive clip boundaries and locators, by holding modifier keys.

To nudge a clip or selection to the next or previous clip boundary or locator:

- Hold **OPTION** (Mac) or **CTRL** (Windows) while pressing the **LEFT ARROW** key or **RIGHT ARROW** key on the computer keyboard. The start of the clip or selection will snap to successive start and end boundaries for other clips on the track and any locators in the Set.

You can also use macro-level nudging to extend selections to successive clip boundaries and locators.

To extend a selection to the next or previous clip boundary or locator:

- Hold **OPTION+SHIFT** (Mac) or **CTRL+SHIFT** (Windows) while pressing the **LEFT ARROW** key or **RIGHT ARROW** key on the computer keyboard. The selection will lengthen or shorten by snapping to the next or previous clip boundary or locator.

Undoing Your Work

Often your editing tasks will involve performing a series of related steps to achieve a desired effect. Along the way, you might at times need to revert to an earlier point, either to start over or to do a before-and-after comparison. Fortunately, Ableton Live provides rich undo options that give you the flexibility to work without constraints.

Using Multi-Level Undo

Multi-level undo operations make it possible to return to earlier stages of work during the editing process. This lets you work and experiment with confidence, knowing that you can back out of changes if you are not satisfied with the results.

Ableton Live provides an unlimited number of undo operations. All commands that are undoable are stored sequentially in an undo queue. However, a small number of commands in Live cause changes that are not undoable.

Some actions that *cannot* be undone include the following:

- Closing a Set and/or quitting Ableton Live (Clears the Undo Queue)

- Deleting Clips from the Current Project Folder in the Browser

Using the Undo and Redo Commands

To access the Undo command, choose **EDIT > UNDO** or press **COMMAND+Z** (Mac) or **CTRL+Z** (Windows). The Undo command in the Edit menu lists the action to be undone along with the command name.

Figure 9.12 The Undo command in the Edit menu, showing the action that will be undone

To perform multiple undo operations, repeat the above process as needed.

If you undo an action that you want to keep, you can reinstate the action using the Redo command. To access the Redo command, choose **EDIT > REDO** or press **COMMAND+SHIFT+Z** (Mac) or **CTRL+SHIFT+Z** (Windows). Like the Undo command, the Redo command lists the action that it will affect.

Restoring from Backup Sets

Ableton Live retains the undo queue as long as the Set is running. However, at times you may need to go back far enough that using the undo command hundreds of times simply isn't practical. In these cases, restoring from a Backup Set may be a better option.

The ten most recently saved versions of the current Set are automatically saved in a Backup folder that Ableton Live creates inside the project folder.

 Ableton Live automatically deletes the oldest backup Set once the number of backups exceeds 10 files.

Opening a Backup Set is similar to opening an earlier saved copy of the Set. However, you can recognize a Backup Set because it will have the date it was saved appended to the Set name.

To restore your Set from a backup, do the following:

1. Choose FILE > OPEN LIVE SET and navigate to the Backup folder within your project folder.

2. Select a Backup Set based on the modification date and time.

3. Once the Set opens, verify that the backup file represents the desired stage of the Set.

4. Select FILE > SAVE LIVE SET AS to save the restored Set with an appropriate name.

 You can also open Backup Sets using the Browser by navigating to Current Project > Backup and double-clicking one of the Backup Sets.

Review/Discussion Questions

1. What three scrolling behaviors are available in Ableton Live? (See "Follow Behavior" beginning on page 244.)

2. What does the Arrangement Loop option do? What is the minimum selection length required for an Arrangement Loop? (See "Arrangement Loop" beginning on page 245.)

3. What two Edit Grid Modes are provided in Ableton Live? (See "Using the Edit Grid" beginning on page 246.)

4. How can you configure the Edit Grid value? (See "Configuring the Edit Grid Settings" beginning on page 246.)

5. What happens when you move a clip whose start point falls between Grid lines with the Snap To Grid function enabled? What happens when you move a clip with Snap to Grid mode disabled? (See "Snap to Grid" beginning on page 248.)

6. Name some basic editing commands provided in Ableton Live. (See "Basic Editing Commands" beginning on page 249.)

7. What are some operations that the Split command can be used for? (See "The Split Command" beginning on page 251.)

8. What is the purpose of resizing a clip? How can you resize a clip in the Arrangement View? (See "Resizing a Clip" beginning on page 253.)

9. How can you enable a clip to repeat its contents when resized, creating a looping pattern? Where are the controls for this functionality found for MIDI clips? Where are they found for audio clips? (See "Looping Clips" beginning on page 254.)

10. What additional switch needs to be activated to allow looping for an audio clip? (See "Looping Clips" beginning on page 254.)

11. What keys are used to nudge a clip or selection earlier or later on a track? (See "Nudging Clips" beginning on page 256.)

12. What is the maximum number of operations can you undo in Ableton Live? What are some operations that cannot be undone? (See "Using Multi-Level Undo" beginning on page 258.)

To review additional material from this chapter and prepare for certification, see the Ableton Live 101 Study Guide module available through the Elements|ED online learning platform at ElementsED.com.

Editing Audio

🎧 Activity

In this exercise, you will use the Locators you created in Exercise 8 to add a noise effect. You will also shorten the music tracks to fit within a 45-second target length.

🕒 Duration

This exercise should take approximately 10 to 15 minutes to complete.

◈ Goals/Targets

- Use Locators to add a noise sweep
- Extend the end of song to a specific length

Media Files

To complete this exercise, you may need to use various media files included in the **Media Files 2019-Live101** folder. You should have downloaded the media files in Exercise 4.

If needed, you can re-download the media files by going to www.halleonard.com/mylibrary and entering your access code (printed on the opening page of this book). From there, click the **Download** link for the **Media Files 2019–Live101** listing in your **My Library** page. The Media Files folder will begin transferring to your Downloads folder.

Getting Started

You will start by opening the Live Set you completed in Exercise 8. If that Set is not available, you can use the Ex08 Sample file in the 01 Completed Exercises folder within the Media Files 2019-Live101 folder.

Open the Live Set and save it as Exercise 9:

1. Do one of the following:

    *   Open the Set file that you created in Exercise 8 (**Storage Drive/Folder > Live101-XXX > Exercise08-XXX.als**).

    *   Alternatively, you can use the Ex 08 Sample file (**Media Files 2019-Live101 > 01. Completed Projects > Ex08 Sample.als**).

2. Choose **FILE > SAVE LIVE SET AS** and name the Set *Exercise09-XXX*, keeping the Live Set inside the original Project folder. (Move the Set into your **Live101-XXX** folder if working from the sample file.)

Adding a Noise Sweep

In this part of the exercise, you will use the Locators you added earlier to create a transition using a noise sweep effect.

Configure the Edit Grid Value:

■   Right-click in the Arrangement View and set the Edit Grid value to **FIXED GRID: 1/8** (1/8 note), if not already selected.

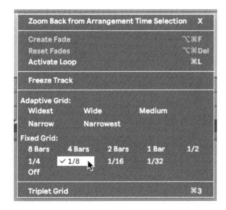

Figure 9.13 Setting the Edit Grid Value to 1/8 notes

Place the noise effect:

1. In the Browser, navigate to **PLACES > 02 EXERCISE MEDIA** and locate the Noise_Sweep_120 clip.

2. Drag the clip onto the Arrangement View so that the start of the clip lines up with the **DRUMS** Locator. Note that the clip placement does not need to be exact.

 Be sure to drag the clip to the "Drop Files and Devices Here" area so that clip will be place on a new track.

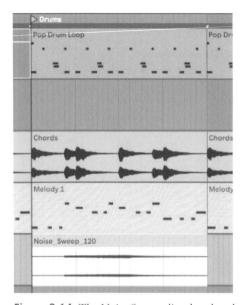

Figure 9.14 The Noise Sweep clip placed at the Drums Locator position

Nudge the noise sweep:

■ With the Noise_Sweep_120 clip selected, use the **LEFT** and **RIGHT ARROW** keys to nudge the clip into position, so that it peaks near the Drums locator position.

 Nudge the clip by Edit Grid increments until the middle of the clip is visually aligned with the Drums locator. Continue to nudge with Snap to Grid turned off, auditioning periodically, to align the clip by ear at the best location.

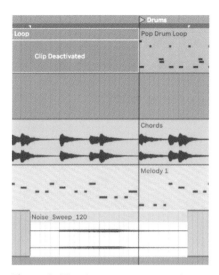

Figure 9.15 The Noise Sweep peaking near the Drums Locator

Extending the Song

In this section of the exercise, you will extend the Drums, Bass, Chords, and Melody tracks so that the song is around 60 seconds in length.

Duplicate the clips:

1. Locate the final clips at the end of the song.

2. Select any one of the clips.

3. Choose **EDIT > DUPLICATE TIME** or press **COMMAND+SHIFT+D** (Mac) or **CTRL+SHIFT+D** (Windows) to duplicate the clips.

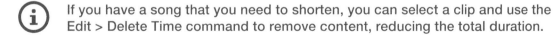

If you have a song that you need to shorten, you can select a clip and use the Edit > Delete Time command to remove content, reducing the total duration.

Resize the Chords clip:

1. Place the cursor near the right edge of the final Chords clip. The cursor will display a bracket icon.

2. While referring to the Time Ruler at the bottom of the Arrangement View, click and drag to resize the end of the Chords clip to around 1:00.

Hold Command (Mac) or Alt (Windows) as needed to trim with the Edit Grid temporarily inactive.

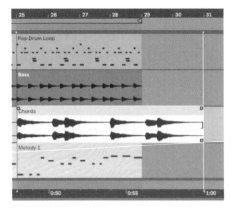

Figure 9.16 The Chords clip resized to end around 1:00

Add a fade out to the end of the Chords clip:

1. Place the cursor near the upper right edge of the clip. The Fade Our Start Handle will appear.

2. Click and drag to the left to create a fade out. Try creating a fade out over approximately one bar.

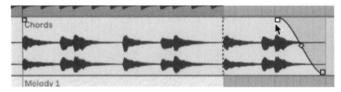

Figure 9.17 The Chords with a fade out

Finishing Up

Using the knowledge you have gained thus far, you can continue to edit and fine-tune this basic musical idea to your liking, if desired. To complete this exercise, you will need to save your work and close the Set.

Review your work:

1. Place the Insert Marker at the start of your arrangement.

2. Press the **SPACEBAR** to play back the Live Set and confirm your results.

3. Press the **SPACEBAR** a second time when finished.

Save your work and close the Live Set:

1. Choose **FILE > SAVE LIVE SET**.

2. Press **COMMAND+Q** (Mac) or **CTRL+Q** (Windows) to quit Live and close the project.

Chapter 10

Mixing and Creating a Bounce

This chapter covers basic mixing techniques and processes as they are performed in Ableton Live. It includes discussions of mixer terminology, mixer configuration (including configuring devices, sends, and returns), basic automation, and real-time processing. The chapter also covers techniques for finishing your work, including creating a project back-up/archive and a final mixdown your project as a stereo file.

 Learning Targets for This Chapter

- Recognize common mixer terminology

- Understand how devices and send-and-return paths are used to add signal processing to your tracks

- Configure the devices and sends in the mixer

- Record and edit basic automation for your mix

- Add devices to your tracks for internal effects processing and sound shaping

- Understand the purpose of the Collect All and Save command and recognize situations in which you should use it

- Select appropriate options for your stereo mix when using Export Audio/Video

 Key topics from this chapter are illustrated in the Ableton Live 101 Study Guide module available through the Elements|ED online learning platform. Sign up for free at ElementsED.com.

With all of your tracks recorded and edited, it's time to start thinking about how to create a good balance between the audio elements, adding emphasis where it's needed and creating the subtle touches required for a professional–sounding result. Setting levels, adding signal processing, and creating dynamic automation are all parts of this process.

Once the mix sounds the way you want it, you will be ready to output the finished product as a stereo file. This chapter outlines the essential concepts and techniques required to complete all of these mixing tasks.

Basic Mixer Terminology

The fundamental job of any audio mixer is to route incoming and outgoing audio via the mixer's inputs and outputs. Additional signal routing and processing can be achieved using the mixer's inserts and send and return functions. These terms are defined in this section as they apply to general audio mixing; specific Ableton Live applications of these concepts are described under "Mixing in the Session View" later in this chapter.

Inputs

The term *input* refers to an audio signal traveling into an audio hardware device, such as a mixer or an audio interface. The inputs available in Ableton Live vary depending on the system and the audio interface(s) in use.

Outputs

The term *output* refers to an audio signal traveling out of an audio hardware device. The outputs available in Ableton Live also vary depending on the system and the audio hardware in use. In a new Set, all tracks will route to the main stereo outputs (left and right) by default.

Inserts (Devices)

Most mixers have a feature known as a *channel insert*. An insert is an audio patch point that allows a signal processor to be placed directly into the signal path of the audio channel. Ableton Live uses the term *device* to describe channel inserts.

Ableton Live provides an unlimited number insert positions per track, allowing you to process a track's signal through multiple software plug-ins and/or external effects loops in series.

Sends and Returns

The term *send* refers to a signal path carrying a mix output of one or more channels (or tracks) routed for parallel processing. The send may route to an external receiving device, such as a hardware effects unit, or to an internal processor, such as a software plug-in.

Pre-Fader versus Post-Fader Sends

Sends can be *pre-fader*, meaning the send level is independent of the source track's Volume slider level, or *post-fader*, meaning the send level will be affected by changes you make to the Volume slider on the source track. In Ableton Live, sends are post-fader by default; however, you can set a send to pre-fader at any time, as needed.

Send and Return Processing

When using a send for external processing, the signal is routed out of the mixer, through an external device where some type of processing is added, and then returned to the mixer through an *auxiliary return* channel. When using a send for internal processing in Ableton Live, effects are added using a plug-in applied to the returned signal on the destination track (known as a Return track).

The return channel in the mixer provides level and pan controls, allowing precise control over how the reintroduced signal combines with other audio in the system.

Mixing in the Session View

Although all of Ableton Live's mixing controls can be viewed in the Arrangement View, mixing operations and functions are typically performed using the Session View. The Session View is similar to a standard mixing console. This view offers a variety of display options, many of which can also be customized.

The Session View can be swapped with the Arrangement View as needed. To switch to the Session View, choose VIEW > TOGGLE ARRANGEMENT/SESSION VIEW.

> You can also press the TAB key to toggle between the Session and Arrangement Views at any time.

Configuring the Session View for Mixing

The Session View includes several component parts and controls. Among the controls that you will use to create your mix are Volume controls, Pan controls, I/O choosers, and Send controls.

> The In and Out section in Live includes choosers for Audio Input Type and Channel and Audio Output Type and Channel, as well as MIDI Input Type and Channel and MIDI Output Type and Channel (MIDI tracks only).

To create a mix, you will set the Volume control for each track to achieve an appropriate blend of audio levels, and set the Pan controls to achieve the desired positioning of sounds within the stereo field. You can make changes in real time during playback, either by manually adjusting the controls or by using automation. (See "Using Basic Automation" later in this chapter.)

The Input and Output choosers are used to route signals to and from your tracks. Often the basic I/O routing for your mix will already be in place, based on the work you have done up to this point. However, if needed, you can use these selectors to configure different signal routing for your mix.

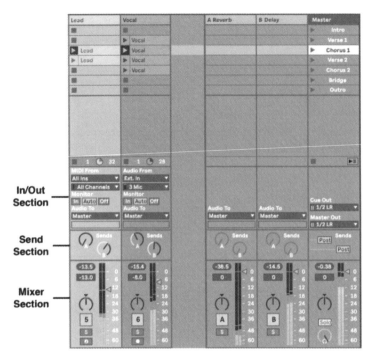

Figure 10.1 Mixing controls in the Session View

Mixing also often involves using devices and sends to add various types of signal processing to the audio on a project's tracks. You can use the Send controls and the Device View in the Session View to achieve these operations.

Showing/Hiding Sections

You can show or hide sections of the Session View using the Show/Hide buttons at the bottom right corner of the Session View. Click a button to toggle the show/hide status of the associated section.

Figure 10.2 The Session View Show/Hide buttons for the In/Out section

The Show/Hide buttons shown in Figure 10.2 are as follows, from top to bottom:

- **I•O** – In/Out Section

- **S** – Sends Section

- **R** – Return tracks

- **M** – Mixer Section

- **D** – Track Delays Section

- **X** – Crossfader Section

Input and Output Choosers

The Session View displays the main Input and Output choosers for each track in the project by default. Though much of your signal routing might have been set up during the recording and editing stages of your project, it is always a good idea to double-check the I/O settings when you begin mixing.

Input Choosers

For tracks that are playing back material already on the track, no input routing is necessary. Tracks that are receiving live input from other sources will need to have their inputs set accordingly.

Output Choosers

Ableton Live enables you to route the output of each track to any available hardware output. For the purposes of creating a stereo mix, you will generally use the main stereo outputs of your audio interface (default).

To set up a basic stereo mix, verify that the Audio Output choosers for the tracks in your Set are routed to the main outputs of your audio interface, as appropriate, so that the audio from each track is included in the stereo playback. This is typically done by assigning each track to the output type labeled Master. This setting routes the track output to the Master track, where the physical output can be assigned using the Master Out chooser.

 Ableton Live 10 introduced the ability to label inputs and outputs with custom names. To do this, go to the Audio tab in Preferences. After selecting the Driver Type and Audio Devices, click the INPUT CONFIG and OUTPUT CONFIG buttons to add labels for the available mono and stereo paths.

If needed, use the Audio Output Type and Channel choosers to select the desired output for your tracks.

Sends Section

The Session View has a dedicated section for the track send controls known as the Send Section. This area can be shown or hidden in the Session View (see "Showing/Hiding Sections" above).

Figure 10.3 Sends Section in the Session View

The Sends Section allows you to access and view up to 12 Send Controls (A – L) in Ableton Live Standard and Suite editions. The default Ableton Live Set is pre-configured with two sends (A and B). Additional send controls are added as you create additional return tracks.

 The Sends Section is part of the Mixer Section in the Arrangement View.

Configuring Devices

You can add one or more signal processing devices to any track in Ableton Live. Audio Effects and Plug-ins provide software-based signal processing, and the External Audio Effect device can be used to create an effects loop for an external hardware device.

To add a device to a track:

1. Locate the device using the Audio Effects or Plug-ins Categories in the Browser.

2. Do one of the following:

   - Drag and drop the device onto the desired track.

   - Select the destination track and then double-click on the device in the Browser.

Software Devices

Audio Effects and Plug-ins route audio through a software add-on inserted onto a track. Using the Browser, you can choose from the Audio Effects or Plug-ins Categories to add a software signal processor, such as an EQ plug-in, directly into the signal path of the channel.

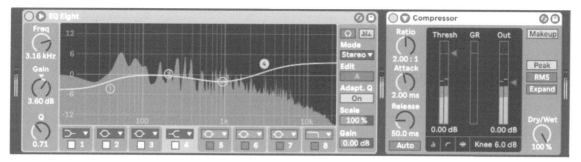

Figure 10.4 EQ Eight and Compressor inserted onto a track

External Audio Effect

The External Audio Effect device routes audio through an external hardware device using parallel inputs and outputs of an audio interface. This option requires an audio interface with sufficient I/O capacity to support hardware inserts in addition to stereo playback through the main left–right outputs.

Configuring Sends and Returns

Sends are used to route a track's signal to a secondary path for parallel processing (internal or external) without interrupting the signal flow through the originating track. To add the processed signal back into the mix, it is returned through a channel strip known as a return track in Ableton Live.

To create a Send to route to an internal processor, such as an Audio Effect or Plug-in, simply create a new return track. A Send to that return track will automatically be created across all of the tracks in the Set.

To create a new return track do one of the following:

- Choose CREATE > INSERT RETURN TRACK.

- Press OPTION+COMMAND+T (Mac) or CTRL+ALT+T (Windows).

To route a send to an external device:

1. Create a return track.

2. Insert the External Audio Effect device on the return track.

3. Set the Audio To chooser and the Audio From chooser in the External Audio Effects device to the appropriate connections on your audio interface.

Automation

For a simple mix, you can often set the Volume and Pan controls as desired and leave them unchanged from the start of the mix to the end. For a more complex mix that requires dynamic changes during the course of playback, you can use Arrangement automation to change control settings throughout a song. Ableton Live allows you to record any real-time changes you make as automation on your tracks. Automatable controls include volume, pan, speaker on/off (mute), send levels, and more.

Arrangement Automation Workflow

In a typical production workflow, the ultimate destination for all automation is the Arrangement View. Aggregating all of the automation in a unified timeline enables a producer to fine tune automation while considering the needs of the entire song.

Automation can be recorded to the Arrangement View in two ways:

- Clip automation created in the Session View can be recorded to the Arrangement using the Arrangement Record function.

- Manual parameter changes can be recorded directly into the Arrangement.

Recording Arrangement Automation

Recording automation in the Arrangement View is quite simple. When the Automation Arm button is enabled, any track control that is moved during an Arrangement Record pass will become Arrangement Automation, regardless of the status of the individual track's Arm button.

To record Arrangement automation:

1. Enable the Automation Arm button in the Control Bar.

Figure 10.5 The Automation Arm button (yellow)

2. Click the Arrangement Record button (solid circle) in the Control Bar.

3. If needed, click the Play button to start the transport.

> **ⓘ** If the START PLAYBACK WITH RECORD preference is enabled, clicking the Arrangement Record button will immediately start playback.

4. Perform any desired control changes in real time during the record pass.

   If Automation Mode is currently enabled (see "Viewing Arrangement Automation" below), you will see the track's main automation lane update in real time. Otherwise, the track will turn red to show that automation is being written.

5. Stop playback when finished.

Automation LEDs

Any control that has automation data on it will display a red automation indicator (or "LED"). The location of this LED can vary depending on the parameter type and the current view. In the Session View, automation LEDs will appear to the upper left corner of most controls, and inside Volume sliders. In the Arrangement View, automation LEDs will appear in the upper left corner of the control.

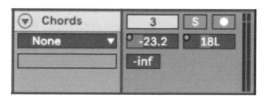

Figure 10.6 Pan and Volume Automation LEDs visible in the Session View (left) and the Arrangement View (right)

Viewing Arrangement Automation

By default, tracks in the Arrangement View show track content and not automation data. To view automation data you must enable Automation Mode.

Toggling Automation Mode

To toggle Automation Mode on or off, do one of the following:

■ Click the **AUTOMATION MODE** button

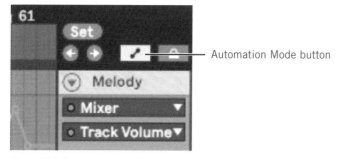

Figure 10.7 The Automation Mode button (blue)

■ Choose **VIEW > AUTOMATION MODE**.

■ Press the **A** key on the computer keyboard (with the Computer MIDI Keyboard disabled).

Viewing Automation Envelopes

With Automation Mode enabled, there are a number of ways to display automation envelopes.

To view the automation envelope for a visible control:

■   Click on any mixer or device control to display the control's envelope on the track. The automation envelope will appear in the track's main automation lane and will be superimposed on top of any audio or MIDI data

To use the choosers to display an automation envelope:

1.   Use the **DEVICE** chooser to select the track Mixer or a Device on the track.

2.   Use the **AUTOMATION CONTROL** chooser to select the particular control that you would like to view. The automation envelope for the selected parameter will appear in the track's main automation lane and will be superimposed on top of any audio or MIDI data on the track.

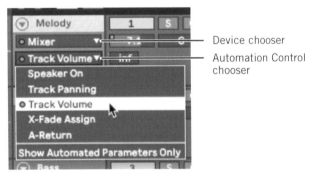

Figure 10.8 Selecting Track Volume from the Automation Control chooser

Oftentimes devices will have dozens of automatable parameters, making the menu in the Device chooser cumbersome to navigate. To simplify the navigation, you can hide all unused parameters in the list, showing automated parameters only.

To limit the Device chooser to devices with automated parameters only:

■   Click the Device chooser and select **SHOW AUTOMATED PARAMETERS ONLY** from the bottom of the menu.

You can also hide all automation lanes on a track to prevent accidental changes to an automation graph while working in Automation Mode on other tracks.

To hide automation envelopes on the track's main automation lane:

■   Click the Device chooser and select **NONE** from the top of the menu.

Using Automation Lanes

In addition to displaying automation envelopes in the track's main automation lane, you can create additional automation lanes below the track.

To display an automation envelope using an automation lane, do the following:

■   Click the **ADD AUTOMATION LANE** button in the bottom corner of the track Title section.

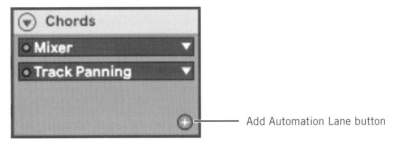

Add Automation Lane button

Figure 10.9 The Add Automation Lane button ("+" symbol in the bottom right)

(i) If the Device chooser is set to None, the ADD AUTOMATION LANE button will not be visible.

To display all automation envelopes in their own automation lanes, do one of the following:

■   Hold **COMMAND** (Mac) or **CTRL** (Windows) and click the **ADD AUTOMATION LANE** button.

■   Right-click on an existing automation lane header and choose **ADD LANE FOR EACH AUTOMATED ENVELOPE**.

To hide an automation lane, do one of the following:

■   Click the **REMOVE AUTOMATION LANE** button ("−" symbol to the right of an automation lane header).

■   Right-click the automation lane header and choose **REMOVE AUTOMATION LANE**.

To hide an automation lane and all subsequent lanes on the same track, do one of the following:

■   Hold **OPTION** (Mac) or **ALT** (Windows) and click the **REMOVE AUTOMATION LANE** button. The current lane and all lanes below it will be hidden.

Drawing Automation Envelopes

In some scenarios, it may be necessary to manually draw an automation envelope in order to achieve a specific result. Ableton Live offers Draw Mode for these situations, which activates a pencil tool for drawing automation on screen.

To enable Draw Mode do one of the following:

■   Click the Draw Mode switch in the Control Bar.

- Press the **B** key on the computer keyboard.

Figure 10.10 The Draw Mode switch (yellow) with Draw Mode active

To momentarily toggle Draw Mode:

- Press and hold the **B** key on the computer keyboard; release to return to Edit Mode.

Drawing Automation

With Draw Mode enabled, you can simply click and drag in a track's Envelope Editor to create new automation data.

Drawing with Snap To Grid Enabled

Drawing with the Snap To Grid enabled will always result in "steps" that are the width of the current Edit Grid Value.

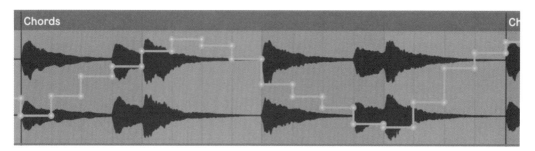

Figure 10.11 "Stepped" automation drawn with Snap to Grid enabled

To draw automation with a finer resolution:

- Hold SHIFT and then click and drag vertically on a segment.

Drawing with Snap To Grid Suspended

With Snap to Grid disabled, you can draw a "freehand" automation curve that is not affected by the current Edit Grid value.

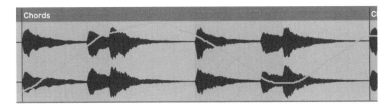

Figure 10.12 "Freehand" automation drawn with Snap to Grid disabled

To disable Snap to Grid, do one of the following:

■ Press **COMMAND+4** (Mac) or **CTRL+4** (Windows).

■ Right-click in the Arrangement View and set the Edit Grid Value to **OFF**.

To temporarily disable Snap to Grid:

■ Hold **COMMAND** (Mac) or **ALT** (Windows) while drawing.

Editing Automation Breakpoints

With Draw Mode off, it becomes possible to use individual breakpoints to create and modify an automation envelope. When creating or editing simple automation moves, it can be convenient to edit the breakpoints directly. As you move a breakpoint, a thin line will appear to show you the position of the breakpoint relative to the beat-time ruler, and a small box will appear to show you the vertical position of the breakpoint.

To add a new breakpoint, do one of the following:

■ Click anywhere on a line segment. A new breakpoint will be added at the clicked location.

■ Double-click anywhere in the envelope display. A new breakpoint will be added at the clicked location and the automation envelope will conform to include the new breakpoint location.

To delete an existing breakpoint:

■ Click on an existing breakpoint. The breakpoint will be deleted and the automation envelope will adjust accordingly.

To move a breakpoint:

■ Click and drag on an existing breakpoint. The breakpoint position will move and the automation envelope will adjust as you drag.

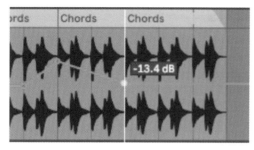

Figure 10.13 Moving a breakpoint

 Moving a breakpoint past a neighboring breakpoint will delete that breakpoint from the envelope. Moving the breakpoint back prior to releasing it will restore the neighboring breakpoint.

To restrict the horizontal or vertical movement of a breakpoint:

■ Hold the **SHIFT** key when dragging the breakpoint horizontally or vertically.

To adjust the breakpoint value with a finer resolution:

■ Hold the **SHIFT** key while dragging the breakpoint vertically.

To suspend grid snapping when moving breakpoints:

■ Hold **COMMAND** (Mac) or **ALT** (Windows) while dragging

To move multiple breakpoints simultaneously:

1. Click and drag in the background of the automation lane, not on the automation envelop, to make a time selection that includes the target breakpoints.

2. Click and the drag on any selected breakpoint to move all of the selected breakpoints.

 You can also nudge selected breakpoints using the Left and Right Arrow keys.

Making Selections in Automation Mode

When Automation Mode is enabled, you can select an automation range using the same methods you would to select time. You can then carry out many editing tasks on the selected automation range, such as duplicating, copying, and moving the automation selection earlier or later in time.

Locking Envelopes

In the default mode, moving a clip to a new position in the Arrangement Timeline will also move all of the automation associated with the clip. However, it is also possible to lock the automation envelopes so that you can move a clip and have its automation remain in its original position in the Arrangement Timeline.

To enable the Lock Envelopes option, do one of the following:

■ Choose **OPTIONS > LOCK ENVELOPES**.

■ Click the Lock Envelopes switch (lock icon) in the Arrangement View

Figure 10.14 The Lock Envelopes switch (red) when enabled

Overriding Automation

In both the Session View and Arrangement View, it is possible to temporarily override automation for a control without modifying the automation data. This can be done by moving a control while not recording automation. The control will be overridden, and its automation LED will turn white. When one or more automation envelopes has been overridden, the **RE-ENABLE AUTOMATION** button (left-pointing arrow) in the Control Bar will light red. Controls will stay overridden until you re-enable automation.

Figure 10.15 The Re-Enable Automation button (red)

To re-enable automation for the entire Live Set:

■ Click the **RE-ENABLE AUTOMATION** button.

To re-enable automation for a single control:

■ Right-click a control displaying a white LED and choose **RE-ENABLE AUTOMATION** from the context menu.

Deleting Automation

Sometimes you may simply want to delete all of the automation data for a particular control, device, or track. Delete operations are available for all of these situations.

To delete all automation data for a control, do one of the following:

■ Right-click on the automated control and select **DELETE AUTOMATION** from the context menu.

■ Right-click on an automation lane header and choose **CLEAR ENVELOPE**.

■ Select an automated control and press **COMMAND+DELETE** (Mac) or **CTRL+DELETE** (Windows).

Once a control's automation data has been deleted, the automation LED will disappear and the control's value will return to a static value for the duration of the Arrangement timeline.

Figure 10.16 A control before deleting automation data (left) and after deleting automation (right)

To delete all automation data for a device:

■ Right-click on an automation lane header and choose **CLEAR ALL ENVELOPES OF <DEVICE NAME>**.

To delete all automation data for a track:

■ Right-click on an automation lane header and choose **CLEAR ALL ENVELOPES**.

Using Devices for Mixing

As you learned in earlier chapters, Ableton's devices include Live's instruments and effects; third-party plug-ins are also available in the VST or AU format. Devices and plug-ins are both types of software add-ons for Ableton Live that provide essential added functionality, such as effects processing and virtual instrument sound sources for tracks.

Devices Provided with Ableton Live

Ableton Live comes bundled with a variety of device options. Among these devices you will find dynamics processors, EQs, reverbs, delays, flangers, choruses, and more. The number of included devices differs significantly depending on the edition of Ableton Live that you are using.

Two commonly used types of processing for audio and MIDI tracks are equalizers (including graphic and parametric EQs) and dynamics processors (such as compressors and gates). Both Ableton Live Standard and Ableton Live Suite feature the following:

- EQ Three

- EQ Eight

- Compressor

- Limiter

EQ Three

EQ Three is a simple, DJ-style equalizer for adjusting the frequency spectrum of audio material in Ableton Live.

To add the EQ Three device to an Ableton Live track, first locate the device in the Browser under **Audio Effects > EQ Three**. Then drag and drop the device onto a track (or double-click the device if the destination track is currently selected). The EQ Three device window will appear in the Detail View.

Figure 10.17 The EQ Three equalizer device

EQ Eight

EQ Eight is an advanced equalizer for adjusting the frequency spectrum of audio material in Ableton Live.

To add the EQ Eight device to an Ableton Live track, first locate the device in the Browser under **Audio Effects > EQ Eight**. Then drag and drop the device onto a track (or double-click the device if the destination track is currently selected). The EQ Eight device window will appear in the Detail View.

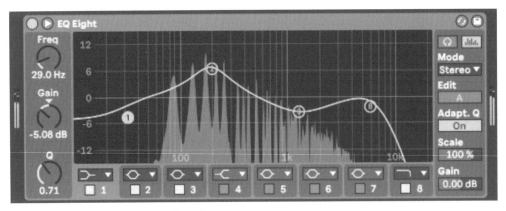

Figure 10.18 The EQ Eight equalizer device

Compressor

The Compressor device can be used to control dynamic levels, using standard attack, release, threshold, and ratio controls.

To add the Compressor device to an Ableton Live track, first locate the device in the Browser under **AUDIO EFFECTS > COMPRESSOR**. Then drag and drop the device onto a track (or double-click the device if the destination track is currently selected). The Compressor device window will appear in the Detail View.

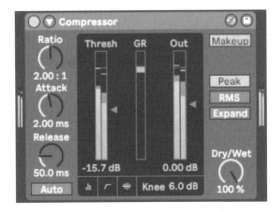

Figure 10.19 The Compressor device window

Limiter

The Limiter device is similar to a compressor, but completely prevents level from going above the ceiling value. It is typically used on complete mixes, but can also be used on individual audio and MIDI tracks.

To add the Limiter device to an Ableton Live track, first locate the device in the Browser under **AUDIO EFFECTS > LIMITER**. Then drag and drop the device onto a track (or double-click the device if the destination track is currently selected). The Limiter device window will appear in the Detail View.

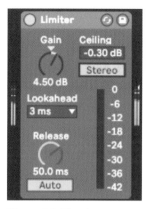

Figure 10.20 The Limiter device window

Backing Up Your Session

Once you've finished crafting your mix with automation and device processing, you can safeguard your work by creating a backup copy. Creating backups is critical for archival and disaster-recovery purposes. Because Ableton Live projects are stored electronically, it is possible to accidentally lose your work by deleting or overwriting files, having a file become corrupt, encountering a virus, or having a drive fail.

Considerations for Backup and Archive Copies

Some of the best protection measures include creating multiple copies of your files, using a separate drive for backup copies, and storing copies in the cloud to protect against disasters such as fire or flood. The more valuable your projects, the more robust your backup plans should be. At a minimum, you should create a backup project upon completing any work that would be difficult or time-consuming to re-create, especially if the recording has significant value or importance to you or your clients.

Whenever creating a backup or archive copy, be sure to include any media files (audio and video) that are referenced by the Set. Keep in mind that these files may not be included in the original project folder.

Saving an Archive Copy

One method you can use to create a copy of your Set with all related files is to follow a two-step process. First, use the **SAVE A COPY** command, which creates a copy of the Set in a new project folder. Then open the copy and use the **COLLECT ALL AND SAVE** command. This command allows you to copy all project media into the current project folder, creating a self-contained archive of the project. This archive project folder can then be stored separately or transferred to a different location, such as on an external drive.

Step 1: Apply the Save a Copy Command

By the time you've completed work on a project, your Live Set will likely include samples that are referenced from many different locations on your system. While this generally does not present a problem for the original project, it does mean that moving the project (or making a copy of it on a separate drive) can inadvertently separate the Set from the associated samples and other referenced media.

To reduce the likelihood of losing files, Ableton Live can copy all of a project's external samples directly into the project folder, using the **COLLECT ALL AND SAVE** command (see below). However, this process will duplicate any referenced media, and can greatly increase the size of the project folder.

To prevent the needless duplication of files on your system, it is best to create a new project folder for your archive prior to using Collect All and Save. This is where the **SAVE A COPY** command comes in.

 Although you could also use the Save Live Set As command for the workflow described here, you would not be able to specify the name of the project folder in the process.

To create a copy of your Set in a new project folder for archiving, do the following:

1. Open the Set that you want to archive.

2. Choose **FILE > SAVE A COPY** to create a new copy of the Set within a new project folder.

3. In the **SAVE A COPY** dialog box, navigate to an appropriate location for your archive, such as an external drive.

4. Provide a meaningful name for the archive copy at the top of the dialog box.

 By default, Ableton Live appends the word "Copy" to the end of the Set name for use as the new project name. It is good practice to replace this default name, using a meaningful naming convention of your own, such as appending the word "Archive" to the name and including the archive date.

5. Click **SAVE** to complete the process.

Ableton Live will create a new Set file, inside of a new project folder, using the name and location that you've specified. Note that you will still be working in the original Set after completing this command.

 Any changes you make to a Set after completing the Save a Copy command will not be included in the copy. To modify the copy, you will need to close the original set and then open the copy you've just created.

Step 2: Apply the Collect All and Save Command

As discussed in Chapter 4, the Collect All and Save command simultaneously saves your current Live Set and packages all of the associated audio files into the project folder. The Collect All and Save dialog box includes a variety options that you can use to specify which media files to copy.

To use the Collect All and Save command for your archive copy, do the following:

1. From within your original Set file, choose **FILE > OPEN LIVE SET**.

2. In the **OPEN DOCUMENT** dialog box, navigate to the location where you saved the archive copy of the Set (within the new project folder of the same name).

3. Select and open the archive Set file (*filename.als*).

(i) You may be prompted to save changes to the original Set, if you've made any unsaved changes to the file. Be sure to keep any important changes you may have made to the original prior to creating the archive copy.

4. With the archive copy open, choose **FILE > COLLECT ALL AND SAVE**. The Collect All and Save dialog box will display.

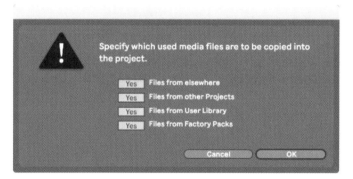

Figure 10.21 The Collect All and Save dialog box

5. Configure the file collection options as desired. (See "File Collection Options for Collect All and Save" below for detailed descriptions of each.)

6. Click **OK** when you are finished configuring the options as desired. Any external samples from the selected locations will be copied directly into the archive project folder.

File Collection Options for Collect All and Save

When using the Collect All and Save command, a number of options will be available that allow you to consolidate external samples into the project folder. The available file collection options are displayed in the Collect All and Save dialog box and include the following:

- **Files from elsewhere.** This option selects media files used in the current project from any locations besides Factory Packs, the User Library, and other projects and then copies them into the current project folder. This is useful to collect any media files you may have imported from an external source (not including samples imported from libraries installed with Ableton Live).

- **Files from other Projects.** This option selects media files used in the current project from any other projects and copies them into the current project folder. This is useful to collect any samples you may have recorded into a Set prior to using the **Save a Copy** command.

- **Files from User Library.** This option selects media files used in the current project from your User Library and copies them into the current project folder. This is useful to collect any media files (samples or clips) you've imported from items you've previously saved in your User Library.

- **Files from Factory Packs.** This option selects media files used in the current project from the Factory Packs installed with Ablton Live and copies them into the current project folder. This can be done to protect imported samples against accidental loss or corruption in their default locations.

Multisampled instruments and libraries can be extremely large. Copying them will greatly increase the size of your project folder. Avoid making duplicate copies of files that are installed with Ableton Live, if possible, as this is generally not necessary for a Set to play back properly from another system.

After collecting the files for your archive, you can reduce the amount of disk space it requires by creating a Pack. This copies the contents of the project folder into a single compressed file.

Creating a Stereo Mixdown

Mixing down is the process of recording the output from multiple tracks to a stereo file. This process is also commonly referred to as *bouncing* the project or *exporting a mix*. Mixing down is often the last phase of music production, although you can export your audio at any time to create a complete mix as a stereo file.

Mixdown Options

The most commonly used mixdown option in Ableton Live is the **File > Export Audio/Video** command. This option is a fast and easy way to create a bounce, requiring little to no setup.

Advanced users also frequently use the *bounce to tracks* technique. Bouncing to tracks is the process of recording the output of any or all of the tracks to a new audio track within the project. This process is also commonly referred to as creating an internal bounce or internal layback.

For the purposes of this course, we will focus on the Export Audio/Video option.

Considerations for Exporting a Mix

When exporting a mix with Ableton Live, it is important to recognize that the exported mix will capture all audible information in your Set just as you hear it during playback.

The following principles apply to exporting a mix:

- **The mix will include only audible tracks.** What you hear during playback is exactly what will be included in the mix. Any tracks that are deactivated will not be included. Conversely, any tracks that are soloed will be the *only* tracks represented in the mix.

- **The created file(s) will be based on the Rendered Track option selected in the Export Audio dialog box.** This chooser in the dialog box lets you select which track or tracks to render. When creating a mixdown, the Rendered Track should be set to Master.

- **The mix file will be a "printed" version of your Set.** Devices, sends, and external effects will be applied permanently in the mix. Listen closely to your entire Set prior to completing a bounce to ensure that everything sounds as it should. Pay close attention to levels, being sure to avoid clipping.

- **The mix will be based on the Timeline selection.** If you have an active selection, Ableton Live will bounce the length of the selection automatically. If no selection is present, the Export command will create a mix from the start of the first clip in the arrangement to the end of the longest track.

Exporting Audio

The Export Audio/Video command allows you to mix your entire Set directly to a stereo file on disk. The corresponding dialog box lets you set the bit depth, file format, and sample rate for the exported file. The export will automatically be rendered offline for faster-than-real-time mixdown.

Supported File Types

The file types that you can create from the Bounce to Disk command include the following:

- **WAV.** This is the default file format for Windows- and Mac-based audio production.

- **AIFF.** This file format is primarily used on Mac systems. Use the AIFF format if you plan to import the bounced audio into Mac applications that do not support the WAV format.

- **FLAC.** This is a lossless file format that can create smaller audio files without a perceptible reduction in sound quality.

- **MP3.** This file format can create smaller audio files for Internet streaming and portable devices. Use this file format to balance file size against audio quality.

Using the Export Audio/Video Command

The Export Audio/Video command combines the outputs of all currently audible tracks routed to the Master (or other selected option) to create a new audio file on your hard drive.

To export a mix of all currently audible tracks, do the following:

1. Adjust track output levels and finalize any automation. Any devices or effects settings that are active on your tracks will be permanently written to the exported media.

2. Make sure that all of the tracks you want to include in the mix are audible. To mix down all tracks in your Set, verify that no tracks are soloed or deactivated.

3. Verify that the output of each track is routed to the same destination (typically the Master track). Use the **OUTPUT TYPE CHOOSER** as needed to set the track outputs.

4. Choose **FILE > EXPORT AUDIO/VIDEO**. The Export Audio/Video dialog box will appear.

Figure 10.22 The Export Audio/Video dialog box

5. Verify that the **RENDERED TRACK** is set to Master (the default).

6. The **RENDER START** and **RENDER LENGTH** fields will already be populated by the current timeline selection (if one exists), or the start of the first clip in the arrangement until the end of the longest track (if no selection is present). You can also manually edit these fields to change the start and length of the exported mix.

7. Choose the desired sample rate for the exported file from the **SAMPLE RATE** pop-up menu. Higher sampling rates will provide better audio fidelity but will also increase the size of the resulting file(s).

> ⓘ **If you plan to burn your mix directly to CD without further processing, choose 44.1 kHz as the sample rate for the bounce.**

8. Enable the **ENCODE PCM** option and choose the desired file type for your exported file from the **FILE TYPE** pop-up menu. Available options include WAV, AIFF, and FLAC.

> ⓘ **When Encode PCM is on, a lossless audio file is created. WAV, AIFF, and FLAC formats are available for PCM export.**

> ⓘ **You can also export to a WAV, AIFF, or FLAC file and simultaneously create an MP3 file. To do so, enable both the Encode PCM option and the Encode MP3 (CBR 320) option.**

9. Choose the desired bit depth for the exported file from the **BIT DEPTH** pop-up menu.

    *   Choose **16** if you plan to burn your mix to CD without further processing.
    *   Choose **24** when you want to create a final mix that will be mastered separately.
    *   Choose **32** for ultra-high-resolution files that will undergo further processing or editing.

> ⓘ **The standard bit depth resolution for compact discs is 16 bits.**

10. Select other options as desired.

11. After confirming your settings, click the **EXPORT** button. A Save dialog box will appear.

12. Specify a file name and save location for your exported file(s). By default, the exported file(s) will be named after the Ableton Live Set.

When performing an export, Ableton Live processes the export without audio playback. A progress window will appear, displaying the percentage of the export that has been completed.

Figure 10.23 The Export Audio progress window

Creating a CD-Compatible Mixdown

Creating a CD-ready mixdown from an Ableton Live Set will require a bit-depth reduction during the bounce, to create a 16-bit file. To maintain the highest possible audio quality when reducing bit depth, it is necessary to apply *dither* to your audio. Dither is a form of randomized noise used to minimize quantization artifacts in digital audio systems. Quantization artifacts are most audible in the lowest parts of a signal's dynamic range, such as during a quiet passage or fade-out.

Introducing dither to a signal helps to reduce quantization artifacts and preserve dynamic range by adding very low-level noise. Dither provides a trade-off between signal-to-noise performance and quantization artifacts. Proper use of dither can create better subjective performance out of 16 bits compared to audio without dither.

Adding Dither to the Mixdown

Dither processing can be added in Ableton Live during the export process when creating a mix at 16 or 24 bits. In these cases, the 32-bit floating-point output from Live will be reduced to create an audio file on disk at a lower bit depth. This in turn will reduce the dynamic range in the file on disk. Adding dither processing will help preserve some of the dynamic range that would otherwise be lost.

To add dither during a mixdown:

1.   Choose **FILE > EXPORT AUDIO/VIDEO**. The Export Audio/Video dialog box will appear.

2.   In the **PCM** section of the dialog box, set the **BIT DEPTH** chooser to 16 or 24.

> (i)   For a CD-compatible mixdown, set the Bit Depth to 16.

3.   Use the Dither chooser to select the desired dither option.

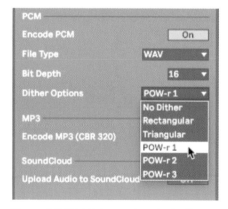

Figure 10.24 Dither options in the Export Audio/Video dialog box

4.   Set other options in the dialog box as desired and click **EXPORT** to complete the mixdown.

Types of Dither

When the dither is active in the Export Audio/Video dialog box, the Triangular option is selected by default. This mode is useful if there is a possibility that additional processing will be applied to the mix file, as it adds very little background noise. Rectangular mode introduces an even less background noise, but at the expense of additional quantization error.

The three Pow-r dither modes are generally the most effective at preserving dynamic range, offering successively higher amounts of dithering, but with the noise pushed above the audible range.

 If you will be sending your mixed file to a mastering house, you'll want to keep it at 32-bit floating-point resolution to retain the highest quality for the mastering process. In this case, you should NOT apply dither.

Uploading a Mix to SoundCloud

Ableton Live lets you upload your exported mix directly to your SoundCloud account during the export process.

To upload your mix to SoundCloud, do the following:

1. Choose FILE > EXPORT AUDIO/VIDEO.

2. Enable the UPLOAD AUDIO TO SOUNDCLOUD option near the bottom of the dialog box.

3. Click EXPORT. The export process will proceed as described above, after which a SHARE ON SOUNDCLOUD dialog box will appear.

Figure 10.25 The Share on SoundCloud dialog box

4. Log in to your SoundCloud account and click SIGN IN AND CONNECT at the bottom of the dialog box. A copy of your mix file will automatically be uploaded to SoundCloud.

Review/Discussion Questions

1.   What term is traditionally used to describe an audio patch point that allows a signal processor to be inserted directly into the signal path on a track? What term does Ableton Live use for this feature? How many of these does Ableton Live support on each track? (See "Basic Mixer Terminology" beginning on page 268.)

2.   What term is used to describe a signal path carrying a mix output of one or more tracks routed for parallel processing? How can this signal be returned to the sending device? (See "Basic Mixer Terminology" beginning on page 268.)

3.   What menu would you use to display or hide the Arrangement View window? What keyboard shortcut can you use to toggle between the Session View and Arrangement View? (See "Mixing in the Session View" beginning on page 269.)

4.   What menu command can you use to display or hide the Sends Section in the Session View? (See "Showing/Hiding Sections" beginning on page 270.)

5.   Which Ableton Live button can be enabled to allow track controls to record automation in real time when playing a Set? (See "Recording Arrangement Automation" beginning on page 274.)

6.   Can you record automation in Ableton Live when the transport is not in Arrangement Record mode? Can you record automation to a track that is not Armed for recording? (See "Recording Arrangement Automation" beginning on page 274.)

7.   What are some ways that you can display automation envelopes on a track? Which mode must be enabled before automation can be displayed? (See "Viewing Arrangement Automation" beginning on page 275.)

8.   What are some ways that you can add, move, or delete automation breakpoints? (See "Editing Automation Breakpoints" beginning on page 279.)

9. What are some Ableton device options that are available for EQ and dynamics processing? (See "Using Devices for Mixing" beginning on page 282.)

10. Why is it important to back up your Ableton Live projects? What are some ways in which your Ableton Live work can be lost accidentally? (See "Backing Up Your Session" beginning on page 285.)

11. What is the recommended process for creating a project archive? How is the Collect All and Save command different from other save options, in terms of the files that are saved? (See "Saving an Archive Copy" beginning on page 285.)

12. What are some considerations for creating a stereo mixdown in Ableton Live? How is the mixdown file affected by soloed or muted tracks? How is it affected by a timeline selection? (See "Considerations for Exporting a Mix" beginning on page 288.)

13. What command lets you mix your entire Ableton Live Set directly to a stereo file? What file types are supported for audio files created with this command? (See "Exporting Audio" beginning on page 289.)

14. How can you upload a mix directly to SoundCloud from Ableton Live? (See "Uploading a Mix to SoundCloud" beginning on page 293.)

To review additional material from this chapter and prepare for certification, see the Ableton Live 101 Study Guide module available through the Elements|ED online learning platform at ElementsED.com.

Automating Shared Effects and Exporting a Stereo Mix

🎧 Activity

In this exercise, you will finalize your project. You will start by creating a shared effect using a delay plug-in on a return track. Then you will automate the delay effect using send automation on the **Noise Sweep** track. Next you will set basic levels for your tracks, and you'll finish by exporting the mix to a stereo file.

🕐 Duration

This exercise should take approximately 15 to 20 minutes to complete.

⊕ Goals/Targets

- Add a return track to create a delay effect

- Use automation to set levels for your mix

- Use a limiter to maximize output levels

- Export your final mix

Media Files

To complete this exercise, you may need to use various media files included in the **Media Files 2019-Live101** folder. You should have downloaded the media files in Exercise 4.

If needed, you can re-download the media files by going to www.halleonard.com/mylibrary and entering your access code (printed on the opening page of this book). From there, click the **Download** link for the **Media Files 2019–Live101** listing in your **My Library** page. The Media Files folder will begin transferring to your Downloads folder.

Getting Started

You will start by opening the Live Set you completed in Exercise 9. If that Set is not available, you can use the Ex09 Sample file in the 01 Completed Exercises folder within the Media Files 2019-Live101 folder.

Open the Live Set and save it as Exercise 10:

1. Do one of the following:

    - Open the Set file that you created in Exercise 9 (Storage Drive/Folder > Live101-XXX > Exercise09-XXX.als).

    - Alternatively, you can use the Ex09 Sample file (Media Files 2019-Live101 > 01. Completed Projects > Ex09 Sample.als).

2. Choose FILE > SAVE LIVE SET AS and name the Set *Exercise10-XXX*, keeping the Live Set inside the original Project folder. (Move the Set into your Live101-XXX folder if working from the sample file.)

Creating a Delay Effect

In this part of the exercise, you will create a return track to function as the delay return. Then you will assign a delay device on the track. Finally, you will use the send controls on the CHORDS and NOISE tracks to create a delay effect for the audio from those tracks.

Adding the Return Track

Use the following steps to add a new return track and add a delay device to the track.

Create a delay return track:

1. If necessary, press TAB to switch to the Session View.

2. Create a new return track by pressing OPTION+COMMAND+T (Mac) or CTRL+ALT+T (Windows). A new return track labeled A Return will appear to the left of the Master track.

3. Click the new return track's Title Bar to select the track.

4. Press COMMAND+R (Mac) or CTRL+R (Windows) to rename the track. Change the track name to Delay and press RETURN or ENTER to commit the change.

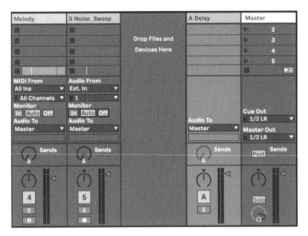

Figure 10.26 The Delay Return track to the left of the Master track

Configure the delay device on the track:

1. Locate the Delay device in the Browser under the **AUDIO EFFECTS** category.

> ⓘ A quick way to find a specific device is to press COMMAND+F (Mac) or CTRL+F (Windows) and type the first few letters of the device name into the search field.

2. Click the disclosure triangle next to the Delay device in the Browser Content pane to reveal the available options; then expand the Clean Delay category to see the available presets.

3. Double-click the **DOTTED EIGHTH NOTE** preset to add the device to the Delay Return track.

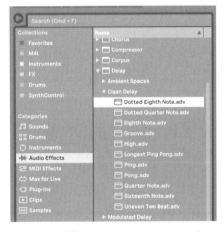

Figure 10.27 Selecting the Dotted Eight Note preset for the Delay device in the Browser

The Delay device window will appear in the Detail View, configured with settings from the Dotted Eighth Note preset.

4. Click on the **FEEDBACK** control and reduce the Feedback amount to 30%.

5. Click on the **DRY/WET** control and increase the Dry/Wet ratio to 100%.

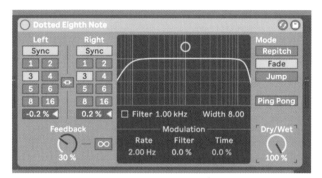

Figure 10.28 The Delay device with the Feedback and Dry/Wet parameters set

Set the Send Levels

Use the following steps to set appropriate send levels for the target tracks in your project.

Raise the send levels on the Chords and Noise tracks:

1. Locate the **SEND A** control for the Chords track in the Session View.

2. Click on the send control for the track and raise the level to around -10.0 dB.

> (i) In Session View, the current Send Level is displayed in the Status Bar area at the bottom of the screen when your mouse cursor is positioned over a Send control.

 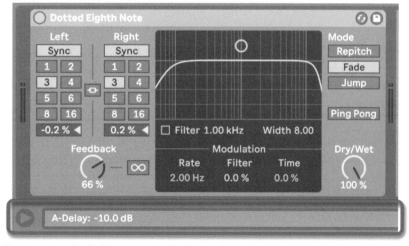

Figure 10.29 Send control set to -10.0 dB (left); Status Bar display (right)

3. Press **TAB** to switch to the **ARRANGEMENT VIEW**.

4. If the Mixer Section is not showing, click the Show/Hide Mixer Section button (**M**) at the bottom right of the Arrangement View to show it.

5. Locate the **SEND A** control for the Noise track. This will be the bottom field in the Mixer section of the track and will be labeled –inf by default.

6. Click on the field and drag up to set the Send level to around -3.0 dB.

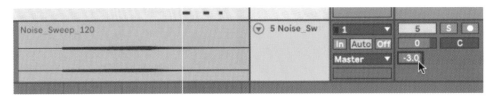

Figure 10.30 Adjusting the Send level in the Arrangement View

Recording Automation and Setting Levels

In this part of the exercise, you will record automation during playback. Then you will set basic levels from the Volume sliders for all the tracks in your mix.

Display automation envelopes in the Arrangement View:

1. If necessary, press the **M** key to disable the Computer MIDI Keyboard.

2. Press the **A** key on the computer keyboard to enable Automation Mode.

3. Click to position the Insert Marker in the last few bars of the Arrangement (just before 1:00) where the final chord clip plays.

Record Automation

In the next series of steps, you will be automating the track volume of the **Delay** return track so that the delay echoes do not extend past the end of the song. You may need to practice the timing a few times to get the desired results.

> To practice the timing without recording Arrangement Automation, you can simply move the control while playing through the Set. After each practice pass, double-click the Track Volume slider to reset the value to 0.

Record volume automation for the Delay return:

1. Click the **UNFOLD TRACK** button (triangle) next to the track name on the Delay Return track to expand the track height for better access to the controls in the Mixer section.

Figure 10.31 The Unfold Track button on the Delay Return track (shown folded in)

2. Verify that the **Delay** return's Track Volume is currently set to **0**. This is displayed in the middle field in the Mixer section.

3. Click the **AUTOMATION ARM** button in the Control Bar to arm automation recording.

Figure 10.32 Automation Arm button in the Control Bar

4. Click a few bars before the end of the song in any track to set the arrangement position.

5. Click the **ARRANGEMENT RECORD** button (solid circle) in the Control Bar and prepare to record your automation.

6. As the playback position approaches the end of the song, fade out the **Delay** return track by gradually reducing the Volume slider control (click and drag downward on the Volume display field) so that the delay echoes do not extend past **1:00** (one minute).

Figure 10.33 Track Volume automated on the Delay return track.

7. Continue recording automation for a few seconds with the track volume pulled down to -inf.

8. Press the **SPACEBAR** when finished to stop playback.

9. Press the **SPACEBAR** again to audition the automation that you recorded. If you are not satisfied with the results, you can click the Arrangement Record button and try again.

Set Relative Levels for the Tracks

In the next series of steps, you will adjust the levels for individual tracks using the tracks' Volume sliders.

Set levels for your mix:

1.   Press **TAB** to return to the Session View.

2.   Begin playback and adjust the levels of each track to achieve a clear, intelligible mix with appropriate levels from the audio tracks, MIDI tracks, and delay return. Following are some suggestions:

     •   Start by lowering all of the Volume sliders to around -6 dB. This will give you room to increase the levels on tracks that are too quiet.

     (i) Any easy way to change the levels of all tracks in the Set is to select them all and then move the Volume slider on any one track.

     (i) You will not be able to affect the volume on the Delay track, since it has been automated. The Volume slider will return to the automated levels on playback.

     •   The drums may be a bit too prominent in the mix. Try lowering the Volume slider on the Drums track by an additional 3 dB.

     •   The Noise sound comes in a bit too quiet. Try raising the Volume slider on the noise track by 4 to 6 dB.

Exporting the Mix

In this part of the exercise, you will maximize the output levels for the mix using a limiter plug-in on the Master track. Then you will use the Export Audio function to create a stereo file from your mix.

Add a Limiter

Use the following steps to add a limiter to the Master track.

Apply a limiter to the mix:

1.   Locate the Limiter device in the Browser under **AUDIO EFFECTS > LIMITER**.

     (i) The Limiter device will not be available when using Ableton Live Lite. In this case, you can use the Multiband & Limiter option instead, found in Audio Effect Rack > Mixing & Mastering.

2.   Drag and drop the Limiter device onto the Master track. The Limiter device window will appear in the Detail View.

3. Press the **SPACEBAR** to begin playback.

4. In the Limiter device window, set the **CEILING** slider to around −0.10 dB. This sets the maximum allowable level for the limiter's output to prevent clipping.

Figure 10.34 The Limiter device with Ceiling set to -0.10 dB

> ⓘ If using the Multiband & Limiter option, start by setting the Bass, Mid, High, and Rack Volume controls to 0 dB. Then set the Limiter Ceiling control to −0.10 dB.

5. While listening to the mix, adjust the **GAIN** slider to achieve a healthy output level without artificially compressing the dynamic range. A setting of around 3 to 6 dB will likely be adequate for this mix.

> ⓘ In the Multiband & Limiter device, use the Multiband Macro Control to set the Master Output level.

Create a Stereo Mixdown

Use the following steps to export a stereo mixdown file for your project.

Export the mix to a stereo file:

1. Press **TAB** to return to the Arrangement View.

2. Make a selection on any track, beginning at the start of the song and extending to slightly past 1:00.

3. Choose **FILE > EXPORT AUDIO/VIDEO** to open the Export Audio dialog box.

4.   Select the following options for your export:

   •   File Type: WAV

   •   Bit Depth: 16 Bit

   •   Sample Rate: 44.1 kHz

5.   Leave the other options set to their defaults (or as directed by your instructor) and click the **EXPORT** button. The Save dialog box will appear.

6.   Name your file **YOURNAME-FINALMIX**.

7.   Navigate to an appropriate save location, making note of the drive location and file path; then click **SAVE** to export your mix.

Finishing Up

Congratulations! Over the course of these exercises, you have created an Ableton Live Set from scratch, imported and edited audio, recorded audio and MIDI, added effects, recorded automation, and exported the result to a stereo file.

1.   When your export completes, save your Set and quit Ableton Live.

2.   Navigate to the location of your exported file and verify that it plays back as intended.

   In classroom settings, your instructor may require that you copy this file and/or your Project Folder to a learning management system, flash drive, or shared network location to submit it for a grade.

For more hands-on experience, see the Final Project section of this book.

Creating a Musical Arrangement

🎧 Activity

In this hands-on project, you will complete a Live Set featuring a roughly 90-second musical arrangement. To complete the project, you will create audio and MIDI tracks, import audio clips, create playable instruments using the Drum Rack and Simpler instruments, record from the Session View into the Arrangement View, and export an audio file from the Live Set

🕐 Duration

This project should take approximately 90 minutes to complete.

◈ Goals/Targets

- Customize the appearance of your Live Set and your tracks

- Work with the Drum Rack and Simpler devices to create MIDI-based drum and bass parts

- Import and work with audio files

- Record from the Session View into the Arrangement View

- Add a Limiter to enhance your mix

- Export your final mix and archive your finished project

The media files for this project are provided courtesy of the artists Haak and Siddhant Bhosle:

- **Song**: The Fall (excerpt)

- **Performed by**: Haak and Siddhant Bhosle

- **Written By**: Haak and Siddhant Bhosle

- **Produced By**: Haak and Siddhant Bhosle ©2018

The audio files provided for this project are strictly for use to complete the exercises contained herein. No rights are granted to use the files or any portion thereof in any commercial or non-commercial production or performance.

Powering Up

To get started on this project, you will need to power up your system. It is important to power up properly to avoid problems that could possibly damage your equipment.

When using audio equipment, you should power up components in the order that the audio signal will flow through them.

The general process for starting up an Ableton Live Set is as follows:

1. Power up external hard drives, if used.

2. Verify connections and power up any audio and/or MIDI interfaces.

3. Start the computer.

4. Launch Ableton Live.

5. Power up your monitoring system, if applicable.

Refer to Chapter 2 for more details on powering up your system.

Getting Started

You will start by opening the Final Project Set file. The Set file is located in the **Final Project Media** folder within the **Media Files 2019-Live101** folder.

Accessing the Media Files for this Project

To complete this project, you will use various files included in the **Media Files 2019-Live101** folder. You can download the media files by going to www.halleonard.com/mylibrary and entering your access code (printed on the opening page of this book). From there, click the **Download** link for the **Media Files 2019-Live101** listing in your **My Library** page.

The Media Files folder will be downloaded and placed in your Downloads folder by default.

Open the Final Project:

1. Do one of the following:

    - Choose FILE > OPEN LIVE SET.

    - Press COMMAND+O (Mac) or CTRL+O (Windows).

2. Locate and open the Final Project file (Storage Drive/Folder > Media Files 2019-Live101 > 03 Final Project Media > FinalProject-Starter.als).

3. Choose FILE > SAVE LIVE SET AS and name the Set *FinalProject-XXX*, where *XXX* is your initials. Save the Set into your Live101-XXX folder or other location of your choosing.

Refer to Lesson 4 for additional information on locating and opening Live Sets.

Adjust the Live Set Display

When the Live Set opens, you will see the starter template in the Session View. This is where you will start, but eventually you will record your work from the Session View into the Arrangement View. You can switch between the two views at any time by pressing TAB.

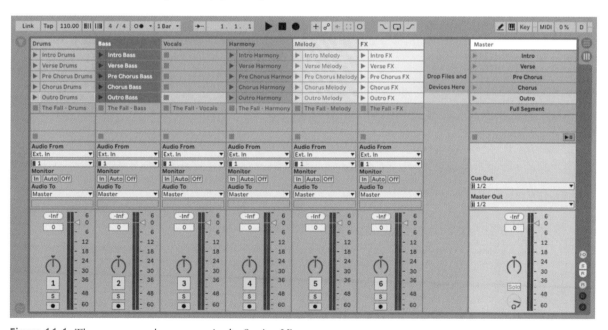

Figure 11.1 The starter template, as seen in the Session View

You may want to adjust the Session View track widths before continuing.

Change track width in the Session View:

1. Hover your mouse cursor over the right-hand edge of a track's title (for instance, **Drums** or **Bass**).

2. When the pointer turns into a bracket, click and drag left and right to contract or expand a track, respectively. (See Figure 11.2.)

3. Adjust the track widths so each track fits comfortably on your screen.

Figure 11.2 Adjusting the width of the Bass track in Session View

You may also want to expand or contract the Mixer section of your tracks. This is a vertical adjustment that can reveal additional Mixer features, as well as add resolution to each track's volume meter.

Expand or contract the Mixer section in the Session View:

1. Hover your mouse cursor over the horizontal divider that separates the In/Out section from the Mixer section.

2. Click and drag vertically to expand or contract the Mixer section, respectively.

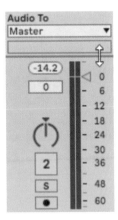

Figure 11.3 Adjusting the Mixer height in Session View

Connect Monitoring Devices

If you have a monitoring system connected to the left and right outputs of your audio interface, you will use that to listen to the Live Set playback. If you do not have a monitoring system, you can listen to the playback using headphones on a compatible interface or on your computer (if using onboard sound output). Plug in your headphones to an available headphone jack and test the output and playback level.

Creating New Tracks

In this section of the project, you will create the new tracks needed for the Live Set. Additional details on the commands and processes used in this section can be found in Chapter 4.

Create, Name, and Color Tracks

You will need to create two new tracks for the Live Set. Both tracks will play back MIDI information using virtual instruments, so both will be MIDI tracks.

The first track you will create will be a Snare Drum track to accompany the existing drums and percussion. The second will be a Bass Instrument track, which will be played during the Intro and Verse scenes.

Create new MIDI tracks:

1. Select the Drums track by clicking on its name.

2. Select **CREATE > INSERT MIDI TRACK** or use the keyboard shortcut **COMMAND+SHIFT+T** (Mac) or **CTRL+SHIFT+T** (Windows). This will insert a MIDI track to the right of the currently selected track.

3. Select the Bass track by clicking on its name.

4. Press **COMMAND+SHIFT+T** (Mac) or **CTRL+SHIFT+T** (Windows) to insert a second MIDI track, placed to the right of the currently selected track.

Live will give the tracks you inserted generic names and colors. This is a good time to customize both qualities of the tracks you have created to help keep your Live Set organized.

Name the new MIDI tracks:

1. Do one of the following to rename the tracks:

    • Right-click the name of the first MIDI track you created and select **RENAME**. (See Figure 11.4.)

    • Select the track and press **COMMAND+R** (Mac) or **CTRL+R** (Windows).

2. Type Snare Drum as the new track name.

3. Press **ENTER** to commit the change.

4.   Repeat this process to rename the second MIDI track you created. Name this track **Bass Instrument**.

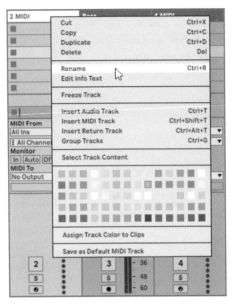

Figure 11.4 Right-click menu for renaming and color-coding tracks in Session View

Color-code the new MIDI tracks:

■   Right-click each track and select a track color of your choice from the pop-up menu.

Save Your Live Set

After making any significant changes to a Live Set, it's a good idea to save your work. Doing so will minimize any rework that you might have to do in the event of a disruption.

Save your progress up to this point by doing one of the following:

■   Choose FILE > SAVE LIVE SET.

■   Press COMMAND+S (Mac) or CTRL+S (Windows).

Working with MIDI Data

For this section of the project, you will add the Drum Rack and Simpler instruments to your MIDI tracks, add audio samples to each instrument to make them playable, and program or record MIDI data using Live's MIDI Note Editor.

Add the Drum Rack to the Snare Drum Track

In the previous section, you created a MIDI track and named it Snare Drum. Now, you will add a Drum Rack instrument to this track. This will allow the MIDI track to play back audio drum samples that are triggered by MIDI data.

Insert Drum Rack on the Snare Drum track:

1. Show the Browser (if it isn't already visible) by selecting **VIEW > SHOW BROWSER** or by pressing **OPTION+COMMAND+B** (Mac) or **CTRL+ALT+B** (Windows).

2. Select the **INSTRUMENTS** category from the Browser.

3. Select the Snare Drum track by clicking on track name.

4. Double-click the Drum Rack instrument in the Browser, or click and drag to place it on the Snare Drum track.

By default, the Drum Rack does not contain any drum samples, so you will need to add a snare drum sample to it in order for MIDI information to trigger sound. This project includes the original snare drum samples used in the song.

Add a snare drum sample to the Drum Rack:

1. In the Browser, select **CURRENT PROJECT**.

2. Click the disclosure triangle to expand the Instrument Samples folder.

3. Click the snare drum samples (Snare Drum 1.wav and Snare Drum 2.wav) to audition them.

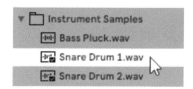

Figure 11.5 Auditioning snare drum samples in the Browser

If clicking on a sample does not trigger playback in the Browser, make sure the Preview button at the bottom of the Browser (next to the waveform display) is enabled and highlighted blue.

4. Click and drag the snare drum sample of your choice to a cell in the Drum Rack. (See Figure 11.6.) Note that each cell is triggered by a specific MIDI note, so pay attention to the note corresponding to the cell where you drop the sample.

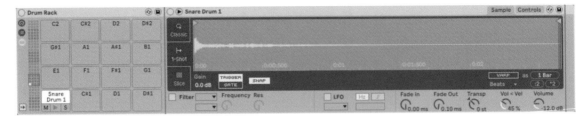

Figure 11.6 Snare Drum 1.wav mapped to MIDI note C1 in a Drum Rack

 You can also put each of the two snare samples in its own cell and trigger them separately from their respective MIDI notes.

You are now ready to play the snare drum sound of your choice using MIDI information. You can experiment with this by enabling the **ARM** button on the **Snare Drum** track and playing the associated note with a MIDI controller. You can also trigger MIDI from your computer keyboard by activating the Computer MIDI Keyboard switch in the Control Bar.

 See Chapter 6 for details on using the Computer MIDI Keyboard function.

Add Simpler to the Bass Instrument Track

While you're in the mindset of loading audio samples into MIDI-based instruments, it is a good time to insert the Simpler instrument on the **Bass Instrument** track and find an audio sample to use for it.

Insert Simpler on the Bass Instrument track:

1. Show the Browser (if not already visible) by selecting **VIEW > SHOW BROWSER** or by pressing **OPTION+COMMAND+B** (Mac) or **CTRL+ALT+B** (Windows).

2. Select the **INSTRUMENTS** category from the Browser.

3. Select the **Bass Instrument** track by clicking on its name.

4. Double-click the **SIMPLER** instrument in the Browser, or click on it and drag it to the **Bass Instrument** track.

By default, Simpler does not contain any samples, so you will need to add a sample to the device in order for MIDI information to trigger a sound. This project includes the original synthesized bass instrument sample used in the song.

Add a bass sample to Simpler:

1. In the Browser, select **CURRENT PROJECT**.

2. Click the disclosure triangle to expand the Instrument Samples folder.

3. Click Bass Pluck.wav to audition the sound.

> (i) This sample may be difficult to hear at when played using the built-in outputs on a computer or laptop. You may need to temporarily increase your computer's speaker volume to adequately hear the low-frequency audio.

4. Click and drag Bass Pluck.wav to the **DROP SAMPLE HERE** indicator within Simpler. Because the original sample is tuned to a C, you do not need to worry about the tuning of the sample.

> (i) In many other cases, you will need to determine the pitch of the original sample and adjust its transposition in the sampler as necessary.

5. Select **1-SHOT** mode using the Playback Mode buttons along the left side of Simpler. Now, even very short MIDI note durations will cause the entire sample to play back, which will work best with this sort of a short, percussive bass sound.

1-Shot mode (active)

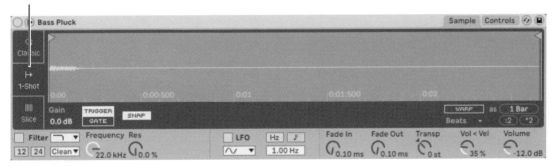

Figure 11.7 An instance of Simpler with the provided Bass Pluck.wav sample loaded in 1-Shot mode

You are now ready to play back the bass sound of your choice using MIDI information. You can experiment with this by pressing the **ARM** button on the Bass Instrument track and playing the sound with a MIDI controller or your computer keyboard with the Computer MIDI Keyboard function enabled.

 See Chapter 6 for details on using the Computer MIDI Keyboard function.

Create a Snare Drum MIDI Clip

Now that your two instruments are created and capable of playing sounds, you can use them to round out this piece of music. You will start by creating a pattern of MIDI notes for the **Snare Drum** track.

Create a MIDI clip on the Verse scene:

1. Find the clip slot on the **Snare Drum** track that corresponds to the **Verse** scene.

2. Do one of the following:

    •   Right-click the empty clip slot and select **INSERT MIDI CLIP(S)**.

    •   Double-click the empty clip slot.

Figure 11.8 Inserting a MIDI clip on the second scene of the Snare Drum track

3. Rename the new MIDI clip as **Snare Drum**.

    Your new Snare Drum clip's parameters and MIDI data should automatically become visible in the Clip View.

4. If not already displayed, double-click the **Snare Drum** clip to show it in the Clip View.

5. In the **Notes** section of the Clip View, set the clip's **LOOP LENGTH** to 8 bars (8 . 0 . 0).

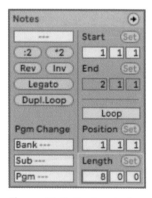

Figure 11.9 Setting the Loop Length parameter to 8 bars in the Clip View

6. Add MIDI notes using the MIDI Note Editor. Each note will cause the Drum Rack to trigger the snare drum sound. For a simple, straightforward snare drum presence, add MIDI notes at the third beat of each of the 8 bars, as seen in Figure 11.10.

> ℹ There are multiple ways to manually create MIDI notes in the MIDI Note Editor. You can pencil in notes using Draw Mode (activate by pressing the B key or clicking the Draw Mode switch), or double-click at a note location in Edit Mode.

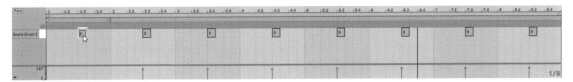

Figure 11.10 MIDI notes at the third beat of each bar

7. Press the **SCENE LAUNCH** button on the Verse scene to audition your Snare Drum track in context with the arrangement.

8. If necessary, adjust the placement and velocity of the MIDI notes to your liking.

Duplicate the Snare Drum MIDI Clip

To save some time, you can copy your snare drum MIDI clip to both the Pre-Chorus and Chorus scenes of the Live Set. That will allow your snare drum pattern to play across all of the applicable parts of the song.

Use one of the following methods to duplicate the Snare Drum clip to additional scenes:

■ Right-click the clip and select **DUPLICATE** to add it to the subsequent scene.

■ Right-click the clip and select **COPY**, then right-click another clip slot and select **PASTE**.

■ While holding **OPTION** (Mac) or **ALT** (Windows), click and drag the clip to another clip slot.

> ℹ Rather than simply duplicating the Snare Drum clip, feel free to create unique snare drum patterns for different parts of the song in this project, as time allows.

Create a Bass Instrument MIDI Clip

Next, you will create a MIDI sequence for your Bass Instrument track by importing MIDI clips that contain the song's original bass line.

Import existing MIDI clips for the bass line:

1. Show the Browser (if needed) by selecting **VIEW > SHOW BROWSER** or by pressing **OPTION+COMMAND+B** (Mac) or **CONTROL+ALT+B** (Windows).

2. In the Browser, select **CURRENT PROJECT**.

3. Click the disclosure triangle to expand the MIDI Clips folder.

4. Click and drag the Intro Bass Clip.mid file to the empty clip slot that corresponds to the Intro scene of the Bass Instrument track.

5. Click and drag the Verse Bass Clip.mid file to the empty clip slot that corresponds to the Verse scene of the Bass Instrument track.

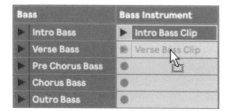

Figure 11.11 Dragging MIDI clips from the Browser to empty clip slots

 Alternatively, you can program your own bass line (using the MIDI Note Editor) or record a bass performance (using a MIDI controller). Be sure to work in the key of C minor and stick to the notes of the scale: C, D, E-flat, F, G, A-flat, and B-flat.

For details on creating MIDI performances, see Chapter 6 in this book.

6. Click the **SCENE LAUNCH** button on the Intro scene to audition your Bass Instrument track in the context of the arrangement. Repeat this process on the Verse scene.

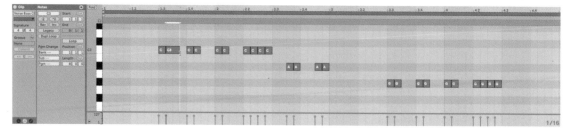

Figure 11.12 The provided MIDI notes, after being imported and displayed in the MIDI Note Editor

7. If necessary, edit the MIDI notes to your liking.

If you find that your new bass line is too quiet, turn up the Volume of Simpler. The default volume is set at -12.0dB. Try increasing that value to -6.0dB (or higher).

Save Work in Progress

As you complete each main portion of the project, you should save your work in progress. This will protect your work while the Live Set is open.

To save your progress up to this point, do one of the following:

- Choose FILE > SAVE LIVE SET.

- Press COMMAND+S (Mac) or CTRL+S (Windows).

Working with Audio Data

In the next section of the project, you will use the Browser to import several audio clips to an existing audio track.

Import an Audio File to a Track

As you've already seen, Live's Browser is a great feature for locating, auditioning, and importing all sorts of instruments and audio files. For this part of the project, you will use the Browser to import audio files containing the vocals of the song.

Locate and import the audio files:

1. Show the Browser as needed by pressing OPTION+COMMAND+B (Mac) or CTRL+ALT+B (Windows).

2. In the Browser, select CURRENT PROJECT.

3. Click the disclosure triangle to expand the folder called The Fall Stems.

4. Click the disclosure triangle to expand the enclosed Vocals folder. In this folder, you'll find the vocals, separated into clips for the verse, pre-chorus, chorus, and outro.

Figure 11.13 The vocals are separated into four audio clips, as seen in the Live Browser.

5. Click and drag the Verse Vocals.wav file to the empty clip slot on the Vocals track that corresponds to the Verse scene. Repeat this process for the remaining audio files: Pre-Chorus Vocals.wav, Chorus Vocals.wav, and Outro Vocals.wav.

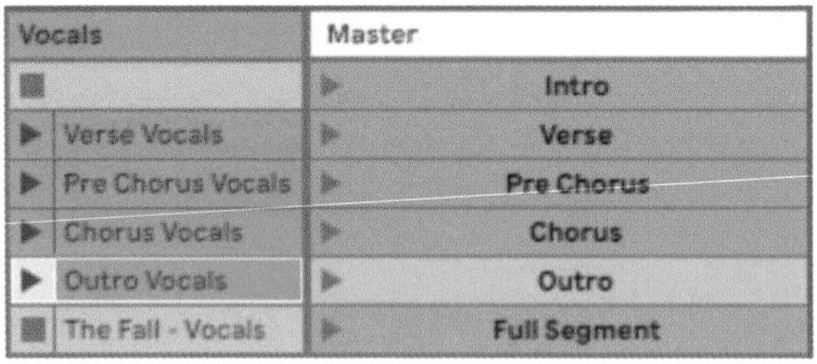

Vocals		Master	
■		▶	Intro
▶	Verse Vocals	▶	Verse
▶	Pre Chorus Vocals	▶	Pre Chorus
▶	Chorus Vocals	▶	Chorus
▶	Outro Vocals	▶	Outro
■	The Fall - Vocals	▶	Full Segment

Figure 11.14 After importing the audio, you will have clips on the Verse, Pre Chorus, Chorus, and Outro scenes.

6. Audition each scene to confirm that the vocal clips are playing back as desired.

When importing audio files, Live may automatically warp the audio clips it creates. Before continuing, you should check on the warp status and loop status of the clips and make any needed changes.

Verify warping and looping status for imported clips:

1. Click on the Verse Vocals clip in the Clip Slot on the Vocals track so that its sample information displays in the Clip View.

2. In the Sample box in Clip View, verify that the **WARP** switch is enabled.

3. Below the Warp switch, ensure the **SEG. BPM** value is set to 110 to match the tempo of the original song. If needed, you can override the current Seg. BPM value by clicking in the field and typing a new value.

4. On the right of the Sample box, verify that the **LOOP** switch is enabled.

5. Repeat the above process for the Pre-Chorus Vocals clip and the Chorus Vocals clip.

6. Next click on the Outro Vocals clip to display its sample information. Since the Outro clips occur at the end of the performance, the clips in this scene should not be set to loop.

7. Verify that the **WARP** and **SEG. BPM** controls are set as above.

8. Verify that the **LOOP** switch is disabled.

(i) You can also experiment with disabling the Warp switch on the Outro Vocals clip. Since this clip has no rhythmic material, it may not need to match the tempo.

Save Work in Progress

You have now imported the audio files needed for the Live Set. Take this opportunity to save your work.

Save your work by doing one of the following:

- Choose FILE > SAVE LIVE SET.

- Press COMMAND+S (Mac) or CTRL+S (Windows).

Recording from Session to Arrangement View

While the Session View is a useful environment for live performances and sketching out song ideas, you will often want to record what you have created in the Session View into the Arrangement View as a linear piece of music. In this section of the project, you will complete this process.

Prepare for Recording into Arrangement View

Before recording the five scenes—Intro, Verse, Pre-Chorus, Chorus, and Outro—as a linear arrangement, take a moment to play through the scenes. When each scene is about to end, press the play button on the following scene. This is the process you'll use when recording to the Arrangement View, so it will help to get some practice in advance.

 When launching clips and scenes in the Session View, your timing doesn't have to be perfect. The Global Launch Quantization value ensures that clips only launch at the specified increment. This will keep your clips and scenes in rhythm with one another by aligning their launch and stop points to a global grid.

 You can change the Global Launch Quantization value in the Quantization menu on the left side of the Control Bar (next to the Metronome switch).

If you want to get creative, you can make changes to the scenes or experiment with having certain scenes play for longer periods of time. For instance, you might want a 16-bar intro rather than an 8-bar intro. If you want to take things further, you can add tracks and instruments to create your own version of the song. Working in Live means it's never too late to make changes; this is a good time to experiment with additional creative choices.

Record into Arrangement View

Use the following general steps for recording from the Session View to the Arrangement View. Although the steps will largely be the same even if you've chosen to modify the Live Set, you can vary the process as needed or desired for your own composition.

Record from Session View to Arrangement View:

1. Before starting a record pass, press the **STOP** button in the Control Bar twice to place the Arrangement Position back to 1 . 1 . 1—the very beginning of bar 1. This will ensure that your recording begins at the start of the arrangement.

2. Before recording, set the **GLOBAL LAUNCH QUANTIZATION** value to 1 Bar (or another value of your choice), as seen in Figure 11.15. This will help avoid rhythmic error when recording from the Session View to the Arrangement View.

Figure 11.15 Setting the Global Launch Quantization value to 1 Bar

3. Click the **ARRANGEMENT RECORD** button (solid circle) in the Control Bar. This will turn the **ARRANGEMENT RECORD** button red and prime the Live Set for recording, but will not initiate recording just yet.

4. Click the **SCENE LAUNCH** button on scene 1, Intro. This will trigger the recording and begin playback of the Intro clips.

5. During the final measure of the Intro scene, click the **SCENE LAUNCH** button on scene 2, Verse. To gauge the timing, watch the Track Status Display indicators (see "Track Status Indicators" below).

6. During the final measure of the Verse scene, click the **SCENE LAUNCH** button on scene 3, Pre Chorus.

7. During the final measure of the Pre Chorus scene, click the **SCENE LAUNCH** button on scene 4, Chorus.

8. During the final measure of the Chorus scene, click the **SCENE LAUNCH** button on scene 5, Outro.

9. At the end of the Outro scene, click the **STOP** button in the Control Bar or press **SPACEBAR** to conclude the recording.

Track Status Indicators

When playing in and recording from the Session View, it can be very useful to watch the Track Status Display indicators (as shown in Figure 11.16) for the currently playing clips. This will help guide you through switching scenes, as you can see how much time remains in a given clip. Looping clips are represented by pie charts, while non-looping clips display a simple countdown timer.

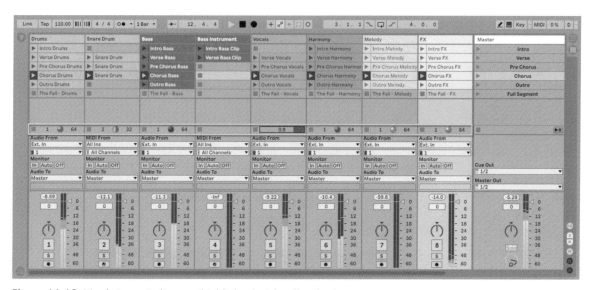

Figure 11.16 Track Status indicators (highlighted with yellow box)

Verify Your Results

Having completed the recording, it's time to switch to the Arrangement View and listen to your results.

Verify your recording in the Arrangement View:

1. Press **TAB** to switch from the Session View to the Arrangement View.

2. Click the red **BACK TO ARRANGEMENT** button at the top-right corner of the Arrangement display. This will cause Live to play back from the arrangement, rather than from the Session View clips.

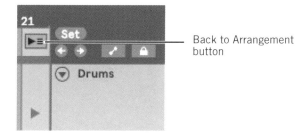

Back to Arrangement button

Figure 11.17 The Back to Arrangement button in the Arrangement View

3.   Press the **STOP** button in the Control Bar twice (or press **HOME** on the computer keyboard) to position the cursor at the start of the Live Set.

4.   Press the **PLAY** button in the Control Bar or press **SPACEBAR** to begin playback.

If you are not satisfied with your recorded arrangement, you can use **EDIT > UNDO** to undo the recording, or you can delete the clips. Then repeat the recording from the Session View as described above.

Clean up the Recorded Arrangement

You may want to fine-tune your arrangement once you've recorded it from the Session View. For instance, if you've extended a section of the song, you might need to smooth out the transition as the section repeats.

Here are some techniques you can use to clean up the arrangement you've created.

■   With the insert marker at the start of the arrangement, choose **CREATE > INSERT SILENCE** or press **COMMAND+I** (Mac) or **CTRL+I** (Windows). Insert 4 bars of silence on the front end of the arrangement.

■   Delete, deactivate, or edit certain clips so that they play back only when you want them to.

■   Trim the end of the arrangement of any unnecessary tails on your audio and MIDI clips.

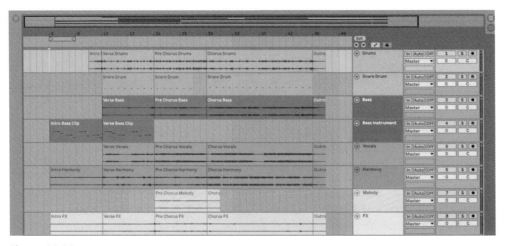

Figure 11.18 An example of an arrangement that has been edited and simplified after recording

Save Work in Progress

You have now created an arrangement for your project. Take this opportunity to save your work.

To save your work, do one of the following:

■   Choose **FILE > SAVE LIVE SET**.

■   Press **COMMAND+S** (Mac) or **CTRL+S** (Windows).

Finishing Your Work

To finish the project, you will add final processing on the Master track, export your arrangement to a stereo audio file, and archive your work. The archive process will allow you to create a backup of your work without consuming excess disk space.

Add a Limiter

First, you will add a Limiter audio effect to the Master track. A limiter is meant to maximize the overall level of a mix, while simultaneously limiting peaks to prevent clipping. Ideally, the end result is a mix that sounds louder while preserving its overall quality.

 Live's Limiter device performs "look-ahead" analysis, anticipating peaks in audio material and preserving attack transients during reduction. This helps makes the results more transparent and maintains the character of the original audio signal without clipping or distortion.

Insert the Limiter effect on the Master track:

1. Show the Browser as needed by pressing **OPTION+COMMAND+B** (Mac) or **CTRL+ALT+B** (Windows).

2. Click **AUDIO EFFECTS** in the Browser.

3. Select the **MASTER** track by clicking on its name.

4. Double-click the **LIMITER** effect in the Browser, or click and drag it onto the Master track.

 The Limiter device will not be available when using Ableton Live Lite.

 See Exercise 10 for suggestions on using the Multiband & Limiter device as an alternative in Ableton Live Lite.

5. Set the **CEILING** parameter in the Limiter to -0.30 dB. This will ensure that your output will never exceed -0.30 dB and will safeguard the mix against clipping.

6. Increase the **GAIN** parameter to around 6.00 dB. During louder parts of the song, you should see some light to moderate activity on the Gain Reduction meter. This indicates the Limiter is working to prevent the signal from exceeding the -0.30 dB ceiling and protecting against clipping, while raising the overall level of the Live Set by 6.0 dB.

Figure 11.19 The Limiter audio effect on the Master track

 Be careful not to increase the Gain too much, as this can introduce distortion.

Export the Song

You can now proceed to export your song as a single stereo audio file.

Export the song:

1.   Select the export range by doing one of the following:

   •   Make a selection spanning the entire length of the arrangement on at least one track.

   •   Create and select a loop region spanning the length of the arrangement, using the loop brace, as illustrated in Figure 11.20.

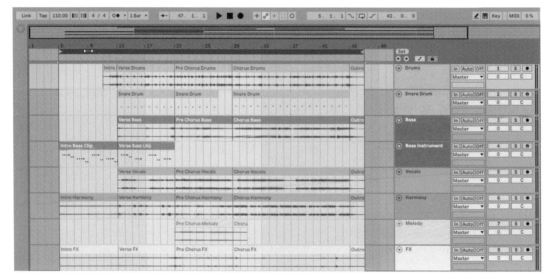

Figure 11.20 A selection of the arrangement made by selecting a loop region

2.   Select **FILE > EXPORT** or press **COMMAND+SHIFT+R** (Mac) or **CTRL+SHIFT+R** (Windows) to open the **EXPORT AUDIO/VIDEO** dialog window.

3.   Verify that the **RENDERED TRACK** is set to Master, and that the **RENDER START** and **RENDER LENGTH** values are an accurate representation of the arrangement start and length. This will help you avoid exporting silence and/or abruptly cutting off audio in the exported file.

4.   Choose the following settings in the Export dialog box:

   • Sample Rate: 44100

   • File Type: WAV

   • Bit Depth: 16

   • Dither Options: POW-r 1

(i)   As a rule of thumb, you should always add dither when bouncing to a lower bit depth.

Figure 11.21   The Export Audio/Video dialog window

5. Click the **EXPORT** button.

6. Navigate to the Final Project directory where your Live Set is saved.

7. Name your file and click **SAVE**. The mixdown will be saved as a .WAV file in your project directory.

Archive Your Work

Now that your project is complete, you have the option to back it up for storage. On a real-world project, you might also need to deliver the work to a client. If you are completing this project in an academic classroom environment, you may be required to submit your work to your instructor for grading.

Because there are often many files associated with a Live Set, something could get lost if the archival process isn't completed properly. In this section, you will use the **COLLECT ALL AND SAVE** command to collect all of your Live Set's media files into the current Live Project directory. This will ensure that your archive includes all of the files you need for the Live Set.

Archive your project:

1. Choose **FILE > COLLECT ALL AND SAVE**.

2. When prompted to specify the files that will be included in the project, choose the following settings:

   - Files from elsewhere: Yes

   - Files from other Projects: Yes

   - Files from User Library: Yes

   - Files from Factory Packs: No

Figure 11.22 The Collect All and Save dialog box

3. Click the **OK** button. This will save your Live Set and copy the audio files used in the project into the current project directory.

This concludes the project. If you are completing this work in an academic environment, please check with your instructor for submittal requirements; be sure to include the exported audio mixdown file with your Live Set archive, as appropriate.

Ableton Live Audio and MIDI Effects

The following Audio and MIDI Effects devices are installed with Ableton Live 10 Suite. Ableton Live Standard and Ableton Live Intro feature a reduced set of these devices.

Audio Effects

- Amp – Features models of seven classic guitar amplifiers.

- Audio Effect Rack – Can be used to combine multiple audio effects into a single device with a shared set of Macro controls.

- Auto Filter – Models an analog multi-mode filter with an envelope follower and LFO.

- Auto Pan – Automatic panning device featuring an LFO.

- Beat Repeat – Repeats portions of drum beats to create new and interesting patterns.

- Cabinet – Features models of five classic guitar cabinets.

- Chorus – Thickens incoming audio using two parallel modulated delays.

- Color Limiter (New in Live 10) – A limiter inspired by vintage hardware limiters.

- Compressor – Workhorse dynamics processor that helps control and maximize levels.

- Convolution Reverb – Ultra-realistic reverb that uses samples of real physical spaces.

- Corpus – Physically models seven types of resonant objects.

- Dynamic Tube – Models analog tube saturation effects.

- Drum Buss (New in Live 10) – A drum-processing device that can add warmth, distortion, drive, compression, transient shaping, and low-frequency enhancement.

- Echo (New in Live 10) – Combines classic analog and digital delay into a hybrid device.

- EQ Eight – Eight multi-mode EQ bands with comprehensive control.

- EQ Three – Classic DJ-style EQ featuring three frequency bands with kill switches.

- Erosion – Can modulate an incoming signal with mono or stereo noise, or a sine wave.

- Flanger – Emulates classic tape flanging effects using time-modulated delays.

- Gate – Can be used to reduce the volume of quieter portions of a single for purposes of eliminating unwanted noises or for rhythmic or processing effects.

- Grain Delay – Uses small "grains" of signal to create delay effects with optional pitch randomization.

- External Audio Effect – Connects external hardware effects into Ableton Live.

- Filter Delay – A delay device featuring three independent delay lines with independent controls for delay time, feedback, pan, and volume.

- Frequency Shifter – Frequency shifting and ring modulation device.

- Gated Delay (New in Live 10) – A delay fed by a gated sequencer that be set to rhythmic patterns.

- Glue Compressor – Bus compressor modeled after the classic SSL bus compressor.

- Limiter – Limits incoming signals to a specific level while maximizing output volume.

- Looper – Emulates classic pedal looping devices and adds modern features such as quantization and tempo control.

- Multiband Dynamics – Features compression and expansion in up to three separate frequency bands.

- Overdrive – Distortion effect based on classic guitar distortion pedals.

- Pedal (New in Live 10) – Features models of classic overdrive, distortion, and fuzz stompbox effects.

- Phaser – Creates a sweeping sound by modulating the frequency and feedback of a multi-pole filter.

- Ping Pong Delay – Delay that bounces from left to right and features a band-pass filter.

- Pitch Hack (New in Live 10) – A delay line with transposition controls. Additional features include reversing audio, randomizing transposition, and recycling signal back into the delay line.

- Redux – Bit-depth and sample-rate reduction for low-fi effects.

- Re-Enveloper (New in Live 10) – A multiband envelope processor that divides the signal into three adjustable frequency bands.

- Resonators – Five tunable resonators that can be applied to any input signal.

- Reverb – Synthetic reverb based on classic analog and digital hardware devices.

- Saturator – A distortion effect featuring waveshaping to add warmth or dirt to a signal.

- Spectral Blur (New in Live 10) – Creates reverb-like sounds and textures within a set frequency range.

- Spectrum – Offers spectral analysis of audio signals.

- Surround Panner (New in Live 10) – Surround panning device for mixing with multi-channel speaker configurations.

- Simple Delay – Basic delay device with feedback and tempo sync.

- Tuner – Simple tuner for tuning real or virtual instruments.

- Utility (Updated for Live 10) – Simple yet useful device for adjusting phase, stereo width, gain, balance, and collapsing signals to mono.

- Vinyl Distortion – Models the noise, distortion, and crackle of vinyl records.

- Vocoder – Offers classic robotic voice effects processed through a bank of bandpass filters.

MIDI Effects

- Arpeggiator – Creates rhythmical patterns from one or more held MIDI notes.

- Chord – Turns MIDI notes into chords with up to six notes.

- Envelope – Can be used to modulate device parameters with incoming MIDI notes.

- Envelope Follower – Can be used to modulate device parameters with any audio signal.

- Expression Control – Can be used to modulate any parameter in your Live Set from a range of MIDI data such as velocity, modwheel, and pitchbend.

- LFO (New in Live 10) – Can be used to modulate up to eight device parameters with one device.

- Melodic Steps (New in Live 10) – A MIDI step sequencer designed to generate evolving patterns.

- MIDI Effect Rack – Can be used to combine multiple MIDI effects into a single device with a shared set of Macro controls.

- MIDI Monitor – Lets users monitor MIDI data including notes, velocity, and continuous controllers.

- Note Echo – Like a delay line for MIDI notes with delay and feedback control.

- Note Length – Can modify the length of MIDI notes or trigger new notes via Note Off.

- Pitch – Can transpose MIDI notes by a specified interval within a user-definable range.

- Random – Can randomly transpose MIDI notes based on chance.

- Scale – Transposes incoming MIDI notes to different outgoing notes based on user-specified scale.

- Shaper (New in Live 10) – An LFO-driven envelope control that can be used to create unique modulation changes.

- Velocity – Can randomize or control the dynamic range of MIDI note velocity.

Ableton Live Software Instruments

The following Software Instruments are installed with Ableton Live 10 Suite. Ableton Live Standard and Ableton Live Intro feature a reduced set of these instruments.

Software Instruments

- Analog – Physically models the sound of vintage analog synthesizers.

- Bass – A monophonic virtual analog synthesizer that emulates a range of vintage and modern sounds.

- Collision – Physically models the sound of mallet instruments.

- Drum Rack – Akai MPC-style 16-pad grid for playing drums, percussion, and other samples.

- DrumSynths – A collection of devices that use synthesis to create drum and percussion sounds.

- External Instrument – Allows you to integrate your external hardware synthesizers into Ableton Live.

- Electric – Physically models the sound of classic electric pianos.

- Impulse – A minimal sampler optimized for playing drum and percussion samples.

- Instrument Rack – Can be used to combine multiple instruments into single device with a shared set of Macro controls.

- Operator – A synthesizer that combines Yamaha-style frequency modulation (FM) synthesis with analog subtractive synthesis.

- Poli – A polyphonic virtual analog synth that emulates the classic poly-synths of the 1970s and 80s.

- Sampler – A comprehensive sampling instrument with multi-sample support.

- Simpler – An intuitive single-sound sample player with deceptively powerful sound manipulation capabilities.

- Tension – Physically models the sound of stringed instruments.

- Wavetable (New in Live 10) – A wavetable synth that combines powerful wavetable oscillators with an elegant and intuitive user interface.

Index

X, Y, Z

About the Authors

This book and associated coursework has been developed by **Eric Kuehnl** and **Andrew Haak**, and is designed to prepare students for Ableton Live certification under the NextPoint Training Digital Media Production program.

Eric Kuehnl is a composer, sound designer, and educator. He is the Director of Partner Programs for NextPoint Training, and the Co-Director of the Music Technology Program at Foothill College. He also teaches game audio and audio post-production courses at Pyramind in San Francisco. Previously, Eric was an Audio Training Strategist in the Avid Education Department, and a Sound Designer for Sony Computer Entertainment America. He holds a Master's degree from California Institute of the Arts, a Bachelor's degree from Oberlin Conservatory, and studied composition at the Centre Iannis Xenakis in Paris.

Andrew Haak is a San Francisco-based producer, sound designer, and engineer who is passionate about the infinite possibilities of digital audio. A graduate of Pyramind's Sound for Pictures and Games program, he's currently pursuing his artist career as an electronic music producer and helping fellow musicians and producers express their creativity as a sound design instructor. Formerly a full-time communications and PR professional, Andrew took a sudden turn into the realm of music after discovering the potential for self-expression and learning that modern music DAWs enable — and hasn't looked back.